INTERNATIONAL BUSINESS AND EUROPE IN TRANSITION

The Academy of International Business series

Published in association with the UK
Chapter of the Academy of International Business

INTERNATIONAL BUSINESS AND EUROPE IN TRANSITION
Edited by Fred Burton, Mo Yamin and Stephen Young

INTERNATIONALISATION STRATEGIES
Edited by George Chryssochoidis, Carla Millar and Jeremy Clegg

International Business and Europe in Transition

Edited by Fred Burton, Mo Yamin and Stephen Young

MACMILLAN
Business

First published 1996 by
MACMILLAN PRESS LTD
Houndmills, Basingstoke, Hampshire RG21 6XS
and London
Companies and representatives
throughout the world

ISBN 0–333–64196–5

A catalogue record for this book is available
from the British Library.

10	9	8	7	6	5	4	3	2	1
05	04	03	02	01	00	99	98	97	96

Printed in Great Britain by
Antony Rowe Ltd, Chippenham, Wiltshire

Published in the United States of America 1996 by
ST. MARTIN'S PRESS, INC.,
Scholarly and Reference Division
175 Fifth Avenue, New York, N.Y. 10010

ISBN 0–312–16041–0

Contents

List of Figures   ix

List of Tables   x

Preface   xiii

List of Contributors   xv

Acknowledgements   xvi

1 Introduction – International Business and Europe in Transition 1
Fred Burton, Mo Yamin and Stephen Young

The Evolution of the EU   1
The Competitiveness of the EU   7
International Business and the European Environment   10
The Structure of the Volume   17

**PART ONE: THE ECONOMY OF THE EUROPEAN UNION –
              BETWEEN VISION AND REALITY**
              Fred Burton   21

2 European Unemployment in a Global Recession   25
Jonathan Michie

A Non-Accelerating Inflation Rate of Unemployment   26
De-industrialisation   27
Full Employment in the Future   29
A Policy Agenda   30
EU Policies for Jobs   33
Conclusions   37

**3 Strategic Opportunities for Retail Financial Service
    Firms in the Single European Market   41**
Kate Prescott

Introduction   41
The Retail Financial Services Industry – A Case for Analysis   42
Foreign Market Servicing – The Challenge for
    Financial Service Firms   44
The European Environment for Retail Financial Services   46
Strategies of European Retail Financial Service Providers   57
Conclusions   61

4 Home Shopping in the Single European Market – Foundering in the Wake of Neo-Liberalism 65
Elke Pioch and Paul Brook

Introduction 65
Retailing – The SEM's Invisible Giant 65
Home Shopping's Place in the EU's Retail Sector 67
1992 – Neo-Liberalism and Globalisation 67
The EU's Vision for Retailing 69
Policies for the European Consumer 69
Towards the Integration of Home Shopping? 71
Distance Selling – the Commission's Objectives 72
Home Shopping and the Data Protection Provisions 76
Conclusions 77

PART TWO: MERGERS, ACQUISITIONS AND COOPERATIVE VENTURES
Mo Yamin 83

5 Foreign Acquisitions in the UK – Impact and Policy 87
Jim Hamill and Pam Castledine

Introduction 87
Foreign Takeovers in the UK 88
Impact of Foreign Acquisitions in the UK 91
Methodology 94
Acquisition Impact – Survey Results 96
Discussion of Results 102
Policy Implications 104
Conclusions 106

6 European Cooperative Ventures between Spanish and UK Firms 109
Fred Burton and Dorothea Noble

Introduction 109
Spanish–UK Cooperative Ventures 110
The Sample 110
Motives for the Choice of Cooperative Ventures 113
Case Study 1: The Initial Configuration of a Joint Venture 117
Case Study 2: Strengthening Strategic Positions in EU Markets 119
Conclusions 120

7 **European Cross-border Acquisitions: The Impact of Management Style Differences on Performance** 122
Richard Schoenberg

Introduction 122
Prior Research and Hypotheses 123
Methodology 126
Results 131
Discussion 134
Conclusions – Corporate Policy Implications 136

PART THREE: THE TRANSITION PROCESS IN EASTERN EUROPE
Mo Yamin 141

8 **Buyouts and the Transformation of Russian Industry** 145
Trevor Buck, Igor Filatotchev and Mike Wright

Introduction 145
The Speed of Privatisation and Corporate Governance 146
Privatisation in Russia 153
Employees as Controllers 157
Employees as Owners 158
Russian EBOs – Employees as Owners and Controllers 160
Conclusions 164

9 **Privatisation in Transitional Economies – East and Central European Experience** 168
Paul Cook and Colin Kirkpatrick

Introduction 168
The Scale of Privatisation 168
Private Sector Development 174
Labour and Social Security under Privatisation 176
Foreign Direct Investment 178
Conclusions 182

**PART FOUR: MNE OPERATIONS – STRATEGIC AND
                    REGULATORY ASPECTS**
                    Stephen Young   **185**

**10 US Foreign Direct Investment in the EU – The Effects
      of Market Integration in Perspective   189**
      Jeremy Clegg

      Introduction   189
      The Impact of EC Trade Policy and Integration on FDI   189
      Leading Hypotheses and Findings on FDI Flows into the EC   193
      US FDI Flows to the EC, 1950–91   198
      Conclusions   202

**11 The Creation and Application of Technology by
      MNES' Subsidiaries in Europe   207**
      Marina Papanastassiou and Robert Pearce

      Introduction   207
      Empirical Evidence   209
      A Case Study   224
      Conclusions   227

**12 Transatlantic Perspectives on Inward Investment and
      Prospects for Policy Reconciliation   231**
      Stephen Young, Neil Hood and Cameron Hood

      Introduction   231
      Inward Investment in the EU and the USA   231
      The Impact of Inward Investment in the EU and the USA   234
      Inward Investment Policy in the EU and the USA   238
      US Policy Proposals   240
      Prospects for Transatlantic Inward Investment Policy   244
      Conclusions   249

**13 Regional and Global Issues in
      International Business   253**
      Peter Buckley

      A Simple Model of the World Economy   253
      East and Central Europe   254
      The Excluded – Regions and Developing Countries   255
      Conclusions   255

Index   257

List of Figures

1.1 Comparative economic performance in the EU,
    USA and Japan, 1980–94   6
1.2 Priorities for a competitiveness policy for the EU   11
3.1 Branch structure and ATM density, 1990   48
3.2 Productivity and wage levels of EU banks, 1990   49
3.3 Concentration and Profits, 1990   56
3.4 Pros and cons of joint ventures   60
5.1 Potential effects of foreign acquisitions in the UK   92
10.1 US FDI in the EC (6) as a percentage of the world,
     for all industries, 1950–91   199
10.2 US FDI in the EC (6) as a percentage of Europe,
     for all industries, 1950–91   200
10.3 US FDI in the EC (9) as a percentage of Europe,
     for manufacturing industry, 1950–91   201
13.1 Internationalization of firms – conflict of markets   254

List of Tables

1.1 Market share as percentage of world exports of manufactures, 1980–92   7

1.2 Balance of trade among Triad members, 1991–3   8

1.3 R & D spending as percentage of GNP, 1991   8

1.4 Percentage share of world patents registered, 1975–9 to 1985–9   8

1.5 Inward and outward FDI of the EU, 1987–91   9

1.6 Educational expenditure as a percentage of GDP/GNP, 1980–9   9

3.1 Personal finance   43

3.2 Relative cost/price positions, banking products   47

3.3 Life and non-life insurance, geographical breakdown, 1988   52

3.4 Insurance products, relative cost/price positions   53

3.5 Key characteristics of the housing market, 1987   54

3.6 Changing age structure of the EU population, 1991–2010   55

3.7 The most appropriate forms of foreign market servicing   57

5.1 Value of world-wide cross-border acquisitions and FDI inflows to developed countries, 1989–92   88

5.2 Twenty largest foreign acquisitions in the UK, 1985–92   89

5.3 Foreign acquisitions in the UK, by nationality of acquiring firm, 1985–92   90

5.4 Sample characteristics, 1985–92   95

5.5 Acquisition motivations   97

5.6 Post-acquisition change, summary table   98

5.7 Locus of post-acquisition decision-making   102

6.1 Ownership methods and types of cooperative Spanish–UK business ventures   111

6.2 Industry distribution of the cooperative ventures   112

6.3 The timing and duration of ventures, pre-1970 to 1990–2   113

6.4 Primary motives for the choice of a cooperative venture   114

7.1 Regression results showing relationship between management style differences and performance for complete sample of cross-border acquisitions   132

7.2 Regression results showing relationship between management style differences and performance for acquisitions characteristics, by preservation or symbiotic integration   133

7.3 Regression results showing relationship between management style differences and performance for manufacturing and service industry acquisitions   133

8.1 The speed of privatisation   147

8.2	Corporate governance and the rate of privatisation	149
8.3	Privatisation 'variants', Russia, 1992–3	155
9.1	Small-scale and large-scale privatisations 1990–3	170
9.2	Average growth rate of GDP and private-sector output and employment, 1989–92	175
9.3	Unemployment in transitional economies, 1990–3	177
9.4	FDI in transitional countries, 1990–3	179
9.5	FDI, by sector, Eastern Europe and the former Soviet Union, 1991 – March 1994	179
9.6	Joint venture agreements in transitional countries, 1992–3	181
9.7	Gross disbursements by IMF and development institutions to transition economies, 1991–3	181
10.1	Tariff averages on total imports of finished and semi-finished manufactures, before and after the implementation of the Tokyo Round	190
10.2	Industrial country imports from industrial countries subject to 'hard-core' NTBs, 1981 and 1986	191
10.3	US FDI stock in the EC as a percentage of total US FDI in the world and in Europe, 1950–91	199
11.1	Percentage of production exported by MNE subsidiaries in Europe	211
11.2	Sources of technological work carried out for MNE subsidiaries	213
11.3	MNE subsidiaries' evaluation of the importance of various types of work in their laboratories	215
11.4	Sources of technology used by MNE subsidiaries in Europe	218
11.5	Extent of, and motives for, adaptation of MNE subsidiaries in Europe	220
11.6	MNE subsidiaries' evaluation of their collaborative research with local institutions	223
12.1	FDI, inward and outward stock for the EU and the USA, 1980, 1985, 1990 and 1992	233
12.2	FDI, position at year end 1992, EU in USA and USA in EU	233
12.3	Japanese FDI, cumulative total, 1993, Europe and North America	234
12.4	The impact of inward investments in the EU and USA, major areas of divergence	236
12.5	US policy proposals	242

Preface

It gives me great pleasure to introduce *The Academy of International Business Conference Volumes*, a new annual series developed by the UK Chapter of the Academy of International Business (AIB) and published by Macmillan. The purpose of the UK AIB, as a national Chapter of the worldwide organisation, is to promote international business as an academic discipline. In fulfilling this role, the UK AIB provides a forum for the exchange of ideas, for the presentation of research, for professional contact and for discussion of matters of common interest in teaching and research. The major event in the UK AIB calendar is the annual conference, which is held in universities around the country focusing on particular themes which are of research and policy significance in international business. Over the years a number of books have been published on the basis of selected papers (suitably edited) from particular conferences. The aim of the present series is to formalise this process, publishing high-quality research around important and topical international business themes, with a number of principles being adhered to:

- Each book will be planned and produced as an integrated volume, designed to make a significant contribution to research and writing in the field.
- The conference organiser(s) and a member of the Executive Committee of the UK AIB will act as editors for the series.
- The editors are responsible for selection of the articles to be included in the books. Where it is deemed necessary to produce a coherent volume, additional chapters may be commissioned from research experts in the area.
- All articles accepted for presentation at UK AIB conferences are referred. However, papers selected for inclusion in the conference volume will go through a further refereeing process involving the editors of the book and others.

The UK AIB was formed in the 1970s, and its first conference was held at UMIST, Manchester, in April 1974 organised by Dr Michael Z. Brooke, who remained as Chair until 1985. Professor Peter Buckley then held the position until 1991 when I took over. I would like to acknowledge the outstanding contribution that my predecessors have made in building the UK AIB and thereby laying the foundations for this book series. My sincere thanks also go to the members of the Executive Committee and especially Fred Burton, Carla Millar and Jeremy Clegg who have worked tirelessly for the AIB over a good number of years.

Finally my thanks go to Jane Powell of Macmillan who had the vision and foresight to recognise the quality of work being produced by UK academics in international business, and who has been so supportive in bringing this book series to fruition.

University of Strathclyde   STEPHEN YOUNG
Glasgow

Acknowledgements

The editors and publishers acknowledge with thanks permission to reproduce the following copyright material: Beddows and Co., for the data in
Figures 3.1 and 3.3; Oxford University Press, for data in Tables 10.1 and
10.2, from *World Development Report*, 1987 (1987); GATT, for data in Table
10.1, from *The Tokyo Round of Multilateral Trade Negotiations, Volume 2,
Supplementary Report* (1980).

List of Contributors

Paul Brook
Senior Lecturer, Department of Retailing and Marketing,. Manchester Metropolitan University

Trevor Buck
Senior Lecturer, School of Management and Finance, University of Nottingham

Peter Buckley
Professor of International Business, Centre for International Business, University of Leeds

Fred Burton
Senior Lecturer, Manchester School of Management, UMIST

Pam Castledine
Lecturer, Strathclyde International Business Unit, Department of Marketing, University of Strathclyde

Jeremy Clegg
Senior Lecturer, Centre for International Business, University of Leeds

Paul Cook
Senior Lecturer, Department of Economics, University of Manchester

Igor Filatotchev
Lecturer, School of Management and Finance, University of Nottingham

Jim Hamill
Reader, Strathclyde International Business Unit, Department of Marketing, University of Strathclyde

Cameron Hood
FI Group plc; formerly researcher, Strathclyde International Business Unit, Department of Marketing, University of Strathclyde

Neil Hood
Professor of Business Policy, Strathclyde International Business Unit, Department of Marketing, University of Strathclyde

Colin Kirkpatrick
Professor of Development Economics, University of Bradford

Jonathan Michie
Lecturer in Economics, Judge Institute of Management Studies, University of Cambridge; Fellow, Robinson College, University of Cambridge

Dorothea Noble
Lecturer, The Business School, University of Hertfordshire

Marina Papanastassiou
Research Assistant, Department of Economics, University of Reading

Robert Pearce
Reader, Department of Economics, University of Reading

Elke Pioch
Lecturer, Department of Retailing and Marketing, Manchester Metropolitan University

Kate Prescott
Lecturer, University of Bradford Management Centre

Richard Schoenberg
Lecturer, The Management School, Imperial College, London

Mike Wright
Professor, School of Management and Finance, University of Nottingham

Mo Yamin
Lecturer, Manchester School of Management, UMIST

Stephen Young
Professor and Head of Department, Department of Marketing, University of Strathclyde

1 Introduction – International Business and Europe in Transition

Fred Burton, Mo Yamin and Stephen Young

This book provides an integrated collection of research writings around the theme of International Business and Europe in Transition. Like others to follow in The Academy of International Business Conference series, it is designed to contribute to general understanding and debate, to academic research and to policy review and evolution. In addition, this book, as with others in the series, concludes with a brief chapter on future research ideas stimulated by the authors' contributions.

In providing the background and context for the contributions which follow, the present chapter provides an outline of developments in the European Union (EU) and its relations with neighbouring states, identifies some of the major problems and challenges facing Europe in the run up to the new millenium, and reviews some of the range of international business issues which stem from EU enlargement and integration.

THE EVOLUTION OF THE EU[1]

The European Community (EC) was formed under the terms of the Treaty of Rome on 1 January 1958. Initial membership comprised France, the Federal Republic of Germany, Italy, the Netherlands, Belgium and Luxembourg; excluding Italy perhaps, these countries still represent the core of power and influence and provide the driving force for European integration. Since establishment a series of enlargements have taken place, with the following countries joining:

- 1973 Denmark, Ireland, United Kingdom
- 1981 Greece
- 1986 Spain and Portugal
- 1990 (3 October) the former East Germany, as part of German reunification
- 1995 Austria, Finland, Sweden.

By 1995, therefore, nearly all countries in Western Europe had become members of the EU (the term used initially in the Treaty on European Union – see below), forming a huge bloc stretching from the Baltic to the Mediterranean with a population of 370 mn (USA 250 mn, Japan 125 mn), a GDP of ecu 5760 bn in 1992 (USA ecu 4590 bn, Japan ecu 2840 bn), and exports representing 21 per cent of GDP in 1992 (USA 7.5 per cent, Japan 9.2 per cent) (*Eurostat*, 1994). The notable country exceptions in EU membership were Norway, which rejected membership in referenda leading up to both the 1973 and 1995 enlargements, and Switzerland. The EU also signed a series of association agreements for the formation of a free trade area involving Poland, Hungary and Czechoslovakia in 1991, and Romania, Bulgaria and the Slovak and Czech Republics in 1993; plans are now in hand to prepare their economies and legal frameworks for EU accession. A membership of 20 or more countries including the Baltic states of Latvia, Lithuania and Estonia, and Slovenia is therefore likely early in the 21st century. A Euro-Mediterranean Economic Area linking the EU to its North African and Middle Eastern neighbours is also high on the agenda.

These facts, while well known, are repeated in part by way of explaining the slow pace of European integration. Undoubtedly much of the EU's energies have been taken up in complex negotiations over membership – 'deepening' has thus been sacrificed at the expense of 'widening'. Enlargement, too, has brought in Member States with very different backgrounds, levels of wealth and philosophies. Much of the debate-taking place at the present time over the future of the EU is concerned with improving democratic processes in the Union and the workings of the formal institutions to speed up decision-making (Shackleton, 1994). The path to European integration has thus been very hesitant, and four stages can be identified.

Customs Union (1958–69)

During the first stages of the evolution of the EU, the six founder members eliminated internal tariffs and quotas on intra-EU trade in goods and a common external tariff was established, and some preliminary steps were taken to deal with non-tariff barriers.

Common Market (1958–85)

The Treaty of Rome envisaged the establishment of a common market involving the free movement of goods and services, people and capital. During this period a variety of institutional and policy developments took place towards this goal, but progress was hesitant and often misdirected. Van den Bulcke (1993) comments that the achievement of the common agricultural policy, while technically an impressive achievement, also created problems in regard to monetary and budgetary aspects. In its support for inefficient agricultural production, it delayed the pace of needed structural reform. The common competition policy was gradually implemented on the basis of Articles

85 and 86 of the Treaty, and some limited progress was made in the field of trade policy. Mention should also be made of the establishment of the European Monetary System (EMS) in 1979 which introduced the ecu (European Currency Unit) as a reserve asset and a means of settlement; this also initiated an exchange rate mechanism (ERM) with the aim of reducing uncertainty in currency markets by limiting variations in exchange rates (normally ± 2.25 per cent, exceptionally ± 6 per cent) around agreed central parities. This was to become a linchpin in subsequent plans for economic union.

Single European Market (1985–)

To gain new impetus for European integration, the Single European Market (SEM) programme was launched in the mid-1980s to secure free trade in goods, services, labour and capital through the removal of non-tariff barriers. The target date for the completion of the Single Market, involving 282 legislative measures, was 31 December 1992. The vast majority of measures were passed by that date, although some were weaker than envisaged, key issues relating to fiscal harmonisation remain to be negotiated and levels of implementation vary greatly between Member States. The reality is that the programme was grossly over-hyped and has to be regarded as an on-going and long-term one. Acceptance of the principle of 'mutual recognition' (products which conform with the specifications of one Member State must not be excluded from another unless they can be shown to be damaging to health, safety, the environment or other aspects of the public interest) was an important step forward, as was the move to speed up decision-making by allowing approval for single market measures to be taken by a qualified majority of Member States.

Economic and Monetary Union (1990–)

While a new milestone on the road to full integration was reached with the creation of the Single Market, economic and monetary union also required cooperation on research and technology, the environment, social policy and, particularly, economic and social cohesion. The Delors Committee (1989) envisaged a three-stage plan, with a transition to permanently fixed exchange rates and then to a single European currency, issued through a European central banking system with responsibility for EU monetary and exchange rate policies. By the terms of the *Treaty on European Union* (hereafter 'Maastricht Treaty') of 7 February 1992 (Council, 1992), the date for the creation of economic and monetary union with a single currency was set for 1 January 1999, with stages towards this goal as follows:

• *Stage 1 (1990–93)* This stage, which was planned to be completed by the end of 1993, had the objectives of improved coordination of economic and monetary policy with all currencies being brought within the narrow band (± 2.25 per cent) of the ERM, and closer collaboration amongst central banks. However the ERM collapsed in August 1993, following the withdrawal of the UK and Italy almost one year earlier. Reasons put forward included macroeconomic problems caused by German reunification, the wide differences in economic performance in the recession conditions prevailing, and possibly the growth of cross-border capital flows consequent on the abolition of exchange controls in the EU.

• *Stage 2 (1994–97)* The aim (now achieved) was to set up a European Monetary Institute (EMI) as a precursor to a European Central Bank (ECB) during this stage in preparation for full monetary integration. More importantly, countries are to seek to bring their macroeconomic performance more closely into line, with guidelines set by a series of convergence criteria:

a *Price stability* An average rate of inflation not more than 1.5 percentage points higher than that of the three best performing Member States in terms of price stability
b *Public finances* No excessive government deficit, defined as a budget deficit of more than 3 per cent of GDP or a total government debt exceeding 60 per cent of GDP
c *Exchange rates* No devaluation for at least two years prior to 1996, and maintenance of the currency within the ± 2.25 per cent fluctuation margins during the same period
d *Interest rates* Average nominal long-term interest rates not more than 2 percentage points higher than those of the three best performing Member States in terms of price stability.

• *Stage 3 (commencing 1997 or 1999)* If the majority of the 15 EU members met the convergence criteria, Stage 3 could have commenced on 1 January 1997; recognising the problems however, in a ministerial meeting in 1995 the date for the introduction of a single currency was deferred until 1999. The final stage will thus begin on 1 January 1999. At this point the transition to fixed exchange rates and a common currency will be decided upon. The European System of Central Banks (ESCB) will be established, with a transfer of economic and monetary authority to Union institutions. The UK has yet to commit itself to participation in this final stage, a decision to be made in 1996, while Denmark has already withdrawn from progress to Stage 3. Member states which do not fulfil the convergence criteria will be given a derogation, but a consequence is that they will not be able to participate in the principal decisions relating to monetary policy.

The Single Market programme is a continuing one, as already noted, and the Economic and Social Committee (ESC) of the European Parliament has been charged with reviewing progress and monitoring the work of the European Commission. In its Opinion of September 1994 (ESC, 1994), the Committee reported that many obstacles to the free movement of goods, services, people and capital remained, with only about half of the 282 measures being implemented by all Member States (the low figure was principally due to non-implementation by one or two Member States; Denmark at 94 per cent and the UK at 90 per cent had the highest levels of implementation). Principal benefits in the first two years of the single market reported from industry surveys related to substantial cost savings due to the abolition of customs' documentation and border controls and the simplification of VAT procedures, lower costs of transport, insurance and intra-EU banking transactions, and ease of investment due to the liberalisation of capital movemements. However, a range of substantive barriers remain, including:

- *Standards* Failure to implement the principle of mutual recognition of standards, with a wide range of difficulties in areas such as labelling, differences in health requirements, variations in consumer protection standards, etc.
- *Procurement and tender* Problems in public procurement, e.g. difficulties in gaining contracts unless the company is established locally, problems in public tenders such as short delays between publication date and tender date, and translation difficulties
- *Taxation* Despite the comments above, continuing problems exist over different VAT rules, VAT registration procedures, and delays in information on VAT transfers
- *Free movement of people* A large range of barriers remain, from lack of mutual recognition of diplomas and certificates and pension contributions to problems with entitlements from social insurance contributions and loss of State benefits on change of residence
- *Financial services, airlines, energy and telecommunications* Difficulties posed *inter alia* by monopolies, restrictive national legislation, variations in state aid, etc.

A key recommendation of the Committee in its 1994 Opinion was that the Commission should publish annually a list of all complaints received about the inadequate functioning of the single market, and state the action which had been taken or was proposed. Much clearly remains to be done.

In relation to economic and monetary union, the demise of the ERM might appear to have killed off possibilities for the immediate future: for example, only Ireland and Luxembourg had fulfilled the government budget deficit and debt criteria at the end of 1994. On the other hand it has been suggested that the existence of the ERM *per se* was not a requirement, rather that a Member State has simply respected the normal fluctuation margins without severe tensions for at least two years (*Financial Times*, 1994). On this basis and given improved economic conditions, a majority of Member States may

6

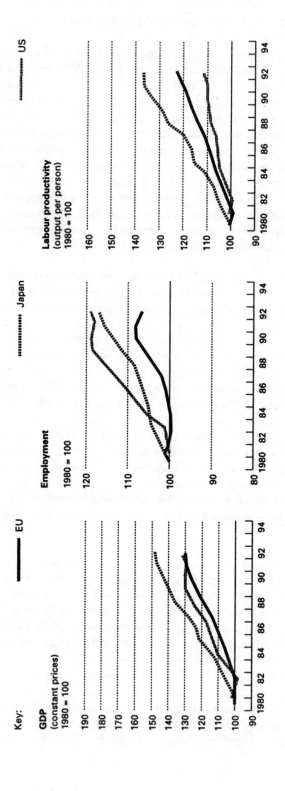

Key: ——— EU   ·········· Japan   ········ US

GDP
(constant prices)
1980 = 100

Employment
1980 = 100

Labour productivity
(output per person)
1980 = 100

Source: Financial Times (1994).

Figure 1.1 Comparative economic performance in the EU, USA and Japan, 1980–94

Table 1.1   Market share as percentage of world exports of manufactures current prices and exchange rates, 1980–92

	1980	1986	1992
EU	29	25	24
USA	18	14	17
Japan	15	18	17
Others	39	43	42

Source: CEC (1994).

well be in a position to commence Stage 3 in 1997. Monetary indicators might well be expected to converge near the peak of the business cycle. The politics of the 1996 inter-governmental conference will be key. In any event technical problems will remain, the European Banking Federation having warned that the banks would require at least five years to plan for a single currency after the EMU starting date was announced.

THE COMPETITIVENESS OF THE EU

While progress towards economic and monetary integration has been slow, in the context of the on-going enlargement progress, and widely differing national economic and political systems, philosophies, and levels of economic development, achievements have been impressive. What needs also to be considered, however, is the growth, competitiveness and employment performance of the Union, given that an improved economic position was a fundamental aim and, indeed, expectation of integration.

Some of the basic statistics on comparative economic performance are summarised in Figure 1.1 and Tables 1.1–1.6. Over the period 1980–92, growth in the EU was very similar to that in the USA, but well below that of Japan (Figure 1.1). Employment and labour productivity show reverse trends in the EU and USA: employment grew by 18 per cent in the USA while labour productivity rose by 12 per cent; the comparative figures for the EU were 6 per cent for employment and 22 per cent for labour productivity. Job creation and hence unemployment is thus a critical problem in Europe, an enigma attributed by some (for example, Henning *et al.* 1994, but rejected by Michie, Chapter 2 in this volume) to a lack of labour flexibility. Turning to international competitiveness, Table 1.1 shows that the EU's share of world exports of manufactured goods has fallen – from 29 per cent in 1980 to 25 per cent in 1986 and 24 per cent in 1992. Investigating this more deeply shows that the EU is less specialised in high technology products, has less of a presence in high growth markets than either the USA or Japan, and since 1986 has had a trade deficit in high technology products. The explanations are complex. One suggestion for the poor

Table 1.2   Balance of trade among Triad members, ecu bn, 1991–3

Trade balance	1991	1992	1993
EU–US	–21.0	–13.0	–2.0
EU–Japan	–30.0	–31.0	–25.0
US–Japan	–35.1	–38.0	–50.7

Source: CEC (1994).

Table 1.3   R & D spending as percentage of GNP, 1991

EU	2.0
USA	2.8
Japan	3.1
Industrialised Asia	2.7
World	2.0

Source: CEC (1994).

Table 1.4   Percentage share of world patents registered, 1975–9 to 1985–9

	1975–9	1980–4	1985–9
EU	43	40	38
North America	29	28	27
Japan	15	20	24
Others	13	12	11

Source: CEC (1994).

performance of manufacturing exports (and one which is highly relevant to the above discussion on integration and to the international business theme of this volume as a whole) is the EU's relative emphasis on internal rather than external liberalisation (*Financial Times*, 1994). This is an important issue: the single market programme was taking place at a time when globalisation was becoming a reality, and when the Asian region was the fastest growing in the world, providing threats (as the trade balance data in Table 1.2 reveal) but also offering big opportunities for EU enterprises.

The technological performance of the EU also provides a part explanation for declining international competitiveness. Total EU expenditure on R & D (Table 1.3) in 1991 was barely equal to the world average; and while still accounting for the largest share of world patents registered, this share was in decline, especially in comparison with Japan (Table 1.4). In turn, there is evidence that the EU's research spending yields a poorer performance in high technology markets than in the market in general. By specialising to a greater extent on medium and low technology products in exports, European industry is inevitably subject to growing competition from the high performing East Asian exporters of labour-intensive manufactures.

Table 1.5 Inward and outward FDI of the EU, ecu bn, 1987–91

ecu bn Year	Inward FDI	Outward FDI	Net Outward FDI
1987	108	201	93
1988	134	253	119
1989	169	275	106
1990	170	275	105
1991	195	297	103

Source: CEC (1994).

Table 1.6 Educational expenditure as percentage of GDP/GNP, 1980–9

	1980	1985	1989
EU	5.3	5.1	4.9
USA	6.7	5.0	5.3
Japan	5.8	5.0	4.7

Source: CEC (1994).

European industry itself has suggested other factors contributing to the relative decline in its competitive position (CEC, 1994). These include more rapid increases in hourly pay rates; a higher tax burden – which averages 40 per cent in the EU compared with 30 per cent for its competitors; major differences in manufacturing productivity – about 30 per cent compared with the USA and 10 per cent compared with Japan; deficiencies in the promotion of physical and intangible investments by companies (especially small and medium sized companies); and weaknesses in management expertise.

This discussion has focused largely on manufacturing industry, but the services sector is the EU's largest source of output and employment (although smaller than in either Japan or the USA). The search for increased competitiveness in this sector is widely recognised, requiring opening up markets to cross-border competition. This means reducing the domination of national monopolies and eliminating the complex regulatory and structural barriers which exist in the industry. Progress in these directions within the framework of the single market programme has been encouraging in financial, professional and business services, but more halting in industries like air transport, telecommunications and energy supply. State aid is pervasive in some countries in these latter sectors.

It is true, of course, that the aggregate position conceals substantial differences between EU Member States. Quoting data from the 1993 World Competitiveness Report, the European Commission (CEC, 1994) suggests a less alarming picture, with Denmark (3rd), Germany (5th), Netherlands (6th) and Belgium/Luxembourg (10th) highly ranked among countries on a world basis. Germany's fall to 5th position from 2nd in 1993 was largely due to the impact of reunification, while France and the UK had improved their positions compared with earlier years. The most fundamental problems existed in the southern States of the EU, where low levels of competitiveness were linked to structural problems and the low value added of a number of basic industries.

The policy paper from the European Commission on competitiveness (*An Industrial Competitiveness Policy for the European Union*, CEC, 1994) accepts that 'most assessments of the state of EU industry continue to emphasise the worrying loss of competitiveness compared with . . . the other members of the Triad' (CEC, 1994, p. A.2).[2] Its conclusions for a way ahead are that there should be four basic priorities for a competitiveness policy designed to redress the problems recognised, namely:

- *Promote intangible investment*, particularly training and learning, the promotion of quality, and R & D
- *Develop industrial cooperation*, both internally and externally
- *Ensure fair competition inside the Union and at international level*: internally, this means reducing overall public aid and controlling state aids, externally, supporting the work of the WTO and developing international rules on competition
- *Modernise the role of the public authorities*, by continuing deregulation processes in telecommunications and energy, redefining public service objectives and simplifying legislative and administrative procedures.

These priorities, and the objectives and proposed Action programmes associated with them are reproduced in Figures 1.2(a)–(d).

INTERNATIONAL BUSINESS AND THE EUROPEAN ENVIRONMENT

In relation to the contents of this book, particular interest attaches to the international business dimensions of the Commission's Industrial Competitiveness Policy. Clearly international business issues are implicit in most of the European Commission's activities, and have always been recognised as the principal mechanism by which the economic gains from integration would be achieved. However, five specific international business themes can be identified:

Cross-border Cooperation, Within and Outwith the Union

Considerable attention is paid to the need to support industrial cooperation, which has chiefly taken the form of strategic alliances and mergers. Accepting that these are the responsibility of businesses themselves, the Commission felt it had a role in the setting-up of round-tables of industrialists in specific countries (e.g. Japan) and for specific industries (e.g. with Central and Eastern Europe on the agri-food and consumer electronics industries). The promotion of partnerships between large and small enterprises (e.g. car makers and component suppliers) was a second area identified. Third, assisting the development of expertise in international financial engineering and countertrade (especially offset) activities. This is especially pertinent to cooperation with Central and Eastern Europe, and reflects the complexity and cost of mounting major industrial cooperation projects in, for example,

Figure 1.2 Priorities for a competitiveness policy for the EU

(a) Promote intangible investment

Objectives	Action
• To adapt vocational training to needs	• Promotion of intangible investment in the general support for investment; examination of ways of taking fuller account of intangible assets, particularly in the context of taxation
• To encourage greater participation by both sides of industry in seeking new ways of organising work	
	• Stepping up of research
• To facilitate the emergence of new markets, of new forms of training and of total quality production	• By proceeding with further action to take fuller account of the needs of the market in R & D policy
• To apply economic intelligence	• By modernising the approaches in order to produce more effective industrial spin-offs from research
• To increase the capacity to keep ahead of changes in technology and on the markets	• By facilitating the establishment of consortia of European companies
	• Promotion of quality
• To ensure expansion and take-up of R&D efforts	• Fuller integration of vocational training schemes in other policies
• To promote sustainable industrial development	• Creation of a legal environment conducive to research
	• Development of clean technologies and economic incentives
	• Introduction of new ways of organising work and improvement of the fiscal environment, particularly for small firms
	• Improvement of the dialogue between the two sides of industry
	• Rational use of statistics

cont. overleaf
Source: CEC (1994).

(b) Develop industrial cooperation

- To bolster the presence of the European Union's industry on high-growth markets
- To take fuller account of the industrial situation of the European Union's partners
- To encourage private cooperation schemes of interest to the Community
- To facilitate transfers of experience and know-how between businesses, particularly small businesses

(a) General measures

- Identification and removal of legal and fiscal obstacles to industrial cooperation
- Development of industrial cooperation tools, using as an example the experience of BC-Net
- Support for the development of trans-national initiatives targeted on growth markets using structural funds
- Industrial round tables
- Recourse to the Working Party of the Heads of Industrial Policy Departments to facilitate industrial cooperation operations and efforts to find information and partners
- Develop a coherent legal approach towards a communal and efficient promotion of European foreign investment

(b) Central and Eastern Europe

- Exploring solutions similar to partial guarantees for investments
- Support for standardisation and certification
- Expertise in international financial engineering and offset activities
- Support for harnessing potential energy resources

(c) Latin American and Mediterranean countries

- Closer technological cooperation
- Participation in the fourth framework programme on R&D activities and in the developments connected with the information society
- Establishment of networks of businesses

(d) Asian countries

- Cooperation programmes
- Scientific and technological cooperation schemes
- Training and dissemination of technology

(c) Ensure their competition

External measures

- To take account of the growing numbers of strategic alliances
- To identify the obstacles to export growth and increased investment
- To put an end to discriminatory bilateral agreements
- To promote more open trade, while encouraging social progress
- To consider the establishment of multilateral rules to reduce distortion of competition caused by businesses themselves
- To establish environmental protection criteria and apply them effectively
- To harness more fully the commercial potential of the region with which the European Union has close ties for historical and cultural reasons

Internal measures

- To define a consistent approach to open up markets and make them more competitive
- To increase discipline within the Union
- To make competition policy more consistent with other policies

External markets:

- Continue efforts to resolve problems not completely dealt with by the end of the Uruguay Round
- Efficiently combat fraud
- Development and effective application of international rules on competition
- Taking account of the European Union's industrial interests, both as an exporter and as an importer
- Establishment of an Industrial Assessment Mechanism
- Continue to improve the structure of the common customs tariff in order to better reflect the industrial interests of producers and users
- Database on the obstacles to smooth operation of the markets
- Improve commercial policy instruments with the aim of making them more efficient and operational
- Consideration of application of commercial policy and defence instruments to services
- Coordination between the measures taken to promote exports and investment and the other policies

Internal market

- Further reduction of State aid, taking account of regional imbalances
- Shortly look at possible changes to the state aid control mechanism
- Re-examination of the aid authorisation criteria
- Improve the coherence between the structural policies and the policies for monitoring State aid
- Improve the coherence between the rules applicable to state aids and the arrangements for Community financing under non-structural policies
- Strengthening of the internal market (in gas, electricity and telecommunications)

cont. overleaf

(d) Modernise the role of the public authorities

- To ensure smooth operation of the internal market
- To improve administrative cooperation between the Member State and the Commission
- To simplify the public mechanisms affecting industrial competitiveness
- To continue deregulation and administrative simplfication
- To modernise the public authorities
- To ensure closer concentration with operators on matters affecting industrial performance
- To bring the administrative departments responsible for research and industry closer together
- To reduce the costs arising from the regulations

- Further deregulation, examining, for example, the expediency of invoking Articles 101 and 102 of the Treaty
- Redefinition of public service objectives
- Use the Structural Funds to support industrial change and to facilitate the development of clusters of competitive activities
- Development of partnerships between big businesses and small firms
- Streamlining and greater transparency of procedures (contribution to the working party set up to simplify administrative procedures and legislation)
- Faster establishment of trans-European networks for the interchange of data between administrations
- Use of the Community instruments to support cooperation projects of Community interest
- Examination of ways of improving decision-making structures

the transport, telecommunications and energy sectors. Fourth, facilitating the establishment of consortia of European companies to exploit synergies in the R & D sector. Fifth, encouraging cooperation programmes on a country to country basis (e.g. the pilot programme between the EU and Japan on parts and components for consumer electronics).

Outward Direct Investment

Although industrial cooperation activity could be a form of outward foreign direct investment (FDI) there is also specific, albeit ambiguous, comment on the latter. On the one hand, it is argued that European companies' export and transplant potential is not fully exploited because of the continued closure of some markets. Action to remove these barriers would make a significant contribution to improving outlets for EU companies' products. On the other hand, there is some concern about the relocation of EU production to low labour cost countries, mitigated by the fact that relocation is still limited to specific sectors (textiles, clothing and footwear; consumer electronics and electronic components) and activities (subcontracting of work with little innovation content). The bulk of outward FDI is directed to high growth markets.

Inward Direct Investment

Data presented by the Commission without comment indicate that in the five years to 1991 outward FDI totalled ecu 1301 bn and inward FDI ecu 776 bn, a difference of 40 per cent. Inward investment received only one other direct mention in the industrial competitiveness policy paper. It is indicated that: 'Steps must be taken to ensure that the European Union remains an attractive site for production and investment, including investment from outside the Union' (p. 13), but that in order to generate jobs a more labour-intensive development model should be employed. There is thus a recognition that in an era of globalisation the EU is in some instance competing for inward FDI with locations in other parts of the Triad. The proviso on the operation of a more labour-intensive development model reflects concerns that the Union's regional aid regime (which sets ceilings on the net grant equivalent aid intensity – for details see Young and Hood, 1993, p. 45) encourages capital-intensive investment, which may not be appropriate, especially in southern European countries. The apparent lack of interest in inward FDI is long standing, witness the fact that in the discussion and implementation of the single market programme, virtually no reference was made to multinational enterprises (MNEs), the assumption being that international production and trade were undertaken by uninational firms (Emerson *et al.*, 1988; Panić, 1991). It could be argued that the limited consideration of inward investment and foreign MNEs reflects a commitment to national treatment (non-discrimination between national and foreign enterprises) in international treaties, but more likely is the difficulty of agreeing an approach which is acceptable to all Member States. Young *et al.* (Chapter 12 in this volume) consider the FDI policy problems of the EU in more detail.

Policies for Trade and Outward FDI

Much of the emphasis was on trade issues, including the need to resolve problems in sectors such as aerospace, steel, audio-visual and financial services which were not finalised in the Uruguay Round negotiations. Trade liberalisation, especially in industrialising countries, together with improvements in social conditions and environmental protection criteria, were also identified as important agenda items for the new World Trade Organisation (WTO). The links with foreign direct investment emerge in services which come within the scope of the WTO, and in anti-dumping where it is recognised that the EU's industrial interests can no longer be approached in purely geographical terms (e.g. EU MNEs may be importing from their subsidiaries in the same countries and sectors against which anti-dumping action is being sought – see Brewer and Young, 1995). In the context of FDI specifically, however, especial attention is paid to international competition policy. It is commented that:

> Account must be taken of the increasing number of strategic alliances in order to avoid the build-up of dominant positions world-wide. Parallel measures must be taken to encourage the development of alliances of industrial and technological interest while at the same time allowing stronger competition on world markets. A balance must be struck between these two objectives. (p. 31)

These problems should be tackled at multilateral level through the OECD and the WTO, an approach which would more generally prevent a proliferation of discriminatory bilateral agreements (the initial phase of the agreement between Japan and the USA on semiconductors is mentioned in this regard).

Policies for the Internal Market

Given that the EU is still far from being a single market, there is a recognised need to continue to eliminate the distortions created by legislative, regulatory or administrative barriers, and to promote deregulation especially in the telecommunications and energy markets.

These broad-brush policy statements can only give a feel of the range of international business issues which have been introduced by the evolution of the EU and which are of interest to students, academics, businessmen and policy-makers. The distinctive international business questions are those which relate directly or indirectly to the effects of integration on international business behaviour. They, therefore, involve cross-border activity in one form or another, and a variety of entry, expansion and reorganisation modes ranging from exporting to joint ventures and strategic alliances, greenfield investments and acquisitions.

From an international business management perspective, interest lies in the choice of corporate and functional management strategies for Europe, and the degree of integration and coordination of operations. Given the problems of implementing the single market programme, alongside structural barriers such as differences in distribution channels, and taste differences, country-centred strategies still predominate in some sectors. In others, examples of pan-European strategies are much in evidence in order to exploit economies of scale in manufacturing, marketing, finance and human resource management. Alternative approaches might involve horizontal specialisation, with concentration of activities in one or a small number of locations to serve the European market; or vertical specialisation, with different stages of value adding activity being located so as to exploit cost differences across Europe.

In the management of cross-border expansion and reorganisation, cultural factors loom large, and have a major influence on success and failure.

Taking an international business economics viewpoint, interest exists, at the broadest level, in the economic consequences of European integration (where early optimistic forecast outcomes of the single market, for example, have now been drastically downgraded – see Mayes *et al*, 1992; Winters, 1993); and more specifically in the interaction between corporate integration and regional integration. The latter issues concern ways in which economic integration helps lower production costs and cross-border transport costs or raises levels of consumer demand, thereby encouraging intra-regional production process specialisation; the processes may facilitate additional economies of scale or scope. Concern also exists (as the Commission document above reveals) about the effects of cross-border activity on the creation of EU-wide monopolies or oligopolies with a concentration of economic power and anti-competitive behaviour. In addition, the country distribution effects of integration and multinational corporate activity are problematic as multinational enterprises restructure across national frontiers: the likelihood of higher value added and decision-making activities being located closer to the market centre has been extensively discussed (Robson, 1993). What follows from all of this are the national and EU-level policy issues relating to competition, industry, foreign direct investment, etc.

THE STRUCTURE OF THE VOLUME

The chapters in the book are grouped into four Parts. Part One on The Economy of the EU is introduced by Fred Burton, with chapters from Jonathan Michie (Chapter 2), Kate Prescott (Chapter 3), and Elke Pioch and Paul Brook (Chapter 4). Michie's chapter has a scene-setting role focusing on one of the most critical problems facing Europe today, namely that of unemployment. The remedies, controversially for many, are seen in terms of less restrictive macroeconomic policies, rather than freeing up labour markets, with fewer limitations on working time, the use of temporary and part-time workers and lower social welfare costs. This issue is right at the heart of debates taking place over the future of Europe. Chapters 3 and 4 consider the progress of the SEM in the EU in two sectors, retail financial services and home shopping, confirming the opportunities which exist but also highlighting how much remains to be done before a genuinely single market is achieved. A theme which runs through the book is indeed the contrast between vision and reality, and a questioning of whether the single market vision is realistic. What is important to preserve, of course, is the diversity of regional languages, cultures and traditions in Europe: there is a thin line at some points between eliminating supposed barriers to stimulate competition and maintaining the medley of European cultures.

Part Two on Mergers, Acquisitions and Cooperative Ventures is introduced by Mo Yamin, and includes chapters from Jim Hamill and Pam Castledine (Chapter 5), Fred Burton and Dorothea Noble (Chapter 6) and Richard Schoenberg (Chapter 7). As earlier comments have revealed, cross-border cooperation by firms has been regarded as one of the main mechanisms for achieving the economic gains from European integration. The methods by which two-way collaboration may occur are revealed in Burton and Noble's study of cooperative ventures between Spain and the UK; the motivation and contribution of these ventures to group strategy are also identified. However Schoenberg illustrates very clearly some of the problems in implementing cross-border acquisitions (and the problems would be shared with joint ventures and strategic alliances) which arise from divergent national cultures and corporate management styles; while Hamill and Castledine question the benefits which accrue to the national economy (using the case of the UK) from inward acquisitions.

In Part Three, also introduced by Mo Yamin, two chapters are presented on The Transition Process in Eastern Europe. The successful transition of Central and Eastern European (CEE) countries to market economies is and will continue to be one of the most important challenges in Europe for at least the next decade. Trevor Buck, Igor Filatotchev and Mike Wright (Chapter 8) review and evaluate employee buyouts (EBOs) in the process of Russian industrial privatisation: the authors provide arguments in support of EBOs, despite their giveaway nature, and speculate intriguingly on the future possibility of Western investors acquiring shares in privatised Russian firms. Paul Cook and Colin Kirkpatrick (Chapter 9) also examine privatisation programmes, but in this case making cross-country comparisons among the states of Central and Eastern Europe. It is concluded that privatisation in itself will ensure neither a rapid nor a smooth economic transition to a market based economy in these countries, with macroeconomic stability and a modern legal framework being pre-requisites for the sustained growth and development of the private sector. A reflective point reinforced by these chapters is the need for the EU to look outwards. The dangers of navel-gazing in a global era have been well illustrated in this introductory chapter. The need for widening and deepening of the EU to go hand in hand is thus emphasised.

Foreign direct investment (FDI) and the operations of MNEs are implicit in much of the discussion in this book, but Part Four on Strategies and Regulatory Aspects deals specifically with these topics, with an emphasis on US FDI. Introduced by Stephen Young, Jeremy Clegg (Chapter 10) reviews US FDI into the EU over a 40-year period and the studies which have been undertaken to explain long-term trends. Marina Papanastassiou and Robert Pearce (Chapter 11), by comparison, provide research results from their continuing work on technology creation and application by MNEs' subsidiaries in Europe; what is highlighted is the growing importance of technology creation by MNE subsidiaries especially in established R & D labs, with multinational affiliates based in the UK having a distinctive and more creative and autonomous technology role. To complete Part Four, Stephen Young, Neil Hood and Cameron Hood (Chapter 12) focus on FDI policy, evaluating prospects for policy reconciliation between the USA and the EU based on the economic impact of multinational activity in the two areas; this issue is of growing importance given the increased attention being paid to multilateral FDI policy in both the World Trade Organisation (WTO) and the Organisation for Economic Cooperation and Development (OECD). The book ends with a concise summary chapter by Peter Buckley, focusing on the conflicts brought about by regionalisation and globalisation in the context of the world economy. Recognising the dangers of introspection, Buckley highlights the fact that a 'Europe in transition' must face the challenges of the cultural and religious diversity of the future EU, as well as its relationships with other regional blocs and developing countries. As he remarks: 'The issues discussed in this book can justly claim to be universal and unresolved.'

Notes

1. Some of material in this section is reproduced from Young and Hood (1993).
2. This report on Industrial Competitiveness Policy is a follow-up to the Commission's White Paper on *Growth, Competitiveness and Employment* (1993) and to its report on *Industrial Policy in an Open and Competitive Environment* (1990).

References

Brewer, T. and Young, S. (1995) 'European union policies and the problems of multinational enterprises', *Journal of World Trade* (forthcoming).

Commission of the European Communities (CEC) (1993) *Growth, Competitiveness and Employment*, COM(93) 700 final (Brussels: CEC) (8 December).

Commission of the European Communities (CEC) (1994) *An Industrial Competitiveness Policy for the European Union*, COM (94) 319 final (Brussels: CEC) (14 September).

Council of the European Communities (1992) *Treaty on Economic Union* (Luxembourg: Office for Official Publications of the EC).

Delors Committee (1989) *Report on Economic and Monetary Union in the European Community* (Luxembourg: Office for Official Publications of the EC).

Emerson, M. *et al.* (1988) *The Economics of 1992: The EC Commission's Assessment of the Economic Effects of Completing the Internal Market* (Oxford: Oxford University Press).

Economic and Social Committee of the European Communities (CESC) (1994) *Opinion on The Annual Report on the Functioning of the Internal Market*, COM(94) 55 final 14–15 September (Brussels).

Eurostat (1994) *Basic Statistics of the Community* (Luxembourg: Office for Official Publications of the EC).

Financial Times (1994) *Can Europe Compete?* (London: *Financial Times* Ltd).

Henning, C.R., Hochreiter, E. and Hufbauer, G.C. (eds) (1994) *Reviving the European Union* April (Washington, DC: Institute for International Economics).

Mayes, D.G. *et al.* (1992) *The European Challenge : Industry's Response to the 1992 Programme* (London: Harvester Wheatsheaf).

Panić, M. (1988) *European Monetary Union* (London: Macmillan).

Robson, P. (ed). (1993) *Transnational Corporations and Regional Economic Integration*, United Nations Library on Transnational Corporations, 9 (London: Routledge).

Shackleton, M. (1994) The Internal Legitimacy Crisis of the European Union, *Occasional Paper*; 1 (Europa Institute, University of Edinburgh) (25 May).

Van den Bulcke, D. (1993) 'The European Community and the Trials of Maastricht: An International Management Perspective', *Discussion Paper* 1993/E/12 (Centre for International Management and Development, University of Antwerp).

Winters, L.A. (1993) 'The European Community : A Case of Successful Integration?', *Discussion Paper*, 755 (London: Centre for Economic Policy Research) (January).

Young, S. and Hood, N. (1993) 'Inward investment policy in the European Community in the 1990s', *Transnational Corporations*, pp. 35–62.

Part One

The Economy of the European Union – between Vision and Reality

Fred Burton

The two themes of Part One of the book focus on the failure of the European Union (EU) to confront directly the problem of chronic and high levels of unemployment (Jonathan Michie, Chapter 2) and on impediments that continue to restrain the integration and convergence of markets across the EU, drawing on the experiences of the retail financial services sector (Kate Prescott, Chapter 3) and retailing, with particular reference to home shopping (Elke Pioch and Paul Brook, Chapter 4).

Market integration was identified in the 1986 Single European Act as the key to employment, a vibrant competitive environment and economic growth. The vision was that a Single European Market (SEM), created from a supply-side attack on formal trade and market entry barriers – physical controls, technical standards, national regulations and fiscal distortions – would capture economies of scale, intensify competition, boost R&D spending and capital investment and reduce industries' costs by stimulating the cross-border movement of goods, services, labour and capital. This mid-1980s' initiative to achieve the single market objective initially identified in the 1957 Treaty of Rome had the backing of European firms, who had grown increasingly apprehensive about a condition diagnosed as 'Euro-sclerosis' – fragmented and highly regulated markets and a declining international competitiveness.

In the short-run period leading up to and beyond the Act, firms responded to the single market initiative (the so-called '1992' programme) with enthusiasm by adopting strategies to re-position their businesses in the EU through cross-border mergers, acquisitions and alliances and by targeting EU markets more than ever before. An initial surge towards integration has since given way to a slow and halting progress, sufficient to suggest that the '1992' programme is unlikely to meet its aims. Many intransigent barriers

21

remain in place that will allow national firms to continue to dominate their home market. Examples include bureaucratic procedures, insider networks, closed distribution channels, public procurement policies and consumer preferences dictated by habit and custom.

The '1992' programme promised a massive supply-side shock, but many of the directives to dismantle formal barriers gained approval only after they had been diluted to satisfy producers' lobbies and then began to be implemented in a feeble spirit. Firms were supportive of measures to lower costs but were less appreciative of those designed to create a more competitive environment. The single market vision has particularly met stiff resistance in the civil aviation, energy and telecommunications sectors, and across most sectors many technical, legal and administrative barriers still exist. These remaining barriers, of which demand-side cultural barriers are particularly impervious to the kinds of legislative action that underpin integration, and the inclination of countries to look after their own, will dictate the pace of further progress towards the integration and convergence of markets across the EU. Many of these obstacles are on display in the services sector. Measures to dismantle formal barriers in financial services, for example, have been laid down, but broken deadlines, remaining differences between national and European norms, and cultural influences form such pervasive barriers that individual suppliers find it impossible to penetrate markets outside their home markets with the range of products they are capable of providing. Similar impediments in the home shopping sector deny opportunities for cross-border expansion. In both sectors, users' charters to protect consumers' rights have been successfully challenged by trade associations.

If the EU exists to promote the welfare of its citizens, this is best achieved by the creation of jobs. The Cecchini Report (1988) predicted that by 1995 up to 5 million new jobs would have been created by the '1992' programme and that unemployment levels would fall by around 1.5 per cent. But the EU's largest producer and employer, the services sector, has failed to create sufficient jobs to compensate job losses in the manufacturing sector caused by de-industrialisation and productivity gains in excess of the growth of output. The contemporary conventional view is that unemployment is a consequence of labour costs and social welfare provision above the market-clearing level, uncompetitive markets and a high burden of taxation, the antidote being more flexible and competitive labour and product markets and smaller public sector deficits. The promise of lower costs and product and process innovations held out by the '1992' programme and the macroeconomic priorities accorded to the convergency requirements of monetary union, presumably, also account for the failure to confront unemployment directly with countervailing employment and industrial policies. The main failure of the EU, post-1986, in consequence, has been an inability to create jobs.

The problem of unemployment in the EU is taken up by Michie in Chapter 2, where he proposes a corporate state model which challenges conventional views, attributing unemployment instead to de-industrialisation, balance of payments constraints and flawed macroeconomic policies. Adopting a neo-Keynesian stance, Michie describes a vicious spiral of low pay, low productivity and low investment best corrected by collective bargaining, minimum employment rights, focused training programmes, controls on cross-border capital movements and a requirement that responsibility for corrections to trade and payment imbalances be taken by surplus countries. The Delors White Paper (1993), belatedly, focused attention on unemployment but failed to pursuade members to introduce schemes for regional development and job creation. The problem of what to do about unemployment is simply not on the EU agenda.

In Chapter 3, Prescott draws attention to cultural differences inside the EU and weaknesses in the '1992' programme which continue to block the access of retail financial services to cross-border markets. The UK made the first move inside the EU towards the deregulation and liberalisation of financial services by permitting formerly specialist firms to operate in product markets that had previously been denied to them. The '1992' programme sought similar effects elsewhere in the EU, but historical, cultural and demographic influences continue to sustain fragmented and insular markets. New products, processes and technologies, accordingly, are being introduced with varying speeds to EU markets, for example in retail banking, mortgages, and insurance and pensions' provision, so that no one country holds a dominant European position across the range of retail financial services. The author's survey of the UK, France, Germany and Spain reveals that firms do not expect a single market to develop by offering the same opportunities to firms as they have in their domestic markets.

A similar theme is pursued by Pioch and Brook in Chapter 4. They argue, additionally, that retailers have succeeded in bringing about changes in legislation sufficient to preserve the primacy of national retail markets. According to the authors, the impact of social, economic and cultural diversity inside the EU has been consciously neglected. The choice instead, as in other sectors, has been to pursue market integration and convergence with supply-side directives. In the home shopping sector, which is dominated by the world's largest mail order firms, the authors predict that the '1992' programme will assist the further globalisation of these firms rather than integrate EU markets. The retention of diverse national rules, for example those which leave consumers unprotected when cross-border shopping, constitutes a severe barrier to market convergence and will allow home shopping firms to continue with their country-focused perspectives.

Reference

Cecchini, P. (1988) 1992 – *The Benefits of a Single Market* (Aldershot: Wildwood House).

2 European Unemployment in a Global Recession

Jonathan Michie[1]

The world-wide growth of unemployment is 'the issue of the 1990s' and represents a 'dangerous potential for human strife' according to the 1993 UN *Human Development Report*. In Europe, unemployment is considered to be the 'most pressing problem' by two-thirds of European Union (EU) citizens.[2]

The first year of the (then) European Community's (EC's) Single Market – 1993 – saw a third year of slow growth, bringing the worst recession for two decades, with 18 million people unemployed in the 12 Member States. Britain saw negative growth rates for 1991 and 1992 from which it only weakly recovered in 1993 and 1994; this made Britain the only major EU country not in recession in 1993 – thanks to the interest rate cuts and devaluation which followed sterling's departure from the Exchange Rate Mechanism (ERM) in September 1992, despite the horrors which political leaders claimed would result from this.

Overall, employment in the EU fell by about three-quarters of a percentage point in 1992 – the first time since 1983 that the number of people in employment actually decreased. In absolute figures this means that in 1993 2 million fewer people than in 1991 were employed in the 12 Member States. At 11 per cent, unemployment had returned to the peak of 1985 – the gains made during the second half of the 1980s having been lost again in the first three years of the 1990s. This left less than 60 per cent of the EU's population of working age actually in work in 1993 compared with more than 70 per cent in the USA and Japan; there is therefore a pool of hidden unemployment which will still have to be absorbed before numbers on the dole will fall substantially.

Account thus needs to be taken of the 'non-employed': those who do not have jobs but are not registered as unemployed. The OECD prescription for unemployment, of cuts in the level and duration of unemployment benefits, risks simply pushing the unemployed off the official jobless count and into economic inactivity. The alternative of subsidising their employment, in either the private or public sectors, makes more sense than leaving the long-term unemployed to decay.

The rise in unemployment in Europe is not due to 'over-generous' benefits or labour market 'rigidities', but rather to the interrelation between macro economic policy, balance of payments constraints and de-industrialisation. The idea of pursuing active macroeconomic and industrial policies has given way to an adherence to monetarism, privatisation and labour market deregulation. Yet the resulting growth in low pay, poverty and unemployment have, ironically, placed an increasing burden on the public purse. At the same time, productive efficiency is harmed by the resulting instability in the labour market – particularly within the increasingly low-paid sectors – and the loss of incentives for producers to upgrade their productive systems. A vicious circle of low wage, low productivity, low investment activity is generated, leading to loss of competitiveness and growing unemployment, with the increasing burdens on exchequers provoking yet further moves down the recessionary spiral.

The second half of the 1980s was taken by the supporters of deregulation as proof of its economic benefits. Economic growth was relatively rapid, with some fall in unemployment, although this remained high. But at the end of the 1980s the revival came to an end with global recession and a return to mass unemployment, with the early 1990s having witnessed recession and unemployment comparable to the 1930s. Indeed, talk of the need for a 'New Deal' has re-entered the economic policy vocabulary. In April 1993, Japan's government introduced an £82 bn set of economy-boosting measures, including a £53 billion public works programme, while in the USA, Clinton was elected in 1992 on an explicitly interventionist economic platform. In the EU, on the other hand, even in late 1994, several months after the much heralded Delors White Paper, policy was still stuck on the policy path laid down by the Maastricht Treaty[3] – drawn up in the late 1980s era of economic growth, falling unemployment and concerns about rising inflation. Any suggestion that these should give way to fiscal and monetary policies for combating unemployment has consistently raised the spectre of high inflation in the minds of policy-makers.

A NON-ACCELERATING INFLATION RATE OF UNEMPLOYMENT?

This spectre receives its support in the economics literature from the idea that there is a unique 'Non-Accelerating Inflation Rate of Unemployment' (the 'NAIRU'): in other words, the assertion that there is one particular level of unemployment at which inflation stabilises. This NAIRU framework is unhelpful since it rests on the implicit assumption of unchanged and unspecified policies and practices. The relationship between unemployment and changes in earnings variously measured is plotted for Britain in the 1980s in Michie and Wilkinson (1992). The results could not be more at variance with the notion of a predictable relationship between the two variables. The historical evidence for any credible relationship between the level of joblessness and the rate of inflation is thus fragile at best.

This NAIRU theory is a version of Milton Friedman's 'Natural Rate of Unemployment' developed by the economists Richard Layard and Stephen

Nickell. They argue that as unemployment falls, the 'bargaining wage' demanded by workers rises whilst the 'feasible wage' which employers can afford to pay does not rise with output. This failure of the wage which employers can afford to pay to rise as output rises is based on one or both of two seriously flawed arguments.

First, it is supposed that as firms increase their level of output, productivity fails to rise and may fall. But, in fact, the opposite is usually the case: in economic expansions output per head generally rises (it increased 20 per cent between 1984 and 1990). This increase in productivity is explained by the fact that capital is operated at a higher level of utilisation as demand increases, and firms invest in more modern and productive equipment. The more reasonable assumption that productivity and hence the 'feasible wage' increases with output destroys one of the bases for the NAIRU law.[4] If increased capacity utilisation and, over the longer term, an increased and more technologically advanced capacity allows a growth of the feasible wage then there may be no unique 'equilibrium' point (NAIRU) with only that one level of unemployment associated with non-accelerating inflation. Thus, even if the bargaining and feasible wages happened to coincide at a given level of unemployment, if unemployment falls with the feasible wage increasing (due to increased productivity) more than the increase in the bargaining wage, then such a model would actually predict that the reduction in unemployment would result in inflation falling rather than rising.

The second string to the NAIRU bow is the argument that firms have to cut prices to sell more. By enabling firms to lower prices, cuts in wages and other employment costs allow them to sell more and to increase employment. But this argument is also fatally flawed. The size of the market of a firm (and hence the employment it can offer) is determined by its price *and* the price of its competitors. If the workers employed by that firm accept a lower wage so that the firm can retain its monopoly profits at a lower price, it will be able to increase its output and its market share but only at the expense of other firms and the employment they offer. But of course if all firms lower their wages there will be no change in relative prices and no increase in demand. In fact, if this happens, the chances are that demand will decline because a general fall in wages relative to prices will have reduced the purchasing power of wage income.

DE-INDUSTRIALISATION

The rise of unemployment in Europe can thus be more usefully analysed by ignoring such economic orthodoxy and referring instead to the interrelation between macroeconomic policy, balance of payments constraints and de-industrialisation. European unemployment has been accompanied by a relatively rapid decline in manufacturing employment. The share of employment in manufacturing fell in the decade 1976–86 from 22.8 per cent to 19.1 per cent in the USA, from 25.5 per cent to 24.7 per cent in Japan, and from 28.9 per cent to 24.4 per cent for what is now the EU. This relative decline represented an absolute fall, for Europe, of almost 5.5 million jobs. Of the EU countries, only Portugal and Greece avoided a fall in manufacturing employment, with the UK experiencing the most extreme cut (of 16 per cent, representing more than 2 million jobs).

There has been considerable debate over the causes of such 'de-industrialisation'.[5] A shift in employment from manufacturing to other sectors could simply be the result of a shift in consumption patterns away from manufactured goods towards services and/or differential productivity growth between the industrial and service sectors. However, two important points are clear: first, the decline in manufacturing employment in the EU has not been caused by shifts in consumption patterns, nor by other sectors' requirements for labour. The loss of manufacturing jobs has been accompanied by rising manufactured imports and by a rise in unemployment.

And secondly, as stressed by Ajit Singh in his original development of the concept of de-industrialisation (1987), an economy's distribution of output (and employment) between sectors can lead to balance of payments constraints, and hence can impact not just on relative shares of output and employment but also on absolute levels. It is this danger of a balance of payments constraint on economic recovery and the achievement of full employment which should be of concern for the EU in the 1990s.

Exchange rate mechanisms and the Balance of Payments have had two major implications for unemployment in Europe.[6] The ERM imposed requirements for monetary and interest rate policy, and domestic fiscal policy, which have been biased towards imposing deflationary interest rate rises on countries whose currency is under pressure, rather than reflationary policies on economies with strong currencies. Given the level of domestic demand so determined, the Balance of Trade indicates the degree to which this is translated into domestic production and employment.

It might be thought that trade imbalances within the EU could not have deflationary implications as a whole because deficits in some countries would be more or less offset by surpluses in others, so that any deflationary implications of deficits would thereby be balanced by expansionary implications for the surplus economies. The effects are not, however, quite so symmetrical. The key surplus economy has been Germany. The German productive system, stimulated as it has been by good labour and social welfare standards, extensive training and strong centralised collective bargaining, has since the Second World War generated competitiveness and hence the ability to export. The tight monetary policy pursued by the Bundesbank has sterilised the potentially reflationary impact of the resulting trade surplus by restricting domestic demand, translating growth into export surpluses.[7]

As for the deficit countries such as the UK, for any level of domestic demand, the more that is met by net imports, the lower is domestic output and employment. Thus, for example, the rise in consumer demand between 1978–81 and 1989–92 was met by net imports, resulting in a move from current account surplus (of 2.5 per cent of GDP) to deficit (of 3.8 per cent of GDP) – a swing of 6.3 per cent of GDP in real terms and an equivalent export of jobs. The increase in consumer expenditure represented a growing share (from 59.9 per cent to 65.9 per cent) of a GDP whose growth lagged behind. Indeed, although there was a rise in gross investment (from 16.5 per cent to 18.7 per cent of GDP), manufacturing investment actually fell as a share of GDP (from 3.0 per cent to 2.7 per cent).[8] The latest available figures show that even in 1992, at the depths of the longest recession since the 1930s, UK net imports were still equivalent to 1.7 per cent of GDP, with a lower share of GDP devoted to investment (at 15.1 per cent) than in Italy (20.3 per cent), France (20.7 per cent), West Germany (21.2 per cent) and Japan (30.9 per cent).[9]

FULL EMPLOYMENT IN THE FUTURE

Throughout the 1950s and 1960s almost all countries enjoyed full employment, meaning that anyone who wanted a job was generally able to find one. There was of course always some registered unemployment as people changed jobs, but the long-term involuntary unemployment of the inter-war period had gone. All this came to an end in the early 1970s, and the 1990s threaten to be the worst decade yet for mass unemployment. So full employment is certainly possible, but it will not return automatically. A return to full employment will require a fundamental change in government policy globally. Governments cannot be held responsible for everything; but what they can be held responsible for is government policy.

However, there are various arguments that suggest full employment may not even be a desirable objective. First, it has been argued that unemployment may be necessary to make those in employment work harder. But this ignores the rapid economic and social progress made during the 25 years from 1948 to 1973 when there was full employment, when economic growth was actually faster than it has been since, and when the response to wide job opportunities was a progressive workforce upgrading. Compare that with the cost of the enforced idleness and the enormous loss of prospects for those entering the labour market since the mid-1970s. Secondly, not everyone wants a full-time job. But they should be given that opportunity.

Thirdly, there are environmental constraints. This means we should think about the type of economic growth we want, not just the amount. But there is no reason to suppose that environmentally friendly economic progress is less labour intensive than a more environmentally unfriendly path. Nor that the physical environment will in any way be served by a progressive degeneration of the social environment.

There is a separate argument that full employment is no longer possible, however desirable, because new technology is displacing workers at a faster pace than the growth in demand can re-employ them. This is simply wrong. There is no evidence at all of a sea change in output per head. In fact, the rate of increase of labour productivity has slowed in the past two decades. Moreover, even a casual glance at the world today would indicate that public and private needs place few constraints on employment whatever the improvement in technology. There may be problems with the willingness or ability of present forms of political, social and economic organisation to meet even the basic requirements of the majority of the world's population, but that does not disguise the want.

A POLICY AGENDA

The industrial world is in the grip of an unemployment crisis of historic proportions which bears striking resemblance to its 1930s' predecessor. In the 1920s the world economy was highly volatile with unprecedented stock market and currency speculation. Organised labour was on the retreat and wage cutting and labour market deregulation was the order of the day. The consequent under-consumptionist tendencies were exacerbated by the collapse of commodity prices in the early 1920s which benefited industrial profits but ruined agriculture. This unstable economic base collapsed in 1929 when the world financial system was completely disrupted by the Wall Street crash and industry was undermined by the Great Depression against which national governments proved individually and collectively powerless.

Economic orthodoxy, then as now, held trade unions, state labour market regulation and social welfare payments responsible for unemployment and preached against state intervention to counter joblessness and for balanced budgets. When translated into policies these notions, by deepening the recession and multiplying social deprivation, had the opposite to the predicted effect and the consequent widening of the credibility gap led to weak and vacillating governments. In Britain, the Labour Government, split over policies which cut pay, reduced unemployment benefit levels and introduced means testing, policies which were insisted on by international bankers and finally implemented by the National Government led by Ramsay MacDonald. In Germany, 6 million unemployed, widespread poverty and cuts in unemployment pay paved the way for fascism and ultimately to the Second World War.

The lessons learned from this debacle, at the level of economic theory and public policy, laid the groundwork for the post-war prosperity. National governments committed themselves to full employment and a welfare state policy which included health, social security, education and housing. In the labour market, collective bargaining was encouraged, minimum employment rights guaranteed and industrial training strengthened. At the international level agreements on finance and trade were concluded which were designed to encourage international commerce but which were targeted at currency speculation and the problems of chronic surplus countries. These were reinforced at the national level by controls on international capital movements.

Contingency plans were made for the stabilisation of commodity prices, but these made little headway after the end of the Korean War crisis when the collapse of raw material prices turned the terms of trade in the favour of industrial countries. The purpose of these policies was to create a framework of rules for encouraging creativity of free enterprise whilst prohibiting the strong predatory and exploitative tendencies of capitalism.

This national and international collectivist effort created the promise that poverty would at last be lifted. This promise was most fully realised in those countries of Northern Europe which most completely adopted the co-operative state model; no more so than in Sweden where the Social Democratic Party embraced the 'wage solidarity' with 'active labour market' policies formulated by the trade unions so that labour effectively managed capitalism (on which, see Michie, 1994). At the international level the growth in the market of industrial countries helped create new opportunities for economic development. The real failure of the post-war period was at the international level. This can be explained by the dominant economic power of the USA and that country's continued adherence to the notion that capitalism operates at its best when completely unrestricted. This philosophy came to pervade the workings of the international agencies (IMF, World Bank, GATT) and subverted their role as agents working for world economic stability. The cost to the USA itself was great. Its own unrestricted capital moved the production base of the US economy off-shore and came increasingly to be dominated more by short-term speculation on the stock market than long-term industrial investment. This, and the fact that the degenerating industrial relations and labour market conditions in the USA made it incapable of meeting the quality competition from abroad, undermined American competitiveness so that it joined the UK as a newly de-industrialising economy.

This combination of, first, the lack of any effective stabilising international institutions and, second, the progressive decline in the economic power of the USA played a major part in recreating the sort of international finance and trade volatility last seen in the inter-war years. This undermined the ability of national governments to exercise control and destroyed the credibility of the policies which formed the basis for post-war economic prosperity. The return to the pre-Keynesian orthodoxy in macro-economic management completed the circle. Restrictive monetary policies, intensified competition for shares in markets which were growing more slowly than productive potential, and unrestricted currency speculation interacted to re-create world recession.

Unemployment today is not therefore the result of the working of mystical economic laws regulating wages. There is no substance to the claim that if the worst off in society accept a cut in their living standards, long-term prospects would thereby be restored; the opposite is more likely the case. Nor is unemployment the result of there being too little work needing doing to fully employ all those who seek employment. Both private need and public squalor are on the increase. The physical environment needs to be improved; more work should go into education, health and public services generally; housing and other infrastructure work would in almost all countries be welcome. The problem is not a shortage of things which need doing. It is a shortage of political will to do them.

Yet there is continuous pressure for cuts in taxes, for lower wages and for reduced social welfare contributions to be matched by cuts in government expenditure. The argument is that if the rewards to capital are increased then enterprise will be stimulated. But after a decade or more of 'putting capital first' in most EU states, where is the evidence of the renaissance?

A massive shift of income and wealth towards the rich took place on a global scale throughout the 1980s and has continued into the 1990s. Reversing this by increasing employment, cutting unearned speculative gains in the interest of benefiting creative enterprise instead and reducing the differential between the highest and lowest paid would relieve pressure on public finances as people were raised out of state dependency and as the costs of administering the tax/benefit system fell. Increased purchasing power from the developing countries globally, and from the mass of consumers in Europe, would allow demand to grow alongside supply. It is also within this context that the need for training should be seen, as training for jobs which are actually being created in the real economy and which will be sustained beyond the life of the associated training programme. Just as economic development can suffer from skill shortages, so training can suffer from lack of genuine job opportunities.

Job opportunities have to be created to suit people's needs and preferences. Where today there are people in the UK, such as security guards, having to work 80 hours a week to make up their take home pay of £100, that level of pay (and more) should be available for a 40-hour week. And even at that new rate of pay, in other words double the present level on an hourly basis, creating the additional jobs would not be expensive from the point of view of society as a whole since the cost of unemployment pay and so on would be saved and extra taxes would be paid. But while job sharing in this context can be a vital part of progressive advance, where it is achieved as a genuine right which workers can choose to exercise, it is important at the same time to guard against the all too common regressive use of such measures as employer-imposed tactics, often as a way of deliberately undermining employment rights.

It should also be recognised that many people may want to work who are prevented from doing so by the lack of adequate child-care facilities. Providing child-care would thus increase the number of people seeking work, but this should not be seen as a hurdle for the achievement of full employment: first, the disguised unemployment of having someone forced to stay at home to look after children is hardly an achievement, and secondly, the creation and development of a national child-care system – for after school care as well as for pre-school age provision – would itself be a labour intensive activity.

It is important, then, not to allow the progressive right to 'job share', or work flexible hours, to spread the illusion that there is only a given lump of work which has therefore to be spread around. The truth is that there are huge numbers of jobs which need doing which are simply not being done. Nevertheless, as part of a strategy for full employment, a reduction in working hours would help bring down unemployment further and more quickly. Historically the length of the working week has tended to remain more or less static for several decades, with a large reduction then being achieved, setting a new norm. The time for a major reduction is surely here again.

The lessons of history have to be re-learned. Just as today's economic orthodoxy represents a retreat by political commentators and ruling elites back to repeating the free market dogmas of the 1920s, so we need to remember the lessons learned at such enormous costs from the resulting Great Depression and the rise of fascism. At the international level those lessons included the need for really effective international agreements – not to 'set capital free' but rather to stabilise trade flows and restrict speculative activities.[10] At the national level there was not only a commitment in principle to full employment and a Welfare State, there was also a recognition of the need for generally applicable effective labour market and social conditions, including meaningful employment rights.[11]

EU POLICIES FOR JOBS

With Delors warning that even a recovery in growth in 1994 may not prevent the continued rise in unemployment to 20 million or more, the EU's December 1993 biannual summit was billed as the one which was to tackle unemployment. Indeed, Delors warned that the Union's unemployment total could be heading for 30 million by the late 1990s if the policies in his December 1993 White Paper were not adopted:

People who have jobs are being selfish – not only wage-earners, but their trade unions and employers. That must change if we are not to see 30 million unemployed by the end of the century...

Solidarity between people who have jobs and those who have not should be at the basis of society... We need a political and social dialogue

between those with jobs and those without to discuss the gains from productivity.[12]

Similar sentiments were articulated by the EU's social affairs commissioner,
Padraig Flynn, who described the White Paper as a plan for creating 20
million jobs by the end of the decade.[13] But will such measures really do
much more than re-arrange the deck chairs? And in these days of globalised
markets and foot-loose capital, is a proactive policy agenda from governments possible? European Commission president Jacques Delors has warned
against the ultimate horror – of an English-style Europe:

> What I see is a European construction drifting towards a free trade zone,
> that is to say an English-style Europe which I reject and which is against
> the spirit of the founding fathers of the Treaty of Rome . . .

> If we do nothing, this drift will lead in 15 years to a break-up [of the
> EU] . . . I reject a Europe that would be just a market, a free trade zone
> without a soul, without a conscience, without a political will, without a
> social dimension.[14]

At the same time, Mitterrand was calling for a doubling of the EU's spending on infrastructure and growth projects, as was Delors who was proposing
in particular a widening of the programme to include investment in labour
intensive sectors such as housing, as well as subsidising borrowing for small
and medium sized enterprises. Even these rather modest proposals were scorned
by the German and British governments. Indeed, less than half the £5.6
billion earmarked for recovery projects by the European Investment Bank
had been committed by the end of October 1993, with Commission officials
blaming the low take-up on the lack of commercially viable investment projects
– hardly surprising in a recession – and because companies were failing to
provide the matching finance required from the private sector.

  While the Delors White Paper (CEC, 1993) was therefore welcome inso-
far as it went some way towards shifting the focus of policy onto the problem of unemployment, it remained hopelessly compromised by its failure to
break from the policy strait-jacket within which the Maastricht Treaty has
trapped governments.[15]

  The jobs initiative debated at the EU's previous summit, in Copenhagen
in June 1993, involved radical changes in the Union's tax and social security
systems. The Commission wanted member states to reduce employers' national
insurance contributions, shifting the tax burden onto others. The rationale
for such policies is that non-wage costs such as firms' social security payments add far more in the EU states on average than they do in Japan or the
USA. Yet such non-wage costs are already down to Japanese and US levels
in Britain, so there is clearly no automatic link between this and low unem-

ployment. Indeed, employment in manufacturing – which should be particularly sensitive to factors affecting competitiveness – is lower in Britain as a percentage of the population in work than it is in Germany or France, despite the far higher indirect employment costs in those countries.

An additional policy idea from the Commission has been to introduce such reductions in employer taxes on unskilled labour in particular. On the general idea of an employment subsidy, expanded public employment would be a more effective method of tackling unemployment, particularly if there are either inflation or balance of payments constraints. The specific idea of a differential subsidy for unskilled work – generally defined in these contexts as low paid work, which raises a rather separate issue of why skills such as cooking or cleaning tend not to be recognised as skills – risks reducing firms' incentives to improve productivity and upgrade productive techniques.

Indeed, investment in R&D is already lower in the EU than in Japan or America. In 1987 the EU went into a deficit on international trade of high-tech goods – a deficit which has been deepening since. Yet while both Japan and the USA announced public measures in 1993 to boost spending on R&D, the EU remained preoccupied with Maastricht.

As for Maastricht itself, despite its ratification, no Member State other than Luxembourg met its convergence criteria in 1993 – and even Luxembourg failed the inflation test. It is vital that these convergence criteria give way to policies for recovery. Quite apart from the short-term damage which adherence to the convergence criteria would cause, the longer term aim of monetary union is ill-conceived without major political and economic changes not envisaged in the Delors Report or Maastricht Treaty. Thus, for example, the MacDougall Report (CEC, 1977) suggested that a Community budget equivalent to 7 per cent of GDP would be necessary just to tackle 40 per cent of existing inequalities, yet the budget at present is set at 1.27 per cent and the more ambitious proposal rejected at the 1992 Edinburgh summit was for this to have risen to only 1.38 per cent. And the Treaty's specific provisions, such as the requirement for an independent Central Bank, with an over-riding objective of achieving price stability, would risk locking the Union into recession.

Behind the present talk of jobs packages, therefore, lies the longer-term agenda of economic and monetary union. What has been amply demonstrated in the academic and policy literature is that measured against the criteria for being an 'optimum currency area', even the present 12 Member States (never mind a Union with additional members) falls some way short, and this shortfall would have to be made up – if the process of integration is to proceed, and to do so without straining cohesion to breaking point – by active industrial and regional policies to ensure the continual (not just one-off) economic adjustments to so-called 'shocks', and more generally, to different levels and growth rates of output and productivity.[16]

With talk today of the possibility of a 'two-speed Europe' – with Germany and the Benelux countries (with or without France) moving more rapidly to monetary union – it is worth recalling that the ill-fated Gold Standard did not collapse in one go in the 1930s: some countries attempted to maintain the fixed exchange rate system, thus heralding a two- (or multi-) tier system (see Kitson and Michie, 1994a). The ones who stuck with the system grew more slowly, those who left first grew fastest. Hence the 'speed' with which countries move towards fixed exchange rate systems should not be confused with the speed at which their economies will grow. In a two-speed Europe the 'slow' lane may be preferable.

Of course, one of the stock responses to any call for growth is to refer to the expansionary policies of the Mitterrand Government in 1981, and subsequent U-turn of 1983. The orthodox interpretation of this experience is that the Keynesian policies were discovered to be unsustainable because of balance of payments and exchange rate constraints and hence had to be abandoned. This is (as argued by Halimi *et al.*, 1994) simply false: these difficulties were not learned from the 1981–3 experience in France but were perfectly well understood and stated quite explicitly by, amongst others, the French Socialist Party before taking office. The problems which any government pursuing such expansionary policies would encounter were documented in advance, as were the additional policies which would be necessary to see through the expansion – including the use of trade policies to ensure that imports grew only in line with exports. The point is that no attempt was, in fact, made to actually introduce these additional, necessary policies; the government instead chose the beggar-my-neighbour route of 'competitive disinflation'.

While coordination is preferable (as pointed out by Kalecki in 1932), there are nevertheless viable programmes for raising employment in a single country; indeed, the only way of building support for an EU-level expansion may be through the contagious impact of a successful expansion of employment in one country first.

Indeed, the 'cooperative' route – of completing the internal market and pursuing economic and monetary union – has tended to increase industrial concentration and exacerbate regional disparities, and an active industrial policy is instead needed to ensure the development of industrial activity outside the European core. To consider the nature which such an interventionist strategy to bolster industrial performance might take, it is necessary to draw a distinction between the notion of a developmental state, organised and concerned to promote economic and industrial development, on the one hand, and a regulatory state on the other, concentrating instead on competition policy. A broadly conceived industrial strategy (as opposed to just a 'policy') is needed to offset the forces of cumulative causation which otherwise will increase disparities and exacerbate the under-utilisation of resources in backward regions in particular.

A range of exchange rate issues also need further analysis, including how to overcome the 'fault lines' of the ERM. Problems caused by currency speculation could be tackled by taxing foreign exchange market transactions, simply reducing the profitability of such activity. Speculators might move 'off-shore', but in that case their transactions could be exempted from legal status so that unpaid debts would not be backed by the force of law.

In the short term, changes in the conduct of monetary and fiscal policies are needed so that they support rather than impede growth, and structural policies need strengthening to boost development and job creation in those regions which are most in need. Longer-term policies are then also needed for boosting investment – and developing mechanisms for funding public investment – as well as for developing specific job creation measures.

Current levels of unemployment are a reflection of the political priorities attached to different objectives of economic policy. The low demand created by monetarist and restrictive economic policies has eroded the capacity to produce: plant capacity, management structures, sales organisation, skilled and experienced labour, and the number of firms have all settled down at a level consistent with 9–10 per cent unemployment. Higher demand is therefore needed, but it would have to be sustained if capacity is to be rebuilt. This is unlikely with an independent European Central Bank dedicated to the achievement of price stability. The emphasis has to be shifted towards restoring full employment.

CONCLUSIONS

Even the IMF believes that labour market policies 'have been unsuccessful in addressing persistently high unemployment, especially in Europe'. Much of the criticism from the IMF's spring 1993 *World Economic Outlook* was reserved for the EU countries; despite cuts in short-term German interest rates monetary conditions were held to be tight, exacerbated by 'substantial interest rate differentials relative to Germany, associated with recent exchange rate turbulence'; the weakness of the German economy was said to justify further cuts in interest rates; and economic recovery was predicted for Britain only because of the lower interest rates coming from sterling's departure from the ERM.

And the OECD's 1993 *Annual Report* on labour market trends stressed the importance of long-term commitments in the workplace and active labour market management – with the *Financial Times* noting the irony of the OECD, usually associated with a more pro-market approach than the European Commission, emphasising long-term human resource development at a time when the EU was considering further deregulation.[17]

Unemployment in the EU can in large part, then, be attributed to restrictive macro-economic policies, and its distribution between Member States by a failure to develop balance of payment adjustment mechanisms which do not throw the burden of adjustment on the deficit countries. Persistent unemployment is creating increasing pressure for the abandonment of minimum social welfare levels, labour market standards and employment rights, orchestrated by free marketeer theorists who mystify real world processes by reference to immutable economic laws which load the responsibility for economic stagnation onto its principal victims.

With its escalating internal problems there is every danger that the EU will drift towards poverty, low wages and poor employment conditions for a large and growing section of its workforce. The economic, social and political dangers in this cannot be overemphasised and their avoidance depends on the ability of the countries of Europe to come together to produce expansionary policies which have at their core full employment and high and equitable social welfare and labour standards. In economic terms a strong welfare state is essential for a healthy, well educated and well trained work force; high wage and employment standards are essential for inducing the most effective use of such a workforce; and full employment is the guarantee that no part of the workforce is diverted into non-productivity. To achieve this collectively the European states require two essential safeguards regulating their relationships: first, measures are needed to deal with countries with persistent balance of payments surpluses so as to prevent deficit countries adopting deflationary policies, thereby beggaring themselves and their neighbours; secondly, centrally enforced common labour and social standards are required to prevent companies and nation states competitively devaluing their workers.

Notes

1. This chapter reports work done with Frank Wilkinson (Michie and Wilkinson 1992, 1993, 1994, 1995; Deakin, Michie and Wilkinson, 1992) and by the various authors of Michie and Grieve Smith (1994).
2. Gallup poll published by the European Commission, reported in the *Guardian* (19 October 1993).
3. See Michie (1993) for an analysis of the dangers which implementation of the Maastricht Treaty's provisions could pose for social and economic welfare.
4. For a discussion of wages and productivity in the business cycle, see Michie (1987).
5. See, for example, Singh (1987) and Rowthorn and Wells (1987).
6. For an analysis of the political economy of trade and trade policy in this context, see Kitson and Michie (1994b, 1995a).
7. See Joan Robinson (1966) – her inaugural lecture entitled 'New Mercantilism'.
8. For an analysis of Britain's relative economic decline which argues that underinvestment in manufacturing has been particularly damaging, see Kitson and Michie (1995b).
9. Datastream and WEFA, reported in the *Financial Times* (26 April 1993). The figures for France and Italy are the latest available, referring to 1991.

10. For a discussion of economic and employment policy in the context of international business and foreign direct investment, including the influence of multinational enterprises, see Porter (1994) and the various authors in Michie and Grieve Smith (1995), and in particular Kozul-Wright (1995); Porter challenges the idea that globalisation has made geography unimportant, and Kozul-Wright, in addition to making similar points to Porter, reports a wealth of new data on multinational investment and other activities and discusses the policy implications of these developments. For an analysis of the 'globalisation' of multinational firms' activities, see Archibugi and Michie (1995a, 1995b).
11. On which, see Sengenberger and Wilkinson (1995).
12. Jacques Delors, quoted in the *Guardian* (14 October 1993).
13. Padraig Flynn, quoted in the *Guardian* (20 October 1993).
14. Jacques Delors, speaking on Luxembourg radio (17 October). His remarks were published by the Commission on 18 October, as reported in the *Guardian* (19 October 1993).
15. For a full critical assessment of the Delors White Paper, see Grieve Smith (1994).
16. Similar concerns about the North American Free Trade Agreement (NAFTA) are reported to have played a part in the greatest parliamentary defeat in world history, suffered by the Canadian government in October 1993 (whose representation fell from 169 seats to 2).
17. See the report in the *Financial Times* (21 July 1993).

References

Archibugi, D. and Michie, J. (1995a) 'Technology and innovation: an introduction', *Cambridge Journal of Economics*, (1) (February).

Archibugi, D. and Michie, J. (1995b) 'The globalisation of technology: a new taxonomy',*Cambridge Journal of Economics*, (1) (February).

Commission of the European Communities (CEC) (1977) 'Report of the Study Group on the Role of Public Finance in European Integration', *Economic and Financial Series* 13, vol. I and II ('The MacDougall Report'), Luxembourg.

Commission of the European Communities (CEC) (1993) *Growth, Competitiveness, Employment: The Challenges and Ways Forward into the 21st Century* (Luxembourg: Commission of the European Communities) (December) ('The Delors White Paper').

Deakin, S., Michie, J. and Wilkinson, F. (1992) *Inflation, Employment, Wage-bargaining and the Law* (London: Institute of Employment Rights).

Grieve Smith, J. (1994) 'The Delors White Paper on Unemployment', *International Review of Applied Economics*, (3) (September), pp. 341–7.

Halimi, S., Michie J. and Milne, S. (1994) 'The Mitterrand Experience', Chapter 6 in J. Michie and J. Grieve Smith (eds), *Unemployment in Europe* (London: Academic Press).

International Monetary Fund (IMF) (1993) *World Economic Outlook* (Washington, DC: IMF).

Kalecki, M. (1932) 'Is a Capitalist Overcoming of the Crisis Possible?', and 'On the Paper Plan', in J. Osiatynski (ed.), *Collected Works of Michal Kalecki* (Oxford: Oxford University Press, 1990).

Kitson, M. and Michie, J. (1994a) 'Depression and Recovery: Lessons from the Interwar Period', Chapter 5 in J. Michie and J. Grieve Smith (eds), *Unemployment in Europe* (London: Academic Press).

Kitson, M. and Michie, J. (1994b) 'Conflict, Cooperation and Change: The Political Economy of Trade and Trade Policy', European Association of Evolutionary Political Economy (EAEPE), *Conference Papers* (October) (Copenhagen: EAEPE).

Kitson, M. and Michie, J. (1995a) 'Trade and Growth: A Historical Perspective', Chapter 1 in J. Michie and J. Grieve Smith (eds) *Managing the Global Economy* (Oxford: Oxford University Press).

Kitson, M. and Michie, J. (1995b) 'Britain's Industrial Performance Since 1960: Underinvestment and Relative Decline' (Cambridge) (mimeo).

Kozul-Wright, R. (1995) 'Transnational Corporations and the Nation State', Chapter 6 in J. Michie and J. Grieve Smith (eds), *Managing the Global Economy* (Oxford: Oxford University Press).

Michie, J. (1987) *Wages in the Business Cycle: An Empirical and Methodological Analysis* (London: Frances Pinter).

Michie, J. (1993) *Maastricht – Implications for Public Services* (Manchester: UNISON).

Michie, J. (1994) 'Global Shocks and Social Corporatism', in R. Delorme and K. Dopfer (eds), *The Political Economy of Complexity* (Aldershot: Edward Elgar).

Michie, J. and Grieve Smith, J. (eds) (1994) *Unemployment in Europe* (London: Academic Press).

Michie, J. and Grieve Smith, J. (eds) (1995) *Managing the Global Economy* (Oxford: Oxford University Press).

Michie, J. and Wilkinson, F. (1992) 'Inflation Policy and the Restructuring of Labour Markets', Chapter 9 in J. Michie (ed.), *The Economic Legacy: 1979–1992* (London: Academic Press).

Michie, J. and Wilkinson, F. (1993) *Unemployment and Workers' Rights* (London: Institute of Employment Rights).

Michie, J. and Wilkinson, F. (1994) 'The Growth of Unemployment in the 1980s', Chapter 1 in J. Michie and J. Grieve Smith (eds) *Unemployment in Europe*, (London: Academic Press).

Michie, J. and Wilkinson, F. (1995) 'Wages, Government Policy and Unemployment', *Review of Political Economy*, 7(2) (Special Issue on 'High Unemployment in Western Economies).

Porter, M.E. (1994) 'The Role of Location in Competition', *Journal of Economics of Business*, 1(1) (February), pp. 35–9.

Robinson, J. (1966) 'The New Mercantilism', *An Inaugural Lecture* (Cambridge: Cambridge University Press), reprinted in *Collected Economic Papers*, vol. 4 (Oxford: Blackwell, 1973).

Rowthorn, R.E. and Wells, J. (1987) *Deindustrialisation and Foreign Trade* (Cambridge: Cambridge University Press).

Sengenberger, W. and Wilkinson, F. (1995) 'Globalization and Labour Standards', Chapter 5 in J. Michie and J. Grieve Smith (eds), *Managing the Global Economy* (Oxford: Oxford University Press).

Singh, A. 1987, 'De-industrialisation', in J. Eatwell, M. Milgate and P. Newman (eds), *The New Palgrave Dictionary of Economics* (London: Macmillan).

3 Strategic Opportunities for Retail Financial Service Firms in the Single European Market

Kate Prescott

INTRODUCTION

The removal of physical, fiscal and technical barriers and the introduction of a common competition policy designed to establish a 'level playing field' are the central tenets of the Single European Market (SEM) initiative. The underlying aim of these initiatives is to provide a more open and competitive environment for firms operating within the European Union (EU) – a 'single market' devoid of inter-country market imperfections which have, to date, stunted the development of firms within the fragmented European arena.

What these policies do not address, however, is the vast cultural differences between the 12 Member States which continue to dog the firms attempting to secure wider business coverage in the new unified Europe. It is barriers such as these which demonstrate the wide gulf between the notion of a 'single market', based on free market entry, and a 'homogeneous market' in which product standardisation and the promise of greater scale economies and efficiency may be achieved. The architects of the Single Market envisage that, in time, as firms expand their activities across Europe, common strategies will emerge and greater harmonisation be realised. This suggests that firms will be the key 'change agents' in the process of harmonisation, and thus much depends on their ability and/or willingness to become major pan-European players (Welford and Prescott, 1994).

Through an assessment of the European environment for financial services (particularly at the outset of the SEM initiative) and the international business strategies open to financial service firms in their attempts to Europeanise, this chapter questions whether European expansion is viable and, if so, to what extent it will permit greater harmonisation of business practices across the EU. The chapter begins by analysing why the retail financial service provides an interesting case for analysis, addresses some of the main theoretical issues (drawn from extant international business literature on the internationalisation of services), reviews the nature of the European business environment and then proceeds with a review of some of the strategic considerations of a sample of retail financial service firms. This information is drawn from a survey conducted in the summer of 1989, at a point when most retail financial service firms were considering the implications of European integration and the potential for European expansion. The sample includes 29 European institutions from the UK, France and Germany. The chapter concludes by attempting to predict the future direction of the industry in terms of harmonisation and market homogeneity.

THE RETAIL FINANCIAL SERVICES INDUSTRY – A CASE FOR ANALYSIS

The retail financial services industry, as distinct from multinational and corporate banking, may be defined as the provision of financial products to individual customers and small firms. This involves a broad group of financial institutions (including banks, insurance companies, housing finance suppliers, credit companies, brokers and investors) and a myriad of product types from simple savings and investment instruments through credit facilities and on to the growing range of personal equity plans, life assurance products, and stocks and shares. For ease of analysis, this report concentrates on the dominant suppliers across Europe, the banks, housing finance suppliers and insurance companies.

The Cecchini Report (1989), commissioned by Lord Cockfield, then President of the Committee of the European Communities, undertook a major review of the benefits of the Single Market. The report focused on a number of industries on which the Single Market initiative was expected to have greatest impact. Among these was the retail financial services sector, which the report suggested would expand rapidly post-1992 as firms took advantage of the wide cost/price differentials and broad market differences pertaining in the Europe-wide industry.

At the time of writing, the authors could not have foreseen the impact on the financial services sector of the recession of the late 1980s and early 1990s which resulted in a downturn in consumer demand and thus a fall in the demand for some financial service products. Nevertheless, in 1991, European lending totalled $4705.1b and consumer spending on housing stood at $523399m, compared with a GDP rate of approximately $6940.2 billion (*Eurostat*, 1994). There are also grounds to suggest that there is potential for further penetration in many EU markets. Table 3.1 highlights statistics on personal finance usage in the 12 Member States and demonstrates that (in theory at least) market saturation in certain areas has not been reached.

Table 3.1 shows that the UK is one of the most developed markets in Europe in terms of usage of banking products. However, in Europe, as elsewhere in the world, the banks are losing their share of households' financial

Table 3.1 Personal finance, per cent of persons in each Member State

Country	Bank Account	Cheque Book	Card	Use card instead of cash
Belgium	81	56	51	18
Denmark	94	43	43	15
France	88	84	53	39
Germany (W)	89	57	38	10
Greece	56	3	2	8
Ireland	63	33	30	14
Italy	57	39	16	6
Luxembourg	87	70	40	31
Netherlands	87	65	61	19
Portugal	68	53	22	7
Spain	69	22	30	13
UK	81	70	60	41

Source: Eurostat (1994).

assets to non-bank institutions such as housing finance providers and insurance companies. In the USA, for example, banks' share fell from 27 per cent in 1977 to 23 per cent in 1987. In the UK the figure fell from 12.5 per cent in 1980 to 9 per cent in 1987. This reflects a trend across the developed markets for financial service liberalisation which has opened up new financial service instruments for customers.

The UK's relatively developed position is partly attributable to market liberalisation. The Financial Services Act 1986 and the Building Societies Act 1986 changed the nature of the UK market place with banks, building societies and insurance companies permitted to operate in each others' business sphere for the first time. The greater competition this engendered led to far greater choice for consumers, both in terms of price and product variety, and the development of new, innovative products and services. The packages set out by the European Commission for liberalisation across Europe are designed to produce a similar effect. For retail financial services there are four main directives concerned with:

- The freedom to establish branches and sell services in other Member States
- Some harmonisation of activities (in particular the form of public accounts, reserve ratios and credit guarantees)
- The introduction of a single banking licence permitting all European based firms to operate freely on foreign soil
- Reciprocity provisions by non-Community financial institutions operating in Europe.

Full harmonisation of standards across the Community is not possible. The broad differences in legislation (discussed in the following section) militate against establishing a single set of rules for controlling all institutions which are, to a great extent, integral to individual Member States' economic welfare. As is the case in many other industries, the rulings of the Council of Ministers favour the notion of 'mutual recognition', which asserts that products accepted for sale in their own domestic market should be automatically accepted by the legislators of the remaining 11 Member States. The only grounds for refusing access to products and services from other countries is on the basis of their posing a threat to national health and safety or 'the public good'. Scope for protectionism at a national level is therefore severely limited, although there have been cases in the retail financial service sector where governments have questioned product access on the basis of national welfare. The Belgian government, for example, were reluctant to accept the products of a UK life insurer providing pensions on the grounds that the levels of risk associated with the product were deemed to be potentially damaging to consumer welfare. Their claim did not, however, stand up in the European Courts, where it was ruled that the risks associated with the product were adequately communicated to consumers.

Less obvious barriers, however, still remain: host country authorities are permitted to impose a three month delay before a branch can be established (in addition to a three-month delay for home country approval). A month's notice is also required before the introduction of a new service. This constrains response times to changes in market conditions in an industry which is characterised by rapid new product development, potentially putting foreign entrants at a disadvantage.

The new legislation, then, provides a common framework for firms establishing a pan-European coverage. It does not, however, in itself, establish a homogeneous market for financial services or eradicate the strategic barriers of Europeanisation.

FOREIGN MARKET SERVICING – THE CHALLENGE FOR FINANCIAL SERVICE FIRMS

Freedom to offer products across borders or establish foreign facilities to service the needs of overseas consumers not only assumes that the environment for such activity is favourable, it also demands that strategies can be easily developed to take advantage of such opportunities.

The pioneering work of Hymer (1960), often believed to be the foundation for modern international business thinking, asserted that firms entering foreign markets need some form of compensating advantage in order to compete abroad with local firms which have innate strengths in terms of their understanding of the local market and their established customer franchise. Thus, the necessary condition for retail financial service firms to exploit the advantages provided by the removal of barriers in the European industry is the existence of some form of comparative advantage which can be transferred across markets. This theme is central to the discussion of environmental differences in retail financial services across the 12 Member States of Europe.

The literature on foreign market servicing, which is principally based on the experience of manufacturing firms, typically accepts that firms can choose between three generic groups of strategy: exporting, licensing and foreign direct investment (FDI) (a full review is presented in Young *et al*, 1989). The literature also refers to foreign market servicing as a dynamic process which most usually involves firms shifting from the least cost/risk options of exporting to more committed forms of foreign direct investment (Vernon, 1966; Johanson and Widershiem-Paul, 1975; Buckley and Casson, 1981), with some examples concentrating on the practicalities of within-mode shifts such as those from exporting via a foreign agent to the establishment of a company dedicated sales/marketing office (Buckley *et al.*, 1992a). In the area of retail financial services, however, certain factors pertinent to the specific nature of services produce a range of available options (and motivations) which differs somewhat from the received theory.

Most services cannot be transported (exported) (Rathmell, 1966; Berry, 1980; Thomas, 1978) and their production and consumption – the inseparability factor – frequently take place simultaneously (Regan, 1963; Lovelock, 1981). These effects can be seen in relation to savings and investment products and the provision of financial advice. In other product areas, however, where there is a physical element of transfer and the 'product' is distinct from the production process (Boddewyn *et al.*, 1986), such as credit cards and insurance documentation, it is possible for institutions to service the market from a distance. Similarly, the notion of 'intangibility' features large in the service sector, which makes it difficult for firms operating at a distance to establish a clear image in the market and engender customer confidence as the products and services they offer cannot be judged until they have been consumed. As a result of these factors there is, unsurprisingly, a greater propensity for firms to enter into forms of FDI in many service sectors, the retail financial service industry being no exception.

A further distinguishing feature of services is their 'heterogeneous' nature. This principally stems from the fact that many services are 'people provided', which makes it very difficult to standardise levels of service and quality between the provision of services. People are therefore a critical asset in service industries and no more so than in the financial service sector where shrewd money managers have typically been the mainstay of many firms' business success. In today's environment, as retail financial service firms are increasingly being forced to face up to new competitive challenges as a result of market liberalisation and deregulation, marketing and sales skills are also becoming a critical feature of the industry as firms vie with each other for market share and sales revenue.

Where FDI is a prerequisite of doing business abroad (principally where production and consumption cannot be separated) there are important ramifications for the dynamics of market servicing. With many manufactured goods, there is the potential for suppliers to take an incremental approach to foreign expansion, initially testing out market opportunities through low risk, low investment export strategies, raising their commitment at a later date when they have established a market presence and achieved a certain level of sales. With many services this is not possible, which raises the risks associated with first moves. For many, the only potential means of lowering initial risk and testing out opportunities is through the establishment of a joint venture with a local company (Buckley *et al.*, 1992b). This allows them to overcome the barriers of 'foreignness' and establish a forum for learning about the foreign market and drawing on the experience of indigenous firms.

The main implication of this is that foreign expansion by many financial service firms necessitates up-front investment and a high degree of risk, whether it be in terms of acquiring an existing operation or entering into a joint venture. As industry characteristics preclude gradually moving up the learning curve and deepening overseas involvement in an incremental way, it is also possible to suggest that there are major perceptual barriers for retail financial firms considering venturing abroad for the first time. From this perspective, the move to European expansion is not automatic.

THE EUROPEAN ENVIRONMENT FOR RETAIL FINANCIAL SERVICES

Historical development of retail financial service markets across Europe has given rise to a market which is far from homogeneous. Broad differences exist in terms of supply, demand and competitive conditions across the 12 Member States. Within a chapter of this scope it is not possible to explore all these factors in depth. What follows, therefore, is a brief outline of some of the major differences which help to clarify the nature of heterogeneity in retail financial services as the Single European Market Act begins to take effect.

The Supply of Retail Financial Services

The supply of retail financial service products depends critically on regulatory environments. At a national level, deregulation and privatisation have figured large in the big four European markets (Germany, France, Italy and the UK) in recent years resulting in intensified competition characterised by renewed vigour in price competition, product innovation and the introduction of new financial instruments. Diversification and the genesis of the

Table 3.2   Relative cost/price* positions, banking products

	Belgium	Spain	France	Germany (W)	Ireland	Netherlands	UK
Consumer credit	41	39	105	136	NA	31	121
Credit cards	74	26	–30	60	89	43	16
Mortgages	31	118	78	57	–4	–6	–20

* per cent discrepancies from price of average lowest four producers.
Source: Cecchini (1989).

concept of 'Allfinanz' (financial supermarkets offering a comprehensive portfolio of products, including housing finance and insurance which were, for some banks, outside of their traditional scope), and the pursuit of cost-saving opportunities (often leading to business rationalisation and redundancies) have also become commonplace.

Table 3.2 outlines the relative cost/price data for a range of generic banking products in a number of Member States which formed the cornerstone of Cecchini's (1989) arguments regarding the potential for cost saving advantages in Europe and expansion by the most efficient firms. Many of the differentials are significant, although it is interesting to note that no one country appears to have an advantage in all product groups.

From the perspective of international strategic planning, the data suggests that firms from particular countries have a comparative advantage, in price terms, in certain areas of retail financial service provision such that in the areas of consumer credit, credit cards and mortgages, the necessary condition for internationalisation (discussed earlier) appears to exist. However, price differences are only one area where markets differ markedly. Over the last decade, the nature of the retail financial service industry has changed dramatically with the introduction of computerised banking services. The extent to which countries have moved towards the provision of automatic teller machines (ATMs) to supplement traditional bank branches provides an indication of the willingness of Member States to embrace new strategic challenges in retail banking, and also raises questions over the extent to which individual Member States' financial institutions are moving away from being money speculators to becoming service providers. Automation implicitly means that financial firms can rely less and less on the 'float', the lag between the time when payments are received and when they are credited to customers, and thus have to pay attention to securing revenue from selling new products and services (*The Economist*, 1989).

Figure 3.1 shows the differences in branch structure (measured by the number of inhabitants per branch) and ATM density between Member States and serves as a proxy measure for levels of automation and focus on service provision.

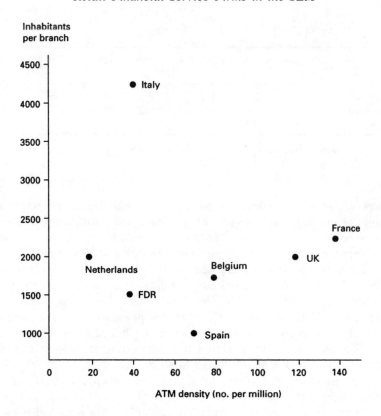

Source: Beddows and Co. data in 1992.

Figure 3.1   Branch structure and ATM density, 1990

Taking the view that ATM density equates with technological sophistica-tion and thus a move towards service related banking, France and the UK lead the field in terms of development. Italy, the Netherlands and Germany show the least developed markets in this respect. It is possible to suggest, therefore, that these markets are ripe for foreign penetration particularly by UK and French firms which have had to develop their skills in service pro-vision and marketing effort to survive. Italy provides and interesting outlier in relation to branch density, lagging far behind the other countries charted in the number of branches per customer. Legislative restrictions, which have resulted in a market dominated by a large number of small regionalised banks with limited branch coverage, principally account for this position although changes in government policy in recent years have fostered national expansion by many small banks and nurtured mergers between institutions. Such dynamism is not reflected in the 1990 data. This suggests that legisla-tive change and market liberalisation has an important role to play in foster-

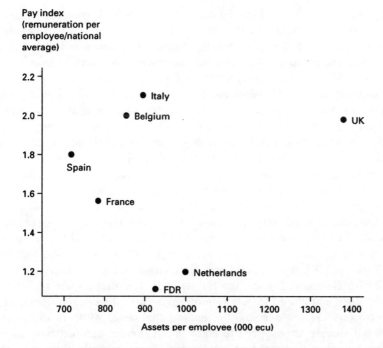

Figure 3.2 Productivity and wage levels of EU banks, 1990

ing the development of service related banking, although it is necessary to question the extent of such change in the light of France's leading position in ATM density. Liberalisation in France took place some years after liberalisation in the UK and yet it has developed a broader network of ATM coverage. French banks, unlike many of their other European counterparts, followed a policy of joint ATM network development at a very early stage in their expansion into technological service provision. As costs of network development could therefore be shared, the expansion rate was rapid.

With people being a critical asset in the financial services industry, it is also useful to consider inter-state differences in productivity and wages. Figure 3.2 presents a comparison of productivity (measured by assets per employee) and wages (measured by dividing the average remuneration of bank employees by the national average). The productivity data may be viewed as a proxy for efficiency. The pay index, on the other hand, may be regarded as a proxy for skilled labour and, in turn, is indicative of the importance placed on the retail financial service sector as a key contributor to national economic returns.

Italy leads the pay index with bank employees being paid 2.2 times the national average. Italy is followed by the UK where employees are paid approximately twice the national average. By attracting highly qualified individuals, the banking sector in these countries possibly benefits from 'skills' assets in the workforce, enhancing competitive potential. Nevertheless, this argument should be treated with a degree of caution. The lowest remuneration levels appear in Germany and the Netherlands where it is likely that greater national emphasis on the manufacturing sector (rather than lesser emphasis on the service sector) accounts for these disparities.

Productivity in the UK stands apart from the rest. Part of the underlying reasoning for this may be the early date of deregulation in the UK, which has forced the banks to rationalise their workforces and substitute people with new technologies where this is practicable. As computer systems are now able to undertake most of the traditional 'back-room' banking activity (paper pushing and processing), scope for rationalisation is significant.

Differences in the supply of mortgage products across Europe are more extreme, principally because there are distinct differences in the way in which mortgages are funded across Europe. There are three basic techniques (Mullender, 1989) – the open system, the closed system and the mortgage bond system – each relating to a specific type of institution, the building society (in the UK), the Bausparkasse (in Germany) and the mortgage bond provider (in Germany, France, the Netherlands, Denmark, Spain and Italy). Both the open and closed system rely on savings. In the open system savers and borrowers are not necessarily one and the same, while in the closed system individuals are required to enter into a savings contract with an institution before a housing loan is granted. More recently, however, the Bausparkasse, recognising the constraint this imposes on buyers (particularly the young first-time buyer), have introduced a bridging loan system which allows customers to borrow a sum of money to be deposited in their savings account so that housing finance loans may be made immediately. By contrast, the mortgage bond system (the most common in Europe) involves loans based on the procurement of long-term capital at fixed rates through the sale of securities at equal interest rates.

Funding systems importantly shape the nature of products offered in the different Member States. For example, as a result of the mortgage bond system being dominant across Europe, fixed interest products prevail. This involves the mortgage institutions adjusting to changes in market conditions rather than consumers, as is the case with variable rate mortgages which dominated the 'open system' of the UK until relatively recently. High inflation and uncertain economic conditions raise the attractiveness of fixed rate products for consumers. The intensity of competitive rivalry in the UK in recent years, and the concomitant threat of European encroachment has forced the UK banks' and building societies' hand to the extent that the greater proportion of new mortgages sold in the UK are now fixed rather than variable rate. This has been facilitated by changes in funding regulations which permit building societies to move from a 'limited' approach to financial management to a 'full' approach, which allows societies to make significant use of hedging instruments (BSC, *Prudential Note*, 1989/3).

A range of other nationally constrained factors play an important role in shaping the types of products offered in the Member States (Davies, 1990). For example, tax incentives on mortgage loans can determine relative product attractiveness. Tax relief on life assurance premiums in the UK prompted the popularity of endowment mortgages, interest-only mortgages where the capital sum is paid off at the end of the mortgage term by a life assurance policy. Likewise, personal equity plan (PEP) mortgages have been encouraged by tax incentives. However, some Member States may learn an important lesson from the UK where tax incentives on mortgages artificially raised the demand for house purchases which, combined with low interest rates in the mid-1980s, led to a dramatic increase in the price of houses. Owner-occupiers took advantage of this boom by raising their mortgage debt, withdrawing equity from their appreciating property assets and going on an inflationary spending spree.

State intervention also has an impact on products. In Greece, Spain, Portugal, France and Germany the state subsidises housing finance. This has tended to dampen competitive pressures and interest rates in the market and thus narrowed the range of products and types of supplier. It has also complicated mortgage lending and resulted in a situation where customers have to deal with more than one institution. Deregulation has also importantly changed supply in most markets. While specialist mortgage institutions continue to prevail in most Member States (Italy, France, Spain, the UK, Germany, Ireland and Greece), a new openness in many markets has resulted in other institutions entering the mortgage market. Commercial banks, in particular, have made important inroads into this sector as they have attempted to maximise their returns from their existing customers through cross-selling. Links between mortgage institutions and commercial banks have also featured large in industry reorganisation following deregulation. The advantages to mortgage lenders from selling through the extensive branch networks of the commercial banks and the scope economies afforded to banks from offering a wider portfolio of products offer clear synergy in the creation of such arrangements (Berger and Hanweck, 1987). Relating back to Table 3.2, it is clear that these differences have given rise to very different cost and price structures for mortgage lending across the Member States of Europe. Spain and France exhibit the highest price levels, the UK the Netherlands and Ireland the lowest.

The insurance industry can be divided into three major sectors: life, non-life/general and reinsurance. Reinsurance, as it does not involve direct sales to customers, cannot be considered part of the retail financial service industry. In life and non-life insurance wide differences between the Member States are similarly apparent. Table 3.3 outlines some of these differences in 1988. While the data is now somewhat outdated, it gives some indication of the nature of the market at the outset of the Single Market initiative. It is clear from Table 3.1 that the Member States listed show broad differences

Table 3.3 Life and non-life insurance, geographical breakdown, 1988

Country	Population (mn)	Life insurance	(%)	General insurance	(%)	Growth life (1988) (%)	Growth general (1988) (%)
France	54.9	F 87 476m	37	F153–742m	63	15.0	6.0
Italy	57.3	L4994 bn	22	L 18 084bn	78	25.0	10.5
Netherlands	15.7	Dfl 13 345m	45	Dfl 16 380m	55	20.0	8.0
Spain	38.9	Pts 424 511m	36	Pts 727 620m	64	35.0	30.0
Germany (W)	61.0	Dm 51 100m	42	Dm 70 830m	58	7.5	6.0
UK	56.6	fi 21 455m	68	fi 10 084m	32	11.0	10.0

Source: UBS Phillips and Drew Global Research Group; *European Insurance Review* (January 1989).

in insurance penetration levels as well as growth levels. With tax incentives on life insurance in the UK, it is hardly surprising that this market shows the highest levels of life insurance cover. Conversely, the UK exhibits the lowest levels of general insurance, although high crime rates and adverse weather conditions in recent years have stimulated demand.

As insurance companies have become the main medium for savings across the EU (*The Economist*, 1990), government intervention is inevitable. Most governments impose price controls, policy wording/prior approval, definitions/restrictions on profits, mortality tables and interest rates to different degrees across the Community. All countries also control insurance reserves and areas of investment, either with the objective of maximising consumer choice or ensuring consumer protection. As a result, the range and type of products in existence across the Community differ quite significantly. In the heavily regulated markets of Germany, Italy, Greece and Portugal, product controls have restricted innovation and new product development. Competition here is mainly centred on price, which has resulted in cut-throat competition and low profitability levels. Conversely, in the least regulated markets of the Netherlands and the UK, aggressive competition has given rise to product innovation and the introduction of new technology systems which have enabled firms to protect profit margins. Table 3.4 outlines the relative cost/price positions for a range of countries. This table confirms the efficiency achieved by UK and Dutch firms, particularly in the field of life insurance.

Demand for Retail Financial Services

It is perhaps in relation to demand conditions across the Community that the biggest differences between markets can be observed. Different cultures give rise to different consumer wants, needs and expectations, which in turn shape the type and volume of products demanded.

Table 3.4 Insurance products, relative cost/price positions*

	Belgium	Spain	France	Germany (W)	Ireland	Netherlands	UK
Life	78	37	33	5	83	-9	-30
Home	-16	-4	39	3	81	17	90
Motor	30	100	9	15	148	-7	-17

* per cent discrepancies from price of average lowest four producers.
Source: Price Waterhouse data in 1989.

The advance of credit card payments in the developed world shows a quite marked difference in levels of penetration. In the UK, for example, there were around 1100 cards per 1000 head of the population in 1990. In Spain, the next largest European market, the number was 750, while in Germany, the corresponding figure was 75. Considering these figures, and the fact that in America there are 2000 cards per 1000 head of the working population, and the fact that by 1987 less than 8 per cent of the $250 billion consumer spending was accounted for by methods of payment other than cheques and cash, there appears to be great room for expansion (*The Economist*, 1989) However, the different rates of penetration are not solely attributable to the competitive environment but are critically shaped by local preferences and cultural quirks. Some observers have argued, for example, that the German market offers false hopes for credit card companies given the German consumer's aversion to credit and preference for saving rather than spending and borrowing. Although there is some evidence that attitudes are changing among the younger generation, the growth of the credit market in Germany is likely to be slow.

Table 3.5 highlights some of the key housing market characteristics for a group of European countries. These factors contribute to differences in individual country demand conditions. France and Germany, by population the two largest European markets, show relatively low levels of owner-occupancy (51 per cent and 37 per cent respectively). Nevertheless, the size of these markets, measured by new advances, puts them among the leading countries. It should be pointed out, however, that the figures for Germany are somewhat misleading. Although only 37 per cent of the population are owner-occupiers, as there is little motivating tax incentive, around 60 per cent own property (mostly for the purposes of investment). In 1987, the Italian and Spanish markets yielded the lowest levels of advance, Italy between £7 and £8 billion and Spain £3 billion, small given their population and owner-occupancy levels. These levels can be explained not by economic conditions but by cultural quirks in the two markets (Davies, 1990). Spanish customers traditionally believed that credit for house purchase was an indication of poverty whereas Italians tended to prefer financing their

Table 3.5 Key characteristics of the housing market, 1987.

	Owner-occupation (%)	Rental market (%)	Subsidised housing (%)	Construction as % of GDP	No. of people per household	Extent of tax advantage
Italy	59	36	6	4.8	2.61	Medium
France	51	41	8	4.6	2.25	Medium
Germany (W)	37	60	3	5.5	2.28	Medium
Spain	77	20	3	n.a	2.51	High
UK	62	10	28	3.6	2.54	High

Source: *International Housing Fact Book*, BAH Analysis.

house purchases from savings and inherited wealth. Times are, however, changing in both countries with consumers becoming less credit-averse and market conditions, notably tax relief in Spain and growing property values, encouraging consumers to consider mortgage credit.

Levels of owner-occupancy also reflect the relative sophistication of the rented property market. In Germany, for example, the rented market for all income levels is well developed, which is clearly not the case in the UK where the rented market is heavily biased towards low income groups. In the UK this tends to engender a high degree of upward mobility as there is a certain stigma attached to renting property on a permanent basis. This is not solely a reflection of supply conditions, the old axiom 'an Englishman's home is his castle' holds true in shaping attitudes towards home ownership.

Customer preference also figures in the insurance industry. For example, the Germans spend up to $25 per head a year on legal insurance compared to less than $2 per head for the British; 'all-risk' insurance is popular in the UK but less so in continental Europe where individuals prefer to itemise specific risks. In the past, these factors have added to national insularity (*The Economist*, 1990).

It is arguable that these differences are more pervasive than differences in supply, which can be changed with shifts in legislation. These cultural quirks are deep seated in the individual societies of the Member States and while attitudes and buying behaviour may change, the time-scale and extent of such change is by no means clear. What this suggests is that there can be no estimable time-frame for greater market homogeneity between the Member States on the demand side, which leaves open the question as to the reality of a trend towards a single market for financial services.

It is important, however, not to overlook certain demand-side factors which are common to the Member States of Europe. Both demographic and social trends across Europe are influencing the range and nature of financial service products. As Table 3.6 highlights, the age structure of the EU is changing. The population is ageing quite considerably, which is raising concerns

Table 3.6 Changing age structure of the EU population, 1991–2010

Age Group	1991 (000)	(%)	2000 (000)	(%)	2010 (0000)	(%)
0–14	58 964	17.9	59 011	17.8	54 170	16.3
15–44	142 878	43.3	139 971	42.1	129 288	39.1
45–64	77 089	23.4	80 092	24.1	89 686	27.1
65+	50 390	15.3	53 053	15.9	57 617	17.4

Source: European Commission.

about the ability of Member States to make adequate pension provisions for their indigenous populations. Governments are therefore actively promoting personal pensions providing enormous potential for EU insurers and persuading banking institutions to diversify into the pensions business.

During each individual's lifetime the demand for financial products changes according to their propensity to borrow, save and consume. The changing age structure of the EU means that there is a changing emphasis on products which are pertinent at different stages in consumers' life cycles. With an ageing population, the emphasis is therefore expected to be on net savings and asset management.

In terms of social trends, younger people are beginning to form households earlier and live alone for longer periods. While this is a declining sector of the population, it is likely that the greater propensity for household formation will more than compensate for this decline. Similarly, as divorce rates continue to climb, new household formation will also emanate from this trend. Finally, increasing longevity of the population will add to housing stock. Whether or not such commonality will lead to greater market harmonisation in terms of supply and demand for financial services is also open to question. Many Member States have shared common social trends for some time and while this may have led to some similarity in the types of products demanded between countries within the EU, the nature of financial services developed to cater for common needs has continued to differ markedly.

Competition in Retail Financial Services

As the previous sections on supply and demand conditions have already demonstrated, changes have taken place in competition in the retail financial service sector. Deregulation and privatisation have intensified competitive pressures and raised the stakes for new product development, innovation and cost cutting programmes. While there are differences in the level of penetration of institutions across the Community (see Figure 3.2), it is generally accepted that most of the markets of Europe are over-banked (and

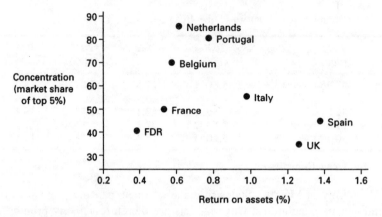

Source: Beddows and Co. data in 1992.

Figure 3.3   Concentration and profits, 1990

over-branched), which suggests that the competitive challenge for the future
will feature the pursuit of new distribution arrangements as well as rationalisation and job cuts. Those countries which were forced to face up to these challenges at an early stage (the UK in particular) may, in the short term, find that
they have a competitive advantage as they have already adjusted to many of
these trends. However, the longevity of such advantages must be questioned.
As is the case with many service sectors, it is not possible to protect new
products with patents and trademarks and the time to copy products is very
short (Dunning, 1989). Equally, as much of the technology on which rationalisation and cost-cutting is based is out-sourced, it is available to all firms and
thus not a sustainable source of advantage (Grubel, 1977; Tschoegl, 1987).

Cross-selling and the establishment of links between financial service firms
to exploit scope economies and maximise returns from existing customer
bases is now a feature of most EU markets. For example, links have been
formed between Commercial Union and Midland Bank (UK), Standard Life
and Halifax Building Society (UK), GAN and CIC Bank (France), AHB and
Bfg Bank (Germany) and Dresdner Bank and a number of regional
Bausparkasse (Germany) in an effort to exploit the potential for extensive
distribution networks.

It is clear that competitive forces and consequent strategic solutions are
similar in many of the markets of Europe. Nevertheless, as the starting point
for institutions from the various Member States differs considerably, some
countries clearly appear to be better placed to take advantage of growth
opportunities than others. For example, in the banking sector, there are clear
differences in levels of concentration and profitability, as charted in Figure
3.3. The highest concentration is in the Netherlands with the five largest
institutions commanding over 80 per cent of the market. Portugal has a similarly high concentration level. The lowest level of concentration is in the

UK. When profitability is considered (measured by return on assets), those countries with a high level of concentration appear to be those which are less profitable. As concentration in these countries is coupled with heavy government control, it is likely that the lack of impetus to innovate, and a tendency to focus competition on price, severely curtails profit margins.

Summary

What is evident from this review of supply, demand and competitive factors across the Community is that the retail financial service sector is far from homogeneous. The situation pertaining in each market is a product of long historical developments in national financial service sectors, culminating in a Europe-wide market where the Member States differ in a number of key respects. The legislative provisions set out in the Single Market initiative to foster greater Europe-wide expansion of players in the industry, at first sight, may permit firms greater opportunities for penetrating each other's markets, and in so doing provide momentum for greater product and service standardisation and thus a move towards market homogeneity in the future. However, this assumes that firms have the strategic arsenal to take on well-developed indigenous competition in markets outside of their own nation state. Therefore, the strategic possibilities for European internationalisation need to be explored in order to ascertain the potential for future encroachment by Europe's leading financial service institutions.

STRATEGIES OF EUROPEAN RETAIL FINANCIAL SERVICE PROVIDERS

Introduction

An exploration of strategies being employed or being considered by European retail financial institutions gives scope to discuss the potential for the establishment of pan-European institutions, and a review of institutions' attitudes towards the Single Market gives some idea of managers' perceptions of the development of the European market in the light of the question of homogeneity.

Firms' Assessment of Foreign Market Servicing Strategies

29 retail financial service firms were interviewed in the UK, France, Germany and Spain in 1989 as part of a project on the relative competitiveness of UK financial service firms in Europe. The following review provides a summary of managers' attitudes towards the Single Market and their strategic response to the opportunities offered by the integration of Europe.

It is possible to split the attitudes of firms towards Europe into two sections: objectives for Europe (which establishes an understanding of the way in which they view the potential for growth offered by the establishment of a Single Market) and policies for Europe (which lays the foundation for the types of strategies which are deemed pertinent to European expansion). In relation to objectives, four different categories emerge:

- Identification and exploitation of niche opportunities
- Exploitation of core strengths
- Broadening of business horizons to the extent that Europe is viewed as the new 'domestic' market
- Adaptation of overall company approach to facilitate overseas operations.

It is apparent from this list that only one group reflects the view that Europe will become a single, homogeneous market which can be exploited in the same way as the domestic market, and even here it was stressed that some markets offer more opportunities than others and sequential targeting of successive markets is viewed as more advantageous than dabbling in several markets at once. As this attitude was only reflected by five firms, the general underlying attitude of most firms appears to be one of 'cherry picking' – pin-pointing profitable opportunities and exploiting niches, adapting to foreign markets where apparent opportunities exist, and extending Europe-wide market share in specific areas of the company's portfolio where competitive strengths are perceived. A sectoral breakdown of these findings shows that the intention to exploit core strengths was only expressed by mortgage lenders, who have traditionally been heavily regulated by governments and have, in many instances (the building societies and Bausparkasse in particular), been regionally oriented. No banks alluded to the search and exploitation of niche opportunities. Diversification in this sector and pursuit of cross-selling opportunities are apparently being transferred to Europe.

In relation to policies, five separate approaches emerged:

- The design of strategies on a market-by-market basis dependent on local business practices and cultural environments
- Expansion based on opportunity
- Pursuit of strategies which allow the maintenance of control by the head office
- Market entry dependent on gaining access to distribution networks
- Choice of strategy which offers a high level of autonomous management by local personnel investment with market knowledge.

Once again, there are clear indications of institutions viewing the divergence between markets as precluding a common approach to pan-European strategic development. The approach that strategies need to be developed on

Table 3.7 The most appropriate forms of foreign market servicing

	Agents	Green-field branches	Takeover branches	Green-field subsidiaries	Takeover subsidiaries	Joint ventures	Total
Banks	-	-	2	-	2	4	8
Mortgage lenders	-	-	-	-	2	9	11
Insurance	-	1	-	3	2	4	10
Total	-	1	2	3	6	17	29

Source: Author's data.

a market-by-market basis, or aiming to develop strategies which allow high levels of autonomy so that local conditions can be reflected in strategic development, are indicative that institutions continue to see the EU as a number of discrete markets which are not homogeneous. Similarly, by viewing expansionary potential on an opportunistic basis, firms do not reinforce any notion of homogeneity. The issue of gaining access to distribution networks reflects the over-branched nature of Europe and the continued existence of barriers to pan-European expansion. This is discussed further in the next section where the strategic implications of institutions entering and servicing foreign markets is assessed with the aim of determining whether the various Member States can be exposed to the same products, services and strategies and exposure which is potentially necessary for the development of a more homogeneous market.

Strategies for Europe

Table 3.7 identifies the forms of market servicing deemed most appropriate by the firms in the sample for penetrating EU markets.

It is eminently clear from Table 3.7 that joint ventures are viewed as the most appropriate means of entering and servicing European markets. This view is supported in practice by the large number of joint ventures and strategic alliances which have taken place in the industry since the inception of the Single Market. Figure 3.4 details the pros and cons of joint ventures voiced by the managers interviewed.

Access to established distribution networks and an extant customer base is, for many firms, the key consideration, although the importance of accessing local 'know-how' figured large in managers' responses. Through such arrangements firms have the potential to expand some of their products and services across Europe, although many firms indicated that adaptation to local markets was critical to secure sales in other Member States. Various reasons were given for adapting products and services to local markets:

Figure 3.4 Pros and cons of joint ventures

Pros	Cons
Access to well-established distribution networks	Dilution of control
Access to an established customer base	Problems of quality maintenance
Lower capital outlay than mergers/takeovers	Competition arising between partners because not equally matched
Rapid returns	Share profits
Good Creation of awareness and brand image	Image confusion
Local partners provide 'know-how' and market understanding	Consumption of management time and effort
Established demand through cross-selling with partner	Communication a problem owing to lack of language skills
Easier to deal with local authorities	Lack of cultural understanding makes liaising with partner difficult

Source: Author's data.

differing customer needs; compliance with local requirements; fit with local business practices and the need to promote a local identity were the most frequently cited. It is the skills developed in innovation and new product development which are being exploited in European markets rather than the products which have been developed to cater for domestic needs. These issues reflect the discussion of supply, demand and competitive factors presented earlier.

Despite the popularity of joint ventures, there are a number of disadvantages cited which point to there being a number of on-going operational difficulties in following such a strategy. These problems are compounded by the fact that many of the joint ventures being entered into are between firms based in more sophisticated markets (in terms of innovation and product development) and in those countries which are at a relatively early stage of deregulation or between institutions specialising in different products in the industry. While these arrangements offer synergy in the short term – in the first case, firms with product advantages joining forces with firms with local market knowledge, and in the second, firms with different product skills combining their skills – the longevity of such synergy is brought into question by the ease with which products and services can be copied in the retail financial service industry. The UK banks' encroachment into the mortgage industry – writing over one-third of all new mortgages only two years after changes in legislation – is testament to this. It is possible, then, that some of the agreements entered into at the outset of the Single Market initiative will not survive in the long term.

Evidence suggests that most cross-border mergers and acquisitions entered into to date have involved large financial organisations acquiring small local institutions (*Euromoney*, March 1992). While this has allowed institutions to extend their branch coverage in certain Member States, the scale of these deals means that few have offered up significant market share opportunities. Between 1988 and 1990 there were over 300 mergers and acquisitions in the EU, 146 of which were cross-border deals. However, most of these involved insignificant shifts in influence and control, being based on cross-shareholdings rather than real strategic expansion. The low levels of strategic investments may be partly explained by the continuance of restrictions on merger and takeover activity. In Germany, for example, banks' shareholdings in industry restricts foreign penetration (Ugeux, 1989) and in the likes of Spain, France, Italy, Greece and Portugal, since a significant proportion of financial institutions' assets remain in the hands of governments, foreign acquisition is not possible. Furthermore, in the run-up to '1992', as firms were intent on jumping on the expansion bandwagon, the demand for takeover opportunities pushed up the price of potential takeover targets and forced firms to look for alternative expansionary means (principally joint ventures).

The sensitivity of financial services means that regulations on mergers and acquisitions remain strict, despite EU legislation. For example, the Bank of England vets all potential mergers between financial institutions, approval being given only where both parties agree to the deal and if the Bank is confident that the foreign acquirers' capital, management and reputation pose no risk to UK consumers. Conversely, in Spain, purchase of more than 50 per cent of an indigenous financial institution is permitted only in exceptional cases – usually where the institution is heading towards collapse (Dixon, 1991). Greenfield strategies have mainly been ruled out due to their inability to secure access to existing distribution networks and customer franchises. While some institutions (principally insurance companies) intent on exploiting niche opportunities in certain of the less developed markets of Europe have begun to develop their own greenfield operations, over-branched markets and the time to profit militate against this approach.

In the banking sector only Deutsche Bank of Germany and Crédit Lyonnais of France have publicly declared their intention to become pan-European retail financial service providers through the acquisition of major stakes in foreign institutions (*Euromoney*, 1992). However, even here there is little evidence of their attempting to exploit a homogeneous market. Their stated aim is to maximise local autonomy and ensure that institutions retain their local character.

CONCLUSIONS

The myth or reality of the SEM has been considered in relation to the European retail financial service industry. No one would deny that the market for financial service products in existence at the outset of the Single Market programme was highly fragmented and characterised by differing supply, demand and competitive conditions. The brief strategic review of managers' attitudes towards the SEM and strategies being employed as part of firms' Europeanisation has attempted to ask the question of the potential for greater industry harmonisation as the policies and directives designed to integrate Europe take effect.

Although strategic alliances have dominated the strategies of firms pursuing European expansion, there appears to be limited scope for these strategies to foster greater harmonisation. This relates back to the idea that firms act as important 'change agents' – and it is only through standardising their products, services and strategies that greater homogeneity may be fostered. Similarly, while the European Commission believes that mergers and acquisitions will become more attractive in Europe as the national character of markets is slowly eroded, they appear to have overlooked the importance of firms playing a role in this erosion process. Finally, greenfield options, mostly restricted to niche opportunities, lack the scale and scope to make any real impact on consumer behaviour. To an extent, then, there is something of a chicken and egg situation involved in the growing homogeneity of the markets of Europe. It is only through exposure to foreign products and services that local market demand conditions may be modified; this process is in turn hampered by profit objectives of firms which, intent on improving market share, see the necessity of adapting their approach to cater for market differences.

As cultural factors lie at the centre of consumer demand patterns, changes in markets and a trend towards greater homogeneity are likely to be slow. While cultural change is endemic in all societies, individuals tend to work hard to protect their own cultures which suggests a degree of resistance to change (Robock and Simmonds, 1989). Ethnocentrism, the natural belief that one's own culture is superior to that of others, tends to perpetuate the existence of cultural barriers. Thus, any active attempt to change consumer behaviour will be met with resistance, while strategies which cater for behaviour nuances in each market are likely to be met with success.

Ultimately, it is hard to confirm the notion of homogeneity given the evidence in this industry. This may preclude institutions pursuing large-scale economies through standardisation and pan-European coverage (the potential for which has been questioned in the financial service sector, see Gilbert, 1984; Lawrence, 1989; Morgan, 1988), and while there are certain opportunities to exploit the diversities apparent across the EU, the strategic hurdles resulting from over-capacity and strict legislation are severely restricting the potential for large-scale expansion in retail financial services. This clearly contradicts Cecchini's predictions for the industry, and brings into question the reality of scale economy cost advantages (in financial services, at least) from the Single Market initiative, a reality which may only be realised through the exploitation of homogeneous markets.

References

Berger, A. and Hanweck, G. (1987) 'Competitive Viability in Banking', *Journal of Monetary Economics*, 26(1).

Berry, L. (1980) 'Service Marketing is Different', *Business*, 30(3), pp. 24–9.

Boddewyn, J.J., Halbrich, M.B. and Perry, A.C. (1986) 'Service multinationals: conceptualisation, measurement and theory', *Journal of International Business Studies*, 16(3), pp. 41–57.

Buckley, P. and Casson, M. (1981) 'The optimal timing of a foreign direct investment', *Economic Journal*, 92(361), pp. 75–87. Reprinted as Chapter 5 in P.J. Buckley and M.C. Casson, *The Economic Theory of the Multinational Enterprise* (London: Macmillan, 1985).

Buckley, P., Pass, C.L. and Prescott, K. 1992a, 'The internationalisation of service firms: a comparison with the manufacturing sector', *Scandinavian International Business Review*, 1(1), pp. 39–56.

Buckley, P. Pass, C.L. and Prescott, K. 1992b, *Servicing International Markets: Competitive Strategies of Firms* (Oxford: Blackwell).

Building Societies Commission (BSC), *Presidential Note 1989/3, Balance Sheet Mismatch and Hedging* (London: BSC).

Cecchini, P. (1989) *1992– The Benefits of a Single Market* (Aldershot: Wildwood House).

Davies, R. (1990) 'Europe's home loans after 1992', *Building Societies Gazette* (February), pp. 29–30.

Dixon, R. (1991) *Banking in Europe: The Single Market* (London: Routledge).

Dunning, J. (1989) 'Multinational enterprises and the growth of services: some conceptual and theoretical issues', *Service Industries Journal*, 9(1), pp. 5–39.

The Economist (1989) 'A Survey of World Banking' (25 March), pp. 3–50.

The Economist (1990) 'European Insurance' (24 February), pp. 3–21.

The Economist (1992)

Euromoney (1992)

Eurostat (1993)

Eurostat (1994)

Gilbert, R. (1984) 'Bank market structure and competition: a survey', *Journal of Money, Credit and Banking*, 16.

Grubel, H.G. (1977) 'A theory of multinational banking', *Banca Nazionale del Lavoro Quarterly Review*, 123 (December).

Hymer, S. (1960) 'The international operations of national firms: a study of direct foreign investment', PhD. thesis (Cambridge, Mass.: MIT Press, 1976).

Johanson, J. and Wiedersheim-Paul, F. (1975) 'The internationalisation of the firm: four Swedish cases', *Journal of Management Studies*, 12(3), pp. 305–22.

Lawrence, C. (1989) 'Banking costs: estimation of economies of scale and scope', *Journal of Money, Credit and Banking*, 21.

Lovelock, C.H. (1981) 'Why marketing management needs to be different for services', in J.H. Donnelly and W.R. George (eds), *Marketing of Services* (Chicago: American Marketing).

Morgan, J. (1988) *Trade in Financial Services*: Washington, DC: Federal Reserve Bank).

Mullender, L. (1989) 'Little by little Europe comes together', *Building Societies Gazette* (March), pp. 35–9.

Rathmell, J.M. (1966) 'What is meant by services?', *Journal of Marketing*, 30(10) pp. 32–6.

Regan, W. (1963) 'The service revolution', *Journal of Marketing*, 47(7), pp. 57–62.

Robock, S.H. and Simmonds, K. (1989) *International Business and Multinational Enterprises* (Homewood, IL: Irwin).

Thomas, D.R.E. (1978) 'Strategy is different in service business', *Harvard Business Review*, 56(4), pp. 158–65.

Tschoegl, A. (1987) 'International retail banking as a strategy: an assessment', *Journal of International Business Studies*, 18(2) (Summer).

Ugeux, G. (1989) 'The integration of financial markets', *Royal Bank of Scotland Review*, 162 (June).

Vernon, R. (1966) 'International trade and international investment in the product cycle', *Quarterly Journal of Economics*, 80, pp. 190–207.

Welford, R. and Prescott, K. (1994) *European Business: an issue based approach* (London: Pitman), 2nd edn.

Young, S., Hamill, J., Wheeler, C. and Davies, R. (1989) *Market Entry and Development* (London: Harvester Wheatsheaf).

4 Home Shopping in the Single European Market – Foundering in the Wake of Neo-Liberalism

Elke Pioch and Paul Brook

INTRODUCTION

Retailing is a large and important element of the European economy, yet it continues to receive scant attention from the European Union (EU). This neglect suggests a disregard for the retail sector's politico–economic significance *vis-à-vis* the 'completion' of the Single European Market (SEM). This chapter, preceded by a brief review of retailing and home shopping[1] within the EU, takes a critical look at the European Commission's policy for this sector, and in the process offers an explanation for the lack of substantive activity relating to the European integration of retailing.

The subject is approached, first, by critically examining the neo-liberal foundations of the SEM project; and, secondly, by assessing the impact of dedicated policy measures for home shopping in two areas: distance selling and data processing.[2] Home shopping is utilised because, according to the logic of the SEM, it is the most conducive of retail forms to rapid and early internationalisation. In particular, the German and Italian markets are discussed as exemplars of the divergent conditions within European retailing. By adopting this dual approach to examining the location and role of retailing, it is possible to make an assessment of its potential for integration into the SEM as currently constituted.

RETAILING – THE SEM'S INVISIBLE GIANT

At the beginning of the 1990s, retailing was one of the fastest growing sectors in the EU (*Eurostat*, 1993; Corporate Intelligence Group, 1991). The distributive trades (retailing and wholesaling) accounted for around 13 per cent of the EU's GDP and more than 30 per cent of all EU firms, 3.3 million of which are in the retail sector. Additionally, retailing provided employment for more than 10 per cent of the Union's total working population.

These overall figures conceal considerable variations across the EU, but it is possible to point to a number of broad based tendencies as measured by the number of retail enterprises per 10 000 inhabitants and employees per enterprise (*Eurostat*, 1993). It is thus possible to see the EU's retail market as divided roughly into two large groups: (1) the Mediterranean member states (excluding France); and (2) the remaining northern European member states. The second group is characterised by fewer outlets per inhabitants but by significantly larger numbers of employees per unit. Throughout the Mediterranean group, in contrast, a high number of predominantly small outlets, many of them family businesses, employ small numbers of people per unit.

Most of the changes in the retail sector during the 1970s and 1980s (such as the proliferation of the French hypermarket concept; the German and Danish discount store format; and the introduction of large 'surface' specialists) originated in the more mature markets of the northern countries. From their origins in northern Europe, the new formats have spread to northern Italy, Spain and Portugal, largely bypassing southern Italy and Greece. However, the Greek government has recently set in motion a process of internal trade liberalisation resulting in rapid retail change (Bennison and Boutsouki, 1995) in line with developments in the northern European markets.

A fundamental aspect of today's retail industry is the increased concentration process, especially in the food sector, alongside growing backward integration into manufacturing. Yet the more rapid concentration and internationalisation of suppliers, particularly in food manufacturing, has had the overall effect of strengthening their bargaining power against retailers. In response, large retailers have entered into alliances, mostly in the food sector, to redress the bargaining 'imbalance'. These alliances, which take the form of voluntary chains, buying groups, franchises and cooperatives can be found at regional, national and European levels.

The growth of large multiples and their economic power has, at least in part, to be seen in conjunction with the proliferating internationalisation of major retail companies, dominated by large northern European food multiples, which has been the subject of a growing debate in the context of global retail expansion (e.g. Hollander, 1970; Waldmann, 1978; White, 1984; Kacker, 1985, 1988; Treadgold, 1988, 1990/91; Burt, 1991; Williams, 1991, 1992; Dawson, 1993). There is common agreement that the '1992' programme will facilitate the continuing internationalisation of retail companies. It will not, however, constitute the driving force, as orientation towards international markets predates the SEM project (Alexander, 1988; Burt, 1989; Treadgold, 1990). Nevertheless, others (e.g. Salmon and Tordjman, 1989) believe that the unified European market will strengthen the internationalisation of retail companies. Yet, surprisingly, detailed studies of the impact of SEM measures on European retailing[3] are scarce (see, e.g., Pioch *et al*, 1992).

HOME SHOPPING'S PLACE IN THE EU'S RETAIL SECTOR

Within the European retail market, home shopping is a growing, if still relatively small, sector, with future growth prospects located primarily in specialist mail order. Geographically, the format is heavily concentrated, with approximately 80 per cent of the EU's home shopping activities occurring in Germany (amounting to 4 per cent of total sales), the UK (3–4 per cent), and France (2–3 per cent). By contrast, in the fourth largest member state, Italy, home shopping accounts for just under 1 per cent of the retail market, ranking it at the bottom of the European league (Home Shopping, 1991, p. 2).

Italian home shopping companies are small and, with the exception of fashion retailer Gucchi, have no international presence. In addition, the major players are in French or German hands (Pioch and Brook, 1992). The German home shopping sector is dominated by some of the largest mail order companies in the world (Otto, Quelle and Neckermann), ranking among the top 20 EU retail groups (*Eurostat*, 1993, p. 23). The largest French, German and British home shopping companies are also among the top international retail players in Europe and are steadily increasing their international activities.

Home shopping companies are thus prominent players in the retail sector's internationalisation process, reflecting the sector's north–south divide and the increasing concentration ratios. These characteristics, combined with home shopping's lack of fixed outlets, flexible distribution systems and the potential for transnational marketing would appear to make its companies early candidates amongst the distributive trades for pursuing the pan-European integration of operations. To establish whether this apparent potential is being realised requires an examination of the neo-liberal foundations of the '1992' programme (Grahl and Teague, 1989) and, within it, the role of retailing.

1992 – NEO-LIBERALISM AND GLOBALISATION

The SEM's neo-liberal foundations imply a supply-side superordination, which is made plain in the EU's seminal analysis, *The Economics of 1992* (Commission, 1988). For example, when referring to the increase in competition brought about by the SEM, it is stated that:

> Throughout the system of industrial interrelationships reductions in cost of *upstream* will reinforce further reductions *downstream* ... these [supply] factors are transmitted via the improvement of the productivity of factors of production. (p. 162, emphasis added)

The key to greater competitiveness and economic growth, then, lies in the facilitation of productive and finance capital. More downstream activities, such as retailing will, it is assumed, benefit through a process of *trickle-down* price reductions.

With this analytic formulation there is an emphasis on the internal deregulation of national markets and the removal of barriers to trade. This assumes, as a result, the freer movement of goods, capital, services and labour, thereby increasing competition and stimulating growth. In practice, this means that there is a logic to the extension and deepening of market dynamics into hitherto state regulated areas of the EU's socio–cultural fabric, such as consumer and employment rights.[4] Accordingly, the SEM, as the principal element in the EU's integration strategy, displays a narrow market economism which is analytically blind to the complexities of the social, economic and cultural dimensions that interrelate to produce change – not least in the case of European integration (Gill, 1992).

The logic which prioritises market dynamics over more complex and historically derived patterns of socio–cultural behaviour and organisation has far-reaching implications for the retail sector. Retailing exists and operates at the interface between the competitive market and a complex of socio–cultural forms, requiring a high degree of sensitivity if it is to survive within a competitive environment. In this way, each retail outlet is simultaneously separated from its host community (*vis-à-vis* its relationship to competitors, and the parent company in the case of chains), yet integral to it, by virtue of its everyday role in interacting with (servicing, reproducing and amending) the existing socio–cultural fabric. The neo-liberal thrust of the SEM pays little attention to this crucial social aspect of retailing, whilst only indirectly effecting changes to its business dimension owing to retailing's prescribed downstream status.

This narrow version of European integration is a recent phenomenon. As Grahl and Teague (1989) have commented, the SEM

> results from the capture by neo-liberal forces of the integration process in Western Europe . . . Today, integration means the unification of national markets, with other definitions of cooperation and interaction either displaced by the neo-liberal formula or subordinated to it. (p. 34)

What can be witnessed is a process of *negative* integration, emphasising the removal of obstacles to the free exchange of goods, capital, services and labour, which inevitably falls short of a comprehensive attack on non-tariff barriers, many of which will remain as long as there exists national differentiation in socio–economic regulation. As a result, the programme is not sufficient to achieve the creation of EU-wide markets for even the majority of goods and services (Grahl and Teague, 1990).

In this light, the SEM cannot be regarded as an intrinsic programme for economic integration, but rather as a process of *globalisation*, primarily concerned with facilitating the continental dominance of a few large globally competitive corporations. Wider socio–economic forms of European integration, therefore will, if at all, tend to come about as a by-product of the subordination of other socio–economic dimensions to the continental dominance of leading international firms – a *trickle-down* effect (Grahl and Teague, 1989). This is an inevitable outcome of the neo-liberal formula which asserts the primacy of market concentration and eschews non-market based integration approaches (Gill, 1992). One implication is that retailing is unlikely to be at the forefront of the integration process, despite the fact that many of its principal companies have internationalised operations.

THE EU'S VISION FOR RETAILING

In line with the SEM's neo-liberal formulation, Whitehead (1992) has argued that the anticipated benefits of integration for the retail sector, as set out in the Cecchini Report (1988), will be predominantly indirect gains filtered through from the supply side as a result of minimal trading regulations. This is because '[n]ational and local regulations affecting commercial activity are extensive and reflect the predominantly national or local character of the sector' (COM (1991), p. 16). It follows, with this rationale, that there is no case for European legislation except in certain very limited cases where differences between national rules threaten to inhibit the internationalisation of the sector – and, in particular, where the marketing method is intrinsically transnational in character (COM 1991, p. 16).

By defining commercial distribution as a generally national or local affair, where the final exchange process with the consumer is not subject to wider international competition, the Commission neglects the fundamental aspects of modern retailing discussed above, such as increased internationalisation and concentration. Furthermore, retailing, unlike manufacturing industries, operates at the interface between the 'end' consumer and the producer, which endows the sector with a unique possibility to extend the internationalisation of production into transnational choice for the consumer. However, to put retailing at the centre of the integration process requires a relaxation of the strict supply-side orientation of the SEM to include a broader approach to integration that counter-balances market deregulation, particularly in the field of consumer policy.

POLICIES FOR THE EUROPEAN CONSUMER

To achieve full benefit from the internal market, it is necessary that its citizens be prepared to use that market by purchasing goods and services available anywhere in it. (COM 1990, p. 3)

This view from the Commission is interesting in at least two aspects. First, it was apparently contradicted by the Commission a year later when the national and local character of retailing was stressed (see above). Second, given the diversity of national rules affecting retailing, consumers may find it difficult to engage safely in cross-border shopping for a variety of non-market oriented reasons, as will be discussed later in more detail. Accordingly, the Commission's statement points to the necessity for a European regulatory framework covering consumer protection:

> the Community has set itself the aim of making the single market operate in a manner which is fully consistent with the interests of the consumer. The measures needed to achieve this aim, by establishing a high level of consumer protection, particularly in the field of health and safety, will have to be carried out at Community level with the support of Member States. A special effort is needed to provide the information needed to increase public confidence and enable the European consumer to take full advantage of the opportunities which the single market offers. (Consumer Rights, 1993, p. 8)

Despite the Commission's objective, and the upgrading of consumer protection to the status of a 'full' Community policy with the accession of the Maastricht Treaty (COM (1993a)), the evidence suggests that it is beyond the scope of the currently constituted integration programme. This is because the

> policy does not seek to replace national policies ... [rather] ... the aim is to complement them as markets have increasingly taken on a European dimension. (Consumer Rights, 1993, p. 5)

Yet, as argued earlier, the continued existence of differing national regulations, as in the case of consumer protection, constitutes a barrier to market integration. Moreover, substantive moves to complement national policies have frequently met with stiff and successful resistance from dominant (neo-liberal oriented) Member State governments and organised business interests. This occurs because consumer policy is viewed as social regulation, which impinges on the flexibility of the market, or more precisely, the discretion of suppliers. This in turn has led to the dilution of initial, more expansive, proposals for regulation both now and in the future, as reflected in the decision to cut the Commission's 1994 consumer budget by more than half. This has led to the abolition of support for consumer information and the removal of financial assistance to promote consumer access to 're-dress', advice and the integration of consumer policy with other EU policies (*European Retail*, 1994e).

Lawlor (1989), however, has argued that there is an inescapable link between consumer policy and economic growth, in that the mutual advantage between supplier and consumer is 'the essence of an efficient and beneficial market' (p. 18). An extensive set of consumer policies, in his view, must recognise that 'consumers are part of the market, not outside it, making claims on it' (p. 19). Lawlor is right to point to the artificial distinction which neo-liberal thought draws between market exchange and the socio-legal structures that foster consumer activity, of which protective and enabling legislation are the most prominent. As will be demonstrated below, the effects on European policy implementation of accepting the logic of such a separation has profound implications for retailing, not least home shopping.

TOWARDS THE INTEGRATION OF HOME SHOPPING?

Home shopping, as discussed, appears to be an ideally positioned sector of the distributive trades for early integration into the single market. Consequently, the Commission, following the neo-liberal logic of the SEM, identified home shopping as the exception to the retail rule of being intrinsically national or local in character. It recognised that home shopping's marketing method is potentially transnational in character and, therefore, saw the need to introduce a regulatory framework of consumer rights, principally the Directive and Recommendation for Distance Selling and the Directive on Data Processing. A detailed analysis of these two directives, set against the background of the diverse markets of Germany and Italy, reveals the contradictions and tensions inherent in the Commission's approach to retailing.

In its rationale for the Distance Selling Directive, the Commission asserts that '[m]arketing at a distance will be one of the areas in which the operation of the SEM will be most obvious and tangible to consumers' (COM (1992a), p. 10). In addition:

> Distance selling restores the initiative in cross-frontier purchasing to the consumer, who, on the basis of a cross-frontier proposal, takes the initiative and approaches a firm located in a country other than his own. (p. 10)

The Commission argues that to bring about such a notion of a single market in services, legal fragmentation should be avoided. However, Member States' regulatory frameworks for distance selling, and by implication home shopping, differ widely. Such fragmentation reflects diverse historical developments and the different stages of retail advancement reached in Member States.

In Germany, distance selling is not a legal category, resulting in the absence of an explicit regulatory framework for home shopping. Court rulings, however, have prohibited distance selling and marketing activities that are considered an intrusion into an individual's privacy, such as telephone calls and the distribution of unaddressed advertising through letter boxes with the proviso that consumers have made their objections known (COM (1992a), p. 10).

Italy has no specific legislation for distance selling, probably due to the underdeveloped nature of the market, although there are voluntary guidelines in force. For example, the home shopping trade association, ANVED, operates a code of business ethics which allows for a seven day withdrawal period after receipt of goods (COM (1992a), p. 10).

The Commission, mindful of disparate national conditions, offered a first draft directive for consultation which, by proposing stringent rules for consumer protection, attracted widespread support from consumer organisations. In contrast, trade associations rejected the proposals as too detailed and restrictive. After intense lobbying by representatives of the sector, the first draft was replaced by a general framework directive which set minimum standards of protection and a recommendation suggesting that codes of conduct should be drawn up by the relevant trade associations in each Member State (Commission Recommendation, 1992). As with other areas of social policy, the predominance of supply-side interests within the decision-making process resulted in the Commission retreating from a regulatory framework in favour of minimalist intervention and voluntarism, despite a half-hearted attempt to move to a consumer-centred approach to the legislative process.

Inevitably, consumer groups criticised the Commission for giving way to pressure from the industry and marketing profession. They also feared that a marker had been put down delineating the limits of a pan-European consumer policy for the foreseeable future (CECG, 1992a), a fear that has been well founded given the recent cuts in the Commission's consumer budget. Paradoxically, this change of direction occurred at the same time as a more vigorous and expansive approach to consumer policy was being agreed as part of the Maastricht Treaty. Nevertheless, distance sellers are still prone to argue that the directive and European-wide legislation are unnecessary as only up to 3 per cent of sales are made 'cross-border' (*European Retail*, 1994c).

DISTANCE SELLING–THE COMMISSION'S OBJECTIVES

The diluted version of the Directive continued to claim that it aimed:

> to provide legal safeguards for the consumer, . . . to safeguard the consumer's right of choice, [and] to ensure repayment to the consumer in the case of non-performance of the contract. (COM 1992a, pp. 11–12)

These broad aims, if not the details, retained the support of consumer groups.

Significantly, two aspects of home shopping are not covered by the Directive: orders placed at 'order centres', which is common practice in eastern Germany; and long-term staged contracts, such as membership of a book club. In the latter case, the initial agreement is covered, but not any further regular sale of goods. This is of importance for Italian consumers, who buy up to 20 per cent of their books through mail order, and for German consumers, who make extensive use of book clubs (Home Shopping, 1991).

As a package, the Directive's array of consumer protection measures are minimal. The principal proposals can be summarised as follows:

1 Offers of sale are subject to a number of provisions concerning consumer privacy, the protection of minors and commercial *good faith* (see below on data protection)
2 The commercial purpose of an offer must be made obvious, and the customer should be given clear and unambiguous information
3 Delivery, unless otherwise stipulated, must be carried out within 30 days of the supplier receiving the order
4 The consumer has a right of withdrawal within seven days after receipt of the goods, or the receipt of documentation, in the case of services.

Other crucial aspects of consumer protection, such as the right not to receive offers, and specific safeguards in relation to special sales promotions, were relegated to the non-binding Recommendation.

As with all directives, Member States have to ensure that effective means exist to enforce compliance with the legislation:

> To this end, Member States shall make provisions, . . . for trade and consumer organisations, which can, according to their national legislation, demonstrate a legitimate interest in the matter, to be entitled, if it is recognised by the Member State of the conflict, to take legal action and/or bring complaints before a competent administrative body. (COM 1992a, p. 82)

The same Article also allows for representation rights in cross-border disputes for consumers and small home shopping traders. Notionally, a consumer has the right to be represented by a fellow consumer or a consumer group, and a small trader may utilise their relevant trade association. However, these rights are subject to Member States' national regulations making provision for representation. Such inconsistency in the provision of rights during disputes is likely to act as a deterrent to consumers and small traders considering cross-border home shopping, whereas larger companies already possess the resources to navigate the national legal fragmentation of the SEM when involved in cross-border disputes. The provisions for representation during disputes reveals the systemic supply-side orientation of the SEM and, in particular, the favouring of large-scale capital.

Article 10 will undoubtedly have the effect of undermining consumer confidence. It stipulates that all necessary information concerning a contract of sale must be in writing, but in the language used for the offer. This means, for example, that an Italian consumer placing an order in response to a German advertisement will receive all written details in German. In many other areas of EU policy, written communication has to be in the dominant language of the country of destination. The Commission addresses this inconsistency by explaining that:

> If the medium is disseminated outside its own language area and the consumer decides to place an order, the language rules must not be an obstacle to this type of cross-frontier contract. (COM, 1992a, p. 20)

Under a so-called 'political agreement' on the distance selling directive drawn up in 1994, this latter article will be amended so as to allow individual EU governments to make their own rules regarding the use of language (*European Retail*, 1994d).

Although the facilitation of cross-border purchasing is central to the proposal's objectives, its provisions are inadequate. The European consumer group, CECG, summarises the basic flaws:

> It is difficult to reconcile the discretionary power granted to Member States to impose unilateral restrictions with the realities of cross-border trade within the Single Market. It assumes an awareness of differing legal requirements which few traders, let alone consumers, possess. It may also lead to market partition. (CECG, 1992b, p. 3)

Even provision for the reimbursement of customers is placed at the discretion of trade organisations. In line with the Directive on distance selling, the non-binding Recommendation advises that suppliers' trade associations should adopt codes of practice. These codes should include provision for the reimbursement of payments made by consumers at the time of placing an order and for a period after the payment has been made. Inevitably, consumer organisations opposed these voluntary arrangements for such a crucial area as reimbursement.

Overall, the Commission's provisions for distance selling contradict its own objectives. Even if it is accepted (as consumer groups and the Commission appear to do) that consumers will only engage in cross-frontier buying once legal fragmentation is eradicated and adequate protection is in place, the SEM's current parameters pose substantial obstacles to these modest objectives. It is a dilemma which has, to date, been settled by opting for predominantly voluntarist solutions rather than regulation. The political realities are neither lost on, nor rejected by, the Commission:

> the Community wants to keep its role as regulator to a minimum. The informal guideline is: *As little regulation as possible, but as much as necessary to protect consumers.* (Consumer Rights, 1993, p. 5)

Voluntary regulations continue to leave the protection of the consumer in the hands of dominant and self-interested suppliers, in this case, the home shopping trade organisations. This downstream, supply-side predominance assumes that home shopping companies will provide the *necessary* and *right* balance in the relationship between customer and retailer.

The home shopping sector quickly grasped the opportunity to establish its own desired guidelines on practice. A European Convention on cross-border mail order and distance sales, introduced in 1993, was signed by companies from fourteen European states (*European Retail*, 1994a). Irrespective of whether such an initiative is perceived by consumers to be effective, the design, operation and enforcement of consumer rights lies with self-interested retailers. This example of supply-side predominance stands in stark contrast to the Commission's belief that 'markets work best when the interests of buyers and sellers are in balance' (Consumer Rights, 1993, p. 1).

The subordination of the consumer to the supplier within the exchange process is likely to result in consumers feeling vulnerable and uncertain of their rights. A *EUROBAROMETER* survey (Consumer Policy, 1993) revealed that consumers perceived four principal difficulties in cross-border transactions: the lack of after-sales services (mentioned by 53 per cent); dealing in a foreign language, which is exacerbated in the case of home shopping by the receipt of conditions of sale in a foreign language (39 per cent); the settlement of disputes (29 per cent); and access to information and advice (27 per cent), an area that has been partly relegated (for sales promotions) to the non-binding Recommendation.

In view of the *EUROBAROMETER* evidence alone, the EU's consumer policies are not conducive to facilitating the integration of retailing. Despite this, the Commission maintains a rhetorical commitment to establishing consumer rights to counterbalance the powerful position of suppliers:

> Individual consumers cannot stand up alone to the might of many of the companies which sell them their goods and services. (Consumer Rights, 1993, p. 2)

Paradoxically, the consequence of voluntary policies is that consumers will have to *stand up alone* to cross-border retailers. The recent budget cuts make it doubtful whether the projected renewal of the consumer policy process, announced in the Maastricht Treaty, will result in a more steadfast and balanced approach. To date, the Commission has shown little determination, and few signs of success, in standing up to the political pressures exerted by the home shopping industry, the marketing profession and their allies in member state governments.

HOME SHOPPING AND THE DATA PROTECTION PROVISIONS

The other large area of legislation that is directly linked to home shopping concerns data protection, an aspect that is central to distance selling with regards to the use of direct mailing. The Commission sees a need for legislation on data processing because of the diversity and inconsistency of approaches to protection within the Union. Germany, Denmark, France, Ireland, Luxembourg, the Netherlands and the UK have data protection legislation, whereas Italy, Spain, Greece, Belgium and Portugal have none.

As with distance selling, the initial draft on personal data processing was greeted with concern by business interests, especially companies involved in direct marketing. Consequently, their intense lobbying led to the proposal being significantly changed (Derek, 1992). Inevitably, the amended proposal (COM (1992b)) contained a shift in the balance of power from the consumer to the supplier – the direct marketer.

Prior to assessing the effectiveness of the proposed legislation on data protection, it is necessary to provide a summary of the relevant sections. In general, the proposed framework directive makes provision for additional national regulation and allows for national codes of conduct to be laid down by trade associations.

The Directive includes the proviso that consumer consent to processing of data is required, unless:

> processing is necessary in pursuit of the general interest or of the legitimate interest of the controller (person or institution that holds the data) or of a third party to whom the data is disclosed, except where such interests are overridden by the interests of the data subject (an individual whose personal data is concerned). (COM, 1992b, p. 72)

Furthermore, consumers must be given the opportunity to have their data erased if it is to be passed on to a third party. This can be done within the course of regular correspondence, that is, it does not require a special mailing.

The processing of sensitive data, such as ethnic origin or trade union membership, is generally disallowed. Where personality profiles of consumers are compiled, these must not be used against the interests of individual consumers, excluding the sending of information such as a brochure. Despite such seemingly stringent regulations on the use of data, direct mail organisations will enjoy widespread derogation. For example, it will be unnecessary to notify the supervisory authority (to be established under Article 30) of the details of correspondence with consumers. Rather, a system of selective monitoring will be established from which direct mail operations will be largely excluded. The overall approach to data protection, once again, reveals a European consumer policy where suppliers' interests are protected at the expense of fundamental aspects of statutory consumer protection.

Despite the minimalist scope and approach of the Directive, the German and Italian home shopping sectors will have to adapt to the new legislation. The strict German legislation will probably have to be loosened, whereas in Italy any new regulation could be potentially restrictive as the provisions for direct mail advertising are currently very lenient. ANVED was quick to voice fears that such legislation could have an adverse effect on the already ailing industry (*European Retail*, 1994b).

As with distance selling, the Commission's approach to data processing has been marked by a retreat from an extensive regulatory framework in favour of minimal legal protection for consumers and self-regulation by companies. The Commission, nevertheless, continues to retain an expansionary vision for European consumer policy despite the political and structural exigencies of the policy process favouring the retailer. In effect, the development of European consumer rights and protection relies, in large measure, on a *trickle-down* process from retailer to consumer.

CONCLUSIONS

The neo-liberal foundations of the SEM project have profound implications for the retail sector in terms of its prescribed location, status and regulatory framework within the EU's political economy. In particular, the whole process is analytically blind to the nature of retailing's interface with socio–cultural, non-market determined aspects of consumption. Even though the Commission has demonstrated a rhetorical, if narrow, appreciation of this dimension, particularly in the area of consumer rights, the political realities of neo-liberal hegemony within the SEM policy-making process have had the cumulative effect of undermining the quality of the all too small number of legislative decisions.

Within the SEM, as currently constituted, retailing as a whole cannot become an integrated pan-European sector at the level of integration that is implied or envisaged by the Commission's public statements. Yet the question remains of whether the sector can be integrated to the point where there is a significant level of cross-border home shopping.

If this latter, narrower, form of integration is to be achieved, the large home shopping companies must, as a prerequisite, develop integrated pan-European activities more extensively, but this would require a far higher level of facilitation by the EU. The German home shopping organisation (BVH) has argued that the SEM will have little influence on the sector as too many obstacles remain. Differences, for example, in the banking and legal environment prevent it from engaging in cross-border deliveries. Instead, it tends to opt for the traditional approach of establishing subsidiaries or joint ventures in target markets, rather than developing integrated pan-European operations (BVH, 1992). The BVH's analysis is supported by BEUC (European Consumers' Organisation), which conclude that:

mail order companies continue to organize along national lines rather than on the basis that there is a single market in which every consumer should have the right to buy from anywhere in the EU. Different currencies and fluctuating exchange rates, moreover, provide a cover behind which cross-border price distortions can be hidden. (*European Retail*, 1993, p. 9)

The BEUC analysis also reveals that major home shopping companies in the EU continue to refuse to meet cross-border orders. Smaller companies, where there are variations in national prices, ignore requests for cheaper, cross-border merchandise, and supply the goods from the usually more expensive national subsidiary. Significantly, this exploitation of national price variations is defended by the European home shopping trade organisation (EMOTA) (*European Retail*, 1993), which may be part of the explanation for the mere 3 per cent of total mail order turnover accounted for by cross-border sales.

The evidence suggests that retail companies will continue to internationalise at a pace, and in forms, largely unaffected by the legislative provisions of the SEM. However, a border-free EU, and with it a truly pan-European distribution system, does not yet seem a realistic proposition, nor does large-scale cross-border shopping. To encourage these developments, there needs to be, at the very least, an unambiguous and extensive statutory framework of rights and protection for consumers. In the case of home shopping, this opportunity was missed by succumbing to the neo-liberal prescription of deregulation and voluntary codes for retailers. As a result, consumers remain disadvantaged *vis-à-vis* the retailers, and the SEM is currently failing to produce mutual benefits for suppliers and customers.

A realistic assessment of the extent and range of intact non-tariff barriers against commercial cross-border distribution, despite the SEM, would reveal that their removal requires an integration process at a level that would have to reach into the heart of the European political economy, directly challenging the very existence of European national states and national regulations.

Notes

We are grateful to Gill Lester, Danusia Malina and Fred Burton for their help.

1. 'Home shopping' is understood here as all ordering of goods and services from domestic premises or order centres and their subsequent home delivery (Baron *et al.*, 1991). It is commonly used synonymously with 'mail order'.
2. A wide range of other EU policy measures could impact indirectly on the home shopping sector: the cabotage regulation with regards to road distribution operations; the VAT agreements on cross-border pricing; the Commission's Green Paper on postal services addressing the varying levels of communication and distribution services amongst national postal systems; and the directive on broadcasting and the proposal on comparative advertising dealing with central as-

pects of home shopping operations. The creation of a single currency would also help facilitate cross-border ordering, delivery and purchasing.
3. A number of authors have commented on the legal implications. Compare for example: CBI (1989), Gibson and Bernard (1989), Hill (1989), Thompson and Knox (1991) and Willis (1991). Others have highlighted relevant legislation, for example, Corporate Intelligence Group (1991), *Euromonitor* (1993) *European Retail* (1994c).
4. Whilst this extended approach is more readily associated with the full-blown Anglo–Saxon model, there is growing evidence that the EU's policy trajectory is increasingly caught within the same logic, most notably revealed in the White Paper on *Growth, Competitiveness, Employment* (COM (1993b)), launched in December 1993.

References

Alexander, N. (1988) 'Marketing the UK's retail revolution post 1992', *The Quarterly Review of Marketing* (Autumn) pp. 1–5.

Baron, S., Davies B. and Swindley, D. (1991) *Macmillan Dictionary of Retailing* (London: Macmillan, 1991).

Bennison, D. and Boutsouki, C. (1995) 'Greek retailing in transition', *International Journal of Retail and Distribution Management*, 23(1), pp. 16–23.

Burt, S. (1989) 'Trends in management issues in European retailing', *International Journal of Retailing*, 4, pp. 1–97.

Burt, S. (1991) 'Trends in the internationalization of grocery retailing: the European experience', *The International Review of Retail, Distribution and Consumer Research*, 1 (4), pp. 487–515.

BVH (1992) Personal Communication from Bundesverband des Deutschen Versandhandels e.V. (January).

CBI (1989) *Marketing: Communicating with the Consumer* (London: CBI).

Cecchini, P. (1989) *1992 – The Benefits of a Single Market* (Aldershot: Wildwood House).

CECG 1992a, Conversation (27 February).

CECG 1992b, *Distance Selling* (November London: CECG).

COM (1990) *Three Year Action Plan of Consumer Policy in the EEC 1990–1992*, COM(1990) 983 (May).

COM (1991) *Communication from the Commission: Towards a Single Market in Distribution. Internal Trade in the Community, the Commercial Sector, and the Completion of the Internal Market*, COM(91) 41 final (11 March).

COM (1992a) *Proposal for a Council Directive on the Protection of Consumers in Respect of Contracts Negotiated at a Distance (Distance Selling)*, COM(92) 11 final. SYN 411 (20 May).

COM (1992b) *Amended Proposal for a Council Directive on the Protection of Individuals with Regard to the Processing of Personal Data and on the Free Movement of such Data*, COM(92) 422 final. SYN 287 (15 October).

COM (1993a), *Consumer Policy – The Commission's Second Three Year Action Plan, 1993–1995*, COM(93) 378 (May).

COM (1993b) *White Paper: Growth, Competitiveness, Employment*, COM(93) 700 final.

Commission (1988) *The Economics of 1992*, Commission of the European Communities, *European Economy*, 35.

Commission Recommendation (1992) *Commission Recommendation of 7 April 1992 on Codes of Practice for the Protection of Consumers in respect of Contracts Negotiated at a Distance (Distance Selling)*, OJ L (19 June).

Consumer Policy (1993) *Consumer Policy in the European Community – An Overview, Background Report ISEC/B2/93* (London: Commission of the European Communities).

Consumer Rights (1993) *Consumer Rights in the Single Market* (Luxembourg: Commission of the European Communities).

Corporate Intelligence Group (1991) *European Retailing in the 1990s – A Manual for the Single Market* (London: CIG).

Dawson, J.A. (1993) 'The internationalization of retailing', in R.D.F. Bromley and C.J. Thomas (eds), *Retail Change – Contemporary Issues* (London: UCL Press), pp. 15–40.

Derek, R. (1992) 'Direct marketers hail EC revised Draft Directive', *Marketing* 29 October), p. 7.

Euromonitor, European Business Legislation Handbook 1993 (London: Euromonitor).

European Retail (1993) 'BEUC calls for cross-border improvements', 89 (EIU), p. 9.

European Retail (1994a) 'Ministers close to agreement', 92 (EIU), p. 11.

European Retail (1994b) 'Fears for mail order market', 96 (EIU) pp. 3–4.

European Retail (1994c) 'Plans and proposals affecting the retail sector', 98 (EIU) pp. 8–9.

European Retail (1994d) 'Compromise reached on regulation', 100 (EIU), p. 10.

European Retail (1994e), 'Consumer protection – Budget cuts 'Deplorable' says BEUC', 105 (EIU), p. 11.

Eurostat (1993) *Retailing in the European Single Market 1993* (Luxembourg/Brussels: Commission of the European Communities).

Gibson, G. and Bernard, P. (1989) 'Consumer trends in the EC – how can retailers respond?', in *Responding to 1992: Key Factors for Retailers* (OXIRM, Coopers & Lybrand) pp. 23–34.

Gill, S. (1992) 'The emerging world order and European change', in R. Miliband and L. Panitch (eds), *The Socialist Register 1992* (London: Merlin), pp. 157–96.

Grahl, J. and Teague, P. (1989) 'The cost of neo-liberal Europe', *New Left Review* 174, pp. 33–50.

Grahl, J. and Teague, P. (1990) *1992 – The Big Market: The Future of the European Community* (London: Lawrence & Wishart).

Hill, M. (1989) 'EC legislative change – impact on retailers', in *Responding to 1992: Key Factors for Retailers*, (OXIRM, Coopers & Lybrand), pp. 18–22.

Hollander, S.C. (1970) *Multi-national Retailing* (East Lansing: MSU International Business and Economic Studies).

Home Shopping (1991) *Home Shopping in West Germany, France and Italy – A Survey of Mail Order and Distance Selling*, Marketing in Europe Special Market Survey (EIU).

Kacker, M. (1985) *Transatlantic Trends in Retailing, Takeovers and Flow of Know-How* (London: Quorum Books).

Kacker, M. (1988) 'International flow of retailing know-how. Bridging the technology gap in distribution', *Journal of Retailing*, 64 (1), pp. 41–67.

Lawlor, E. (1989) *Individual Choice and Higher Growth. The Aim of Consumer Policy in the Single Market* (Luxembourg: Deadline '92 Document).

Pioch,E. and Brook, P. (1992) 'Shopping sans frontieres? European integration and home shopping', *European Business and Economic Development*, 1 (2), pp. 7–12.

Pioch, E. Davis, B. and Bennison, D. (1992) 'Pharmacies: the SEM and retail harmonisation', *International Journal of Retail and Distribution Management*, 20 (7), pp. 29–35.

Salmon, W.J. and Tordjman, A. (1989) 'The internationalization of retailing', *International Journal of Retail and Distribution Management*, 18 (5), pp. 3–14.

Thompson, K. and Knox, S. (1991) 'The single European grocery market, prospects for a channel crossing', *European Management Journal*, 9 (1), pp. 65–72.

Treadgold, A. (1988) *The Internationalization of Retailing* (OXIRM).

Treadgold, A. (1990) 'The developing internationalization of retailing', *International Journal of Retail and Distribution Management*, 18 (2), pp. 4–11.

'Treadgold, A. (1990/91) 'The emerging internationalization: present status and future challenge', *Irish Marketing Review*, 5 (2), pp. 11–27.

Waldman, C. (1978) *Strategies of International Mass Retailers* (New York: Praeger).

White, R. (1984) 'Multinational retailing: a slow advance?', *Retail and Distribution Management*, 12 (2), pp. 8–13.

Whitehead, M. (1992) 'How will retailers compete in an integrated market? Pan-European retailing – myth or reality', presented at the *Studies in the New Europe Conference* (Nottingham).

Williams, D.E. (1991) 'Differential firm advantages and retailer internationalization', *International Journal of Retail and Distribution Management* 19 (4) pp. 3–12.

Williams, D.E. (1992) 'Retailer internationalization: an empirical enquiry', *European Journal of Marketing*, 26 (8/9), pp. 8–24.

Willis, G. (1991) 'The Single Market and national marketing thinking', *European Journal of Marketing*, 25, (4), pp. 148–56.

Part Two

Mergers, Acquisitions and Cooperative Ventures

Mo Yamin

Regional integration in Europe, where it has developed more fully than else-where, and in North America and East Asia, is one of the forces (another being more rapid technological change) that is persuading more and more firms of the potential merit of collaboration through, for example, a joint venture and, frequently, full merger and acquisition (M & A). The choice of cross-border market entry between various modes of operation has been extensively researched within the transaction cost and internalisation litera-tures and many now agree, as Burton and Noble (Chapter 6) point out, that cooperative ventures are not necessarily second-best choices.

The boom in M&As and the increasing number of cooperative ventures between European firms are not merely reactive but also reinforce the proc-ess of European integration, and can thus be considered to be bridging or reducing the 'vision-reality' gap *vis-à-vis* the emergence of a single market, at least on the supply side. Intra-EU M&As and cooperative ventures facili-tate a greater degree of cross-penetration of markets across Europe, and boost the ability of EU firms to compete against US and Japanese rivals by developing pan-European strategies. At the same time, firms outside the EU, anxious to create 'beach-heads', as Hamill and Castledine (Chapter 5) put it, into the Euro-pean market use European acquisitions or alliances, in part, to achieve this.

The three chapters in Part two provide an examination of a number of issues relating to M&As and cooperative ventures. In Chapter 5, Hamill and Castledine, dealing with the impact of foreign acquisitions, both EU and non-EU, on the UK economy, address a relatively neglected issue. In Chap-ter 6, Burton and Noble focus on UK and Spanish cooperative ventures and examine their motives, their role in the strategies of their parents and how these strategies affect the longevity of the ventures. In Chapter 7, Schoenberg deals with the impact of differing management 'styles' on post-acquisition performance. Taken together, these chapters highlight two problem areas that suggest the 'vision–reality' gap will persist. First, there is the issue of the 'unlevel playing field' and the consequent heavy and disproportionate UK involvement in cross-border mergers and cooperative ventures in the

EU. Second, there are questions relating to performance. The overall success of cross-European mergers is not impressive, largely due to the persistence of management style differences between UK and continental firms which reflect deeper structural and cultural differences. As the discussion in Burton and Noble's Chapter 6 shows, the effective operation of a cooperative venture is also largely dependent on the management of style (and other differences) between the parent firms.

For a number of fairly familiar reasons the UK provides a fertile ground for mergers and acquisitions. For example, the relative weight of listed companies, which are both easier to acquire and may have a higher propensity to grow by mergers compared with family owned companies, is far greater in the UK than other EU countries. According to one estimate, the relative weight of listed companies in the UK is nearly three times greater than the average for all EU countries and over 40 per cent of listed companies in the EU are UK companies (CEC, 1989). Other factors helping to produce a more favourable M&A environment in the UK include the greater sophistication of financial markets and a more supportive regulatory structure. As a result, the UK is the leading target country for cross-border acquisition within Europe and has also attracted the largest number of acquisitions by non-EU companies.

The uneven incidence of acquisitions in Europe forms the background to Hamill and Castledine's concern. In a relatively short time-span, 1985–92, there were nearly 1300 EU and non-EU acquisitions in the UK, with a total value exceeding £59 bn. Hamill and Castledine assess the UK impact of acquisitions along a number of dimensions including 'resource', 'trade balance', 'employment' and 'sovereignty' effects. One observation relates to the differential impact of EU and non-EU acquisitions on the UK economy. Non-EU acquisitions appear to have a more beneficial (or less negative) impact on the UK economy, judged by the above dimensions, compared to EU acquisitions. This is not surprising, as one would expect intra-EU acquisitions to be motivated by a desire to rationalise operations on a Europe-wide scale, the short-term consequence being the closure or 'down-sizing' of operations in the UK. Thus, while intra-EU acquisitions may be helping to promote pan-European integration, it may be that the costs of this process fall unevenly on member countries. In this context, Burton and Noble's finding that locally successful ventures may nevertheless be abandoned as part of a broader, market-integrating, strategy is highly pertinent. Of course, many cross-border acquisitions may have less ambitious motives and be focused on 'traditional' issues such as market entry. Nevertheless, a subset of acquisitions is clearly driven by market-integrating and 'regionalising' considerations, possibly as a stepping-stone to globalising. Burton and Noble's observation regarding different motives for cooperative ventures is probably equally applicable to mergers and acquisitions.

Setting aside the impact on individual countries, an important question is whether intra-EU acquisitions add to the population of firms with pan-European capabilities, since the same structural differences that create an uneven incidence of merger pressures across countries can also impede effective post-acquisition integration. For example, while the vast majority of the UK acquirers in Schoenberg's study were publicly quoted companies, the majority of their European target companies had controlling family owners. Differences in ownership structure imply differences in management 'styles' which are reflected, *inter alia*, in risk-taking propensities, decision-making approaches and preferred control and communication patterns.

Schoenberg's finding that differences in national management styles have a clear-cut effect on post-merger performance is particularly relevant so far as market-integrating acquisitions are concerned. In such cases post-merger arrangements are likely to involve a high degree of strategic and hence organisational interdependence, effective management of which can be impeded by differences in management styles unless managers implement specific corrective measures. By contrast, market entry acquisitions may be tolerant of post-merger autonomy and require a lesser degree of integration.

'Style' differences are clearly also relevant when considering the effective operation and longevity of cooperative ventures, and style compatibilities are critical for their 'success'. Parkhe (1991) has pointed out the importance of the notion of 'diversity' for cooperative ventures. Some diversity, in technological competence for example, is actually a necessary condition for meaningful cooperation. However, other types of diversity, of which management style is but one, can undermine the effectiveness of potentially fruitful ventures. Other examples of diversity are differences in societal culture, stages of economic development and political economy characteristics. All three chapters, in different ways, illustrate the prevalence of national and cultural and style diversities within the EU. The management of M&As and cooperative ventures needs to take cognisance of such diversities and implement corrective measures if these strategies are to be effective in contributing to European integration.

References

Commission of the European Communities (CEC) (1989) *Study on Obstacles to Takeover Bids in the European Community* (Luxembourg: Commission of the European Communities).

Parkhe, A. (1991) 'Interfirm diversity, organisational learning, and longevity in global strategic alliances', *Journal of International Business Studies*, 22 (4), pp. 579–601.

5 Foreign Acquisitions in the UK: Impact and Policy

Jim Hamill and Pam Castledine

INTRODUCTION

The years since the mid-1980s have witnessed a boom in cross-border mergers and acquisitions (M & As). Initially, the USA was the main destination for such activity, with the years 1984–1988, in particular, being characterised by 'the foreign takeover of corporate America'; a total of 2055 foreign acquisitions valued at \$126 bn (see Hamill, 1993a). In more recent years, the geographical focus of crossborder M & As has shifted to Europe as companies attempt to strengthen product and geographical market positions in the Single Market. Crossborder M & As have been one of the most important strategies used to achieve pan-Europeanisation. In the period 1989–1992, there were a total of 6446 crossborder acquisitions in Europe valued at approximately £112 bn. These included both crossborder deals within the EU and a large number of European acquisitions by non-EU firms.

Previous papers by the author have examined the strategic motivations underlying the recent wave of crossborder M & As in Europe; issues concerning the planning, negotiation, management and performance of crossborder M & As; and the employment and related effects of post M & A rationalisation (Hamill, 1992, 1993a, 1993b). The recent boom in international acquisitions also raises important issues concerning the host country impact of foreign direct investment (FDI) and the multinational enterprise (MNE). While the economic impact of greenfield FDI has been extensively covered in the literature, far less attention has been paid to the host country effects of FDI in the form of external acquisitions. This is a serious omission in the literature given that crossborder acquisitions were the dominant mode of FDI during the late 1980s. As Table 5.1 shows, over two-thirds of the increase in FDI flows between 1986 and 1992 was accounted for by crossborder takeovers.

This chapter examines the host country impact of the recent boom in international takeovers, based on the experience of the UK. The choice of the UK is particularly relevant, given its pole position as the leading target country for crossborder acquisitions in Europe. Over 40 per cent of the total value of all crossborder acquisitions in Europe have been accounted for by the

Table 5.1 Value of world-wide cross-border acquisitions and FDI inflows to developed countries, 1989–92

Year	World-wide cross-border acquisitions ($bn)	FDI inflows to developed countries	Value of cross-border acquisitions as % of FDI inflows
1986	39	67	58
1987	71	109	65
1988	113	131	86
1989	122	168	73
1990	113	176	64
1991	50	121	41
1992	75	102	74
Total	583	874	67

Source: UNCTAD (1994).

foreign acquisition of British companies. In addition to the economic impact issues examined, the boom in foreign takeovers in the UK raises important policy concerns in the area of merger control which are examined in the final section.

FOREIGN TAKEOVERS IN THE UK

Between 1985 and 1992, foreign companies made a total of 1278 acquisitions in the UK valued at almost £60 bn. The years 1989 and 1990 were particularly active with a total of 558 deals valued at £31 bn. Many of the UK's largest industrial and commercial companies have passed into foreign ownership as a consequence of being externally acquired, with Table 5.2 showing the 20 largest acquisitions by value. In total, there have been 101 foreign acquisitions over the period valued at £100 mn or more; with 21 deals in excess of £500mn. Public interest has quite naturally focused on these mega-acquisitions. Foreign acquisitions of UK companies, however, have not been confined to such mega-deals. A large number of small and medium sized British companies (SMEs) have been externally acquired; with some 548 acquisitions (43 per cent of the total) valued at £1mn or less. This is a legitimate source of concern from an economic impact and policy perspective given the importance attached to SMEs as generators of economic growth.

The nationality of ownership distribution of foreign acquirers in the UK is shown in Table 5.3. US companies have been the most active acquirers, accounting for 22 and 25 per cent respectively of the total number and value of deals; followed by French (13 per cent and 16 per cent) and Australian

Table 5.2 Twenty largest foreign acquisitions in the UK, 1985–92

Acquired company	Acquiring company	Nationality of acquiring company	Sector	Acquisition value (£mn)	Year
Beecham	SmithKline	USA	Pharmaceuticals	4509	1989
Midland Bank	Hong Kong & Shanghai Bank	Hong Kong	Banking	3600	1992
Rowntree	Nestlé	Switzerland	Confectionery	2622	1988
STC PLC	BCE Inc	Canada	Electronics	1836	1990
Jaguar	Ford Motor	USA	Motors	1560	1989
Courage	Elders IXL	Australia	Brewing	1400	1986
Inter-Continental	Saison	Japan	Hotels	1350	1988
Occidental Petroleum	Elf Aquitaine Oil	France	Minerals oil and gas	1350	1991
Pearl Group	Australian Mutual Provident Society	Australia	Insurance	1243	1989
Nabisco, R J R	BSN	France	Crisps, snacks, biscuits	1064	1989
Reedpack	Svenska Cellulosa	Sweden	Packaging and paper	1050	1990
Yorkshire Bank	National Australia Bank	Australia	Banking	977	1990
Morgan Grenfell	Deutsche Bank	Germany	Banking and financial services	950	1989
Smiths/Walkers	Pepsico	USA	Potato crisps	856	1989
Guinness	Louis Vuitton Möet Hennessy	France	Brewing	821	1990
Metalbox Packaging	Carnaud	France	Metal packaging	780	1988
ICL	Fujitsu Ltd	Japan	Computers	743	1990
Mount Charlotte	Brierley Investments	New Zealand	Hotels	644	1990
DRG	Pembridge Associates	USA	Stationery and packaging	641	1989
RTZ Chemicals	Rhône-Poulenc	France	Fine chemicals	568	1989

Source: Acquisition Monthly (various issues).

Table 5.3 Foreign acquisitions in the UK, by nationality of acquiring firm, 1985–92

Nationality	no. of acquisitions	% of total no. of acquisitions	Acquisition value (£mn)	% of total acquisition value
Non-EU				
USA	279	22	14 787	25
Australia	55	4	5505	9
Hong Kong*	17	1	3862	7
Switzerland	51	4	3762	6
Sweden	85	7	3699	6
Japan	58	5	3318	6
Canada	29	2	3107	5
New Zealand	11	1	1715	3
South Africa	15	1	835	1
Other Non-EC	155	11	2083	4
All Non-EU	738	58	42 673	72
EU				
France	167	13	9330	16
Germany (W)	83	6	2634	4
Netherlands	70	5	1891	3
Eire	128	10	1342	2
Belgium	17	1	768	1
Denmark	33	3	419	1
Italy	26	2	192	-
Spain	10	1	149	-
Luxembourg	6	-	97	-
Portugal	2	-	10	-
Greece	-	-	-	-
All EC	542	42	16 641	28
Total	1278	100	59 375	100

* Most of this value due to one acquisition of £3.6 bn, i.e. Hong Kong & Shanghai Banks takeover of Midland.

Source: *Acquisition Monthly* (various issues).

(4 per cent and 9 per cent) companies. A particularly interesting aspect to note from Table 5.3 is that non-EU based companies have been the most active foreign acquirers in the UK. Over 70 per cent of the total value of all foreign acquisitions in the UK during the period covered have been accounted for by non-EU firms. For many of these companies, UK acquisitions have been used as a 'beach-head' into European markets in the run-up to '1992'.

Finally, in terms of industry distribution, foreign acquisitions in the UK have occurred across a wide range of sectors, both manufacturing and non-manufacturing. Almost half of the total value of all deals, however, is accounted for by just three sectors – banking, insurance and financial services; food and drink; and chemicals.

IMPACT OF FOREIGN ACQUISITIONS IN THE UK

The impact of inward direct investment on the UK economy has been the subject of a number of studies spanning four decades (Dunning, 1958, 1976, 1986; Steuer *et al.*, 1973; Brech and Sharp, 1984; Stopford and Turner, 1985; Panić and Joyce, 1980; Panić, 1991; Hood and Young, 1976, 1982, 1983, 1984. While certain negative effects have been identified, the weight of empirical evidence supports net benefits overall; particularly in terms of technology transfer and diffusion, balance of payments, employment, productivity and labour relations.

The above conclusion has been based mainly on an evaluation of the economic impact of inward direct investment in greenfield subsidiaries. Very little work has been done on the effects of inward acquisitions. What little there is largely predates the recent boom in foreign takeovers in the UK (e.g. Hood and Young, 1983). There has been some related work which has examined the impact of external acquisitions on regional economies within the UK. The foreign owned dimension, however, has not been specifically examined in these studies (Ashcroft, 1988; Ashcroft and Love, 1988, 1990, 1993; Ashcroft, Love and Scouller, 1987; Coppins, 1989; Hughes, 1989; Leigh and North, 1978; Smith 1979, 1982). The lack of empirical evidence concerning the impact of foreign acquisitions in the UK is a serious weakness in the literature, given that the balance of positive and negative effects might differ considerably from that of greenfield foreign investments. While positive effects have generally been associated with the latter, the economic impact of foreign acquisitions is less clear. Particular concerns have been expressed regarding the possible negative effects deriving from post-acquisition integration and rationalisation (e.g. employment losses, transfer of HQ functions, etc.).

The host country impact of FDI in greenfield subsidiaries is normally examined in five main areas covering resource transfer effects; impact on market structure, conduct and performance; trade and balance of payments effects; employment; and sovereignty effects (see Hood, Young and Hamill, 1988). These can be used as a basis for hypothesising concerning the impact of foreign acquisitions. Figure 5.1 summarises the range of potential positive and negative effects of foreign acquisitions in the UK in each of the five areas. Thus, foreign acquisitions in the UK would have positive effects when:

- New or advanced technology is transferred to the recently acquired subsidiary

Figure 5.1 Potential effects of foreign acquisitions in the UK

Impact	Positive effects	Negative effects
Resource transfer	Transfer of new technology from acquiring to acquired company	Access to new technology restricted
	Transfer of new management practices	Centralisation of R & D at parent company leading to loss of indigenous technology capability
	Acquired company gains access to new sources of capital	Capital funding restricted to reinvested earnings
Trade and balance of payments effects	Capital account gain through initial purchase price	Subsequent repatriation of profits, royalties, interest, etc.
	Increased exports through access to international distribution channels and international marketing knowledge of parent	Increased imports of intermediary products from other subsidiaries/parent company
	UK subsidiary granted wide product/geographical market mandate, e.g. Europe	Subsidiary role restricted to UK market/narrow product line
Market structure, conduct and performance	Acquisition stimulates competition through breaking existing oligopoly	Acquisition strengthens existing market position of acquirer and increases industry concentration
	Improved efficiency and performance through transfer of resources (as above) and competitive reaction of rivals	Further increase in industry concentration through rival acquisitions
	Increased international competitiveness	
Employment effects	Increased employment and jobs security as a consequence of higher exports, wide product/market mandate, etc.	Large-scale job losses as consequence of post-acquisition rationalisation; reduced job security
	Improved quality of employment through technology transfers, international marketing responsibilities, etc.	Lower quality of employment due to restricted role of subsidiary
Sovereignty and autonomy effects	Transfer of some HQ functions to acquired company	Loss of autonomy through transfer of HQ functions to new parent

Source: Authors' data.

- New management practices are introduced in the areas of finance, marketing, human resources etc.
- The subsidiary gains access to new sources of capital
- The acquisition overcomes market entry barriers, reduces industry concentration levels and stimulates competition
- Subsidiary exports are increased through gaining access to wider international distribution channels and the introduction of new products
- As a consequence of the above (increased exports; new technology, etc.), both the level and quality of employment is enhanced and labour relations are improved
- The recently acquired subsidiary is given enhanced decision-making responsibility, perhaps as a European Regional HQ.

There are, of course, opposing scenarios in each of these areas. Thus, negative effects would occur when:

- Technology transfers are limited and there is a loss of indigenous technology capability through the centralisation of R & D
- The introduction of new management practices leads to conflict between parent and subsidiary
- Access to funding is restricted
- The acquisition strengthens the existing UK market position of the foreign acquirer, thereby increasing industry concentration and reducing competition
- The newly acquired subsidiary is allocated a restricted product/market status, thereby reducing exports
- Post-acquisition rationalisation leads to major job losses and reduced job security
- There is a significant transfer of head office functions from subsidiary to parent resulting in the loss of decision-making autonomy.

The above list covers mainly the first order effects of an inward acquisition. There will, however, be important second order effects associated with foreign takeovers. For example, the foreign acquisition of a UK company may result in reduced local linkages as the newly acquired subsidiary becomes integrated with the global or Euro-wide strategy of the acquirer. Important second order effects may arise, too, in terms of the impact of the acquisition on indigenous companies. Where a foreign acquisition stimulates competition, this may be expected to lead to improved efficiency. On the other hand, a foreign acquisition which results in a dominant market position may have adverse effects on indigenous companies who lack the scale economies necessary to compete with the new industry leader. Finally, it is worth noting that the balance between positive and negative effects may differ considerably, depending on the motivations underlying the acquisition. Hamill (1993a) explained the boom in crossborder mergers and acquisitions since the mid-1980s as an attempt by MNEs to create a sustainable competitive advantage in industries which were becoming increasingly global or regional in scope. Two main types of competitive advantage can be sought through crossborder acquisitions: first, acquisitions which seek to strengthen product and geographical market portfolios; second, acquisitions which seek to achieve lower costs and greater efficiency through resource sharing and scale economies. Clearly, elements of both may be present in any specific deal since acquisitions are multi- rather than uni-causal (Hamill, 1993a).

The importance of this distinction between acquisitions which are primarily product/market expansion driven and those which are cost/efficiency driven is that the nature of post-acquisition change, and therefore the economic impact of the acquisition, may differ radically. Foreign acquisitions in the UK which are primarily cost/efficiency driven are likely to have greater negative effects than those which are product/market expansion driven. The former is likely to be accompanied by significant post-acquisition rationalisation and integration leading to major job losses, reduced subsidiary status, the transfer of HQ functions out of the UK and so on. In product/market expansion driven acquisitions, on the other hand, the UK company acquired may play a much more important role in the overall international market development of the new parent company.

There is an important nationality of ownership dimension to the above argument. Acquisitions in the UK by non-EU based firms are more likely to be product/market expansion driven (i.e. establishing market share in Europe), while UK acquisitions by EU based companies are more likely to be cost/efficiency driven. The research results presented below highlight significant differences in acquisition impact by nationality of ownership.

METHODOLOGY

In order to examine the economic impact issues identified in the previous section, a postal questionnaire was sent to a large sample of British companies externally acquired since 1985. A total of 325 companies were surveyed, covering all acquisitions valued at £20 mn or more. 38 companies replied that the survey was inappropriate, mainly because there had been a further change in ownership since the original acquisition. From the 287 remaining companies, a total of 73 completed questionnaires were returned, giving a response rate of 25 per cent. Given the highly sensitive nature of the topic, this was a very satisfactory response level. The respondent companies were highly representative of the total population by sector, nationality of acquirer, date and value of acquisition (see Table 5.4). Over 90 per cent of the acquisitions examined were described as being friendly rather than hostile takeovers. Again, this is representative of acquisitions in general.

Table 5.4 Sample characteristics, 1985–92.

(a) Companies acquired

Year of acquisition	No. of companies	% of sample
1985	3	4
1986	6	8
1987	4	5
1988	7	10
1989	18	25
1990	19	26
1991	12	16
1992	4	5
Total	73	100

(b) Acquirer nationality

Nationality of acquirer	No. of companies	% of sample
France	18	25
USA	13	18
Germany (W)	9	13
Japan	6	8
Australia	4	6
Sweden	4	6
Finland	3	4
Others	16	20
Total	73	100

(c) No. and % of sample companies, by acquisition value

	£20<£50mn	£50<£100mn	£100<£200mn	>£200mn
No. of companies	43	10	12	8
% of sample	59	14	16	11

(d) Sectoral distribution

	No. of companies	% of sample
Oil, gas, mining water utilities	7	10
Manufacturing	37	51
Non-manufacturing	29	40
Total	73	100

(e) Nature of acquisition

	No. of companies	% of sample
Friendly	67	92
Hostile bid	6	8
Total	73	100

Source: Authors' postal survey.

Despite the extensive media coverage of hostile deals, the vast majority of acquisitions are friendly takeovers.

The questionnaire itself was divided into five main sections, covering background information on the company and the acquisition (company name, principal activities, year of acquisition, acquisition value, nationality of acquirer, friendly or hostile takeover, pre-acquisition and current sales, pretax profits, exports and employment); acquisition motivations (with a list of motivating factors being presented derived from the acquisition literature – see Hamill, 1992); post-acquisition change covering subsidiary product strategy, R & D, export volume and export markets supplied, imports, technology transfers, capital investment, changes in employment levels and personnel; the locus of post-acquisition decision-making covering financial, production, marketing, personal and R & D decisions; finally, general comments covering post-acquisition integration and performance.

Before summarising the main findings of the survey it should be noted that there are a number of methodological problems in attempting to assess the economic impact of takeovers. These have been examined in detail by Ashcroft and Love (1993) and include the appropriate balance between quantitative (financial ratios) and qualitative (structural changes in products/markets supplied, etc.) measures; data sources (e.g. company reports, postal surveys, company interviews, etc.); the choice of indicators; the time period covered; and so on. A particular problem is the counterfactual difficulty of distinguishing between 'what happened after the acquisition' and 'what happened because of it'. Clearly these difficulties apply to the research reported here. The postal survey was the first of a two-stage research programme evaluating acquisition impact, and will be followed up with detailed personal interviews with the companies concerned. The counterfactual position was at least partly established by asking respondents to explain why certain post-acquisition changes had taken place in order to assess whether they were a direct consequence of the takeover *per se*.

ACQUISITION IMPACT–SURVEY RESULTS

As stated previously, acquisition impact may vary significantly with acquisition motivations (e.g. product/market expansion vs cost/efficiency driven acquisitions). Before presenting the main findings of the survey concerning acquisition impact, the motivations underlying foreign acquisitions in the UK need to be examined. These are summarised in Table 5.5. The results support the proposition advanced earlier that the boom in crossborder mergers and acquisitions since the mid-1980s has been a consequence of the attempt by MNEs to improve their competitive position in increasingly global markets. For foreign acquisitions in the UK, 76 per cent of the companies surveyed stated that improving international competitiveness was a

Table 5.5 Acquisition motivations

	Very important/important		
	% of total sample	% of EC acquirers	% of non-EC acquirers
Improve international competitiveness	76	68	83
Extend geographical market coverage in Europe	73	78	66
Acquire large market share in UK	69	73	60
Product/market diversification	67	59	74
Gain foothold in UK market	65	73	60
Gain access to management/marketing skills	61	58	60
Acquire products or brands	59	51	60
Achieve instant growth	56	68	40
Strategic response to competitors actions	55	54	51
Acquire large market share in EC	51	54	46
Gain access to technology	47	51	43
Gain foothold in EC	46	49	43
Economies of scale in marketing/distribution	43	38	46
Increase short-term profits	42	49	31
Economics of scale in R & D	36	41	29
Exchange rate influences	34	22	9
Acquire under-valued assets	28	27	26
Economies of scale in production	26	19	31
Increase share price	26	35	11
Acquire a competitor	22	16	29
HQ economies of scale	16	16	11
Other economies of scale	11	8	6

Source: Authors' postal survey.

'very important' or 'important' reason underlying the acquisition. Significantly, this increases to 83 per cent for the non-EU based firms surveyed. Table 5.5 also shows that product/market expansion driven acquisitions were more common than cost/efficiency driven acquisitions. A much higher proportion of the sample companies claimed that factors such as 'extending geographical market coverage in Europe'; 'acquiring market share'; 'product/market diversification', and 'acquiring products, brands, marketing and management skills' were important motivating factors compared to cost/efficiency motivations such as economies of scale in marketing, distribution, R & D, production and HQ activities. The relative importance of product/market expansion motivations needs to be borne in mind when considering the results presented below.

The following subsections present the main findings of the survey covering the five impact areas identified earlier. The sections draw from Tables 5.6a and 5.6b which provide a concise summary of the main findings.

Table 5.6 Post-acquisition change, summary table

(a) % of Sample

	Significant increase	Some increase	No change	Some reduction	Significant reduction
R & D expenditure	14	25	52	5	4
Product range	14	33	13	11	29
Export markets supplied	17	28	45	6	4
Export volume	13	31	48	4	4
Import volume	12	26	59	2	2
Employment levels	4	16	12	30	37

(b) % of sample claiming significant change in:

	Yes	No
Technology transfer	40	61
Management practices transfer	55	45
Capital transfers	44	56
Executive changes	69	31
Market structure changes	45	55
Personnel and industrial relations practices	58	42

Source: Authors' postal survey.

Resource Transfer Effects

Figure 5.1 identified a range of potential positive and negative resource transfer effects associated with the foreign takeover of British companies. The results of the survey support net overall benefits in this area, particularly in terms of increased subsidiary R & D and technology transfer.

39 per cent of the sample companies claimed a 'significant' or 'some' increase in UK R & D expenditure post-acquisition. This increases to 47 per cent in the case of manufacturing companies. Only 9 per cent of the sample (2 per cent of the manufacturing companies surveyed) stated a post-acquisition reduction in subsidiary R & D. Therefore, the evidence does not support the often expressed fear that foreign acquisitions in the UK will lead to a loss of indigenous technology capability through the transfer of R & D activity to the new parent company. Indeed, the evidence supports the opposite case, with 40 per cent of the sample (Table 5.6b) reporting significant transfers of technology from the new parent company to the UK subsidiary post-acquisition. This increases to 51 per cent for manufacturing companies.

In addition to increased subsidiary R & D expenditure and technology transfer, other resource transfer effects associated with foreign acquisitions in the UK include the transfer of management practices and capital. As regards the former, 55 per cent of the sample stated that new management practices had been transferred post-acquisition (Table 5.6b). This increases to 61 per cent for the manufacturing companies surveyed. The areas in which management practices were transferred were wide ranging, including financial reporting and planning procedures; quality control techniques; new product development and production planning; distribution and logistics systems; communication procedures; and management culture. Regarding capital transfers, 44 per cent of the sample (45 per cent of the manufacturing firms surveyed) had received a significant injection of capital investment post-acquisition.

The general conclusion emerging from the evidence presented above is that the resource transfer effects of foreign acquisitions in the UK have been in many cases positive, and in others neutral. In very few cases has the resource transfer impact been negative. It is worth noting, however, that there are significant variations in the results by nationality of ownership of the acquiring company supporting the argument developed earlier concerning the differential impact of EU and non-EU acquisitions in the UK. 49 per cent of the non-EU based acquiring companies, compared to only 30 per cent of EC based parents, claimed a 'significant' or 'some' increase in R & D post-acquisition. For management and capital transfers the respective percentages were 60 and 57 per cent for non-EU based parents compared to 51 and 32 per cent for EU firms. Thus, the positive resource transfer effects are greatest in non-EU acquisitions of UK companies. Such nationality of ownership differences are examined in more detail later.

Trade and Balance of Payments Effects

As in the case of resource transfer effects discussed above, both positive and negative hypotheses can be established concerning the trade and balance of payments effects of foreign acquisitions in the UK. These relate to the nature and extent of post-acquisition integration of the newly acquired subsidiary into the overall global operations of the new parent company (see Figure 5.1). Positive trade effects would arise when increased subsidiary exports result from access to the wider international distribution channels of the new parent and/or the UK subsidiary is granted a wide product/geographical market mandate. Negative effects would arise from increased imports of intermediary products and, in cases where the newly acquired UK subsidiary is granted, a narrow product/geographical market mandate.

Several questions in the survey addressed these issues covering changes in the product role of the subsidiary post-acquisition; export volume and markets supplied; and subsidiary imports. The empirical evidence highlights significant changes in each of these areas post-acquisition (i.e. significant changes in product/market responsibilities). For example, only 13 per cent of the companies surveyed stated that the acquisition had no effect on the product role of the UK subsidiary. By contrast, 47 per cent stated that there had been a 'significant' or 'some' increase in the product range of the subsidiary post-acquisition, with 40 per cent claiming a 'significant' or 'some' decrease. The evidence, therefore, highlights important subsidiary product role changes post-acquisition. Concerning export markets, 45 per cent of the sample stated a broadening of geographical markets supplied, compared to only 10 per cent stating a narrowing of geographical focus. As a consequence, 44 per cent of the sample claimed a 'significant' or 'some' increase in export volume post-acquisition, compared to only 8 per cent stating a 'significant' or 'some' reduction in exports. The survey estimated the direct impact of these changes on the total value of exports in the sample companies. The post-acquisition value of exports in the 73 companies was £623mn compared to pre-acquisition exports of £458mn, i.e. an increase of 36 per cent in value terms.

As in the case of resource transfer effects examined in the previous section, the evidence presented above supports net benefits overall in terms of the trade and balance of payments impact of foreign acquisitions in the UK; especially in terms of increased export volume and access to wider geographical markets. There are, however, two main qualifications to this conclusion. First, the increase in subsidiary export propensity post-acquisition must be balanced against a much higher import propensity. 38 per cent of the companies surveyed claimed a 'significant' or 'some' increase in post-acquisition imports compared to only 4 per cent stating a decrease. This is consistent with post-acquisition integration of the UK subsidiary into the wider global operations of the parent company, and implies reduced local linkages. Second, there were significant variations in the results discussed above by nationality of ownership of the acquiring company. As in the previous section, the trade and balance of payments effects of foreign acquisitions in the UK were generally more favourable in the case of non-EU based acquirers compared to EU companies. 49 per cent of non-EU acquirers claimed a 'significant' or 'some' increase in export markets supplied post-acquisition, compared to only 28 per cent for EU acquirers. In terms of export volume, 57 per cent of non-EU acquirers claimed a 'significant' or 'some' increase post-acquisition compared to only 31 per cent of EU acquirers. This is consistent with the UK acquisition being used to gain entry into EU markets. For imports, 36 per cent of non-EU firms, compared to 40 per cent for EU firms claimed an increase. Thus, it may be concluded that UK acquisitions by non-EU firms have generally positive effects on UK trade; the opposite is the case for EU acquisitions of UK companies.

Market Structure, Conduct and Performance Effects

A detailed analysis of the market structure effects of the recent wave of foreign acquisitions in the UK is largely outwith the scope of this chapter, since this would require an in-depth study of changing industry concentration levels. In order to gather some preliminary evidence, however, respondents were asked to state whether there had been any significant change in the competitive structure of their UK industry in recent years as a consequence of mergers and acquisitions. 44 per cent of the sample claimed that significant changes in market structure had taken place. The two principal changes identified were first, increased competition from non-UK based companies as a consequence of foreign acquisitions in the UK (especially in the water supply, electronics and financial services industries) and second, an increase in industry concentration levels as a consequence of M & As (especially in chemicals, financial services, publishing, food and drink).

Employment and Related Effects

The employment and related effects of foreign acquisitions in the UK have become an issue of major concern given the persistence of high UK unemployment.

As in previous sections, both positive and negative propositions can be advanced in terms of employment impact. Negative employment level effects would arise from post-acquisition production rationalisation and from the transfer of certain functions out of the UK. On the other hand, to the extent that the foreign acquisition widens export distribution channels (see earlier), total employment levels may increase post-acquisition. Foreign acquisitions of UK companies may have other significant employment effects on UK managers and workers through changes in executive personnel post-acquisition and the transfer of parent company personnel and industrial relations practices.

Regarding employment level effects, two-thirds (67 per cent) of the companies surveyed reported a 'significant' or 'some' decline in employment levels post-acquisition. Total pre-acquisition employment in the sample was 101 826 employees compared to 91 061 employees currently, i.e. an 11 per cent reduction in employment pre- and post-acquisition. Leaving aside the 20 per cent of firms who reported 'some' increase in employment, the 47 firms reporting an employment decline recorded job losses from 80 087 to 70 653 employees, i.e. a reduction of 12 per cent. Clearly, not all of these job losses were a direct consequence of the acquisition *per se*, with other causes being the recession, technology change and so on. It was clear from the explanations given that approximately 80 per cent of the jobs lost were a direct consequence of post-acquisition rationalisation. The conclusion to be drawn from the above results, therefore, is that foreign acquisitions in the UK have, in general, a net negative effect on employment levels. There was only minor variations by nationality of acquirer. 72 per cent of EU based acquirers compared to 63 per cent of non-EU based acquirers reported employment losses.

Table 5.7 Locus of post-acquisition decision-making, % of sample

	Very centralised			Very decentralised	
	1	*2*	*3*	*4*	*5*
Financial decisions	20	27	31	14	8
Production decisions	8	3	12	28	48
Marketing decisions	3	7	23	23	43
Personnel/industrial relations decisions	3	1	13	37	46
R & D decisions	9	17	17	27	30

Source: Authors' postal survey.

Regarding the other employment and related effects identified earlier, foreign acquisitions of UK companies are generally accompanied by major changes in executive personnel post-acquisition. 69 per cent of the sample reported major changes in this area. In the majority of cases, this involved the appointment of new senior executives (often from the parent company) and non-executive directors across a range of functional areas. The survey also highlighted significant transfers of personnel and industrial relations practices post-acquisition. 58 per cent of the companies surveyed reported 'significant' or 'some' transfers in this area, with the main reason given to achieve standardisation of practices across subsidiaries.

Sovereignty and Autonomy Effects

A major concern relating to the boom in foreign takeovers of UK companies is the potential loss of national sovereignty associated with the transfer of decision-making power out of the UK. The survey examined the locus of post-acquisition decision-making across a range of functional areas with the results summarised in Table 5.7. Clearly, UK companies which have been externally acquired are granted a large degree of decision-making autonomy in terms of day-to-day operational issues covering production, marketing and personnel decisions. A much higher level of centralisation is evident in financial decision-making, consistent with the transfer of long-term strategic control out of the UK. R & D decisions were also centralised in a significant proportion of the companies survey.

DISCUSSION OF RESULTS

The problems involved in attempting to evaluate the host country impact of external acquisitions were discussed earlier. With these in mind, the evidence derived from the postal survey at least allows some preliminary conclusions to be drawn concerning the economic impact of foreign acquisitions in the UK, and these are summarised below.

The survey highlighted a mix of positive and negative effects. There was little evidence to support fears that foreign takeovers will lead to a loss of indigenous technological capability. Only 9 per cent of companies (2 per cent of manufacturing companies) reported a reduction in post-acquisition R & D expenditure. A significant proportion of the sample (40 per cent overall and 51 per cent for manufacturing companies) reported an increase in R & D expenditure post-acquisition. The position regarding other resource transfer effects (management practices, capital) was also generally positive.

Probably the most important area of impact concerns changing subsidiary product/geographical market roles post-acquisition. The evidence highlights significant post-acquisition integration of acquired UK subsidiaries into the overall global operations of the new parent, resulting in major changes in products and markets supplied. The positive trade and balance of payments effects associated with the subsequent increase in export volume need to be balanced against increased imports of intermediary products and reduced local linkages. The most significant negative effects of foreign acquisitions relate to post-acquisition employment losses, (some) loss of decision-making autonomy and increased industry concentration levels.

Significant variations emerged in acquisition impact by nationality of ownership. Generally, UK acquisitions by non-EU firms have a more favourable (less negative) effect than acquisitions by EU based firms. These differences are related to the initial motivations underlying the acquisition. For non-EU based companies, UK acquisitions have acted as a major channel for establishing market share in the Single European Market (SEM). As argued earlier, such product/market expansion driven acquisitions may have positive effects if the acquired UK operation is given an important role to play in the overall European strategy of the parent company. This is much less likely in the case of UK acquisitions by EU based firms which are more cost/efficiency driven. Such acquisitions will have certain negative effects on the UK, particularly concerning increased imports and employment losses.

Finally, reference was made earlier to the large number of studies which had examined the economic impact of greenfield FDI. A major conclusion of the present study is that the economic impact of foreign acquisition is different from that of FDI in greenfield subsidiaries. The empirical evidence supports net positive effects in the case of greenfield FDI, especially in terms of technology transfer and diffusions, balance of payments effects, employment, productivity and labour relations. The evidence presented in this chapter shows that the impact of foreign acquisitions may also be positive in some of these areas – increased R & D expenditure post-acquisition, transfer of management practices, capital investment, and increased exports. In contrast to greenfield FDI, however, foreign acquisitions are likely to have negative effects on employment, increased imports and industry concentration levels.

POLICY IMPLICATIONS

Previous sections of this chapter have shown that the boom in foreign takeovers of British companies since the mid-1980s raises important issues concerning the impact of external ownership on the UK economy. The results of the survey highlight a mix of both positive and negative impacts. These are of sufficient magnitude that the overall net impact of external acquisitions should be a legitimate area of concern for policy-makers. This, however, has not been reflected in the conduct of UK merger policy, which has been characterised by an almost total lack of concern with the effects of external acquisitions. There is a residual power under the Industry Act 1975 to block foreign takeovers of UK companies of strategic importance (e.g. national security and defence). While never invoked, the national security argument has been used on occasions (e.g. Westland Helicopters). Generally, however, the issue of foreign ownership has not been in the forefront of the debate on merger control in the UK.

Three main phases in the evolution of UK merger policy relevant to the debate on the impact of external acquisitions can be identified. Prior to the early 1980s, the public interest criteria predominated. The Monopolies and Mergers Commission assessed proposed mergers referred to it by the Secretary of State on the grounds of whether the merger would operate against the public interest. The latter was defined in extremely broad terms to include the potential impact of the proposed merger on competition; on consumers in terms of the price, quality and variety of goods available; questions of industrial efficiency, costs, technology and international competitiveness; employment and related effects; and issues concerning the regional distribution of industry.

This broad definition of the public interest was both a strength and a weakness of UK merger policy during the 1970s. The major strength was that it allowed a detailed investigation to be made of all aspects of the proposed merger, taking into account both macroeconomic and microeconomic effects. The major weaknesses were the length of time taken to investigate, proposed deals (six to nine months on average) and the absence of clearly defined criteria on when a deal was or was not against the public interest. By the early 1980s, UK merger policy had degenerated into a confusion of 'ad hoc' and inconsistent precedents. This led to the second main phase in policy evolution, namely, the 'Tebbit dictum' under which the sole criteria for assessing mergers became their impact on competition. For most of the last decade or so, proposed mergers have been defined as being against the public interest only when they restrict, distort or prevent competition. This reflects the Conservative Government's belief in the benefits of free competition and the use of market forces over government intervention. The main strength of this policy is its clarity and certainty deriving from an unambiguous definition of the public interest as being equal to competition.

The main weakness is the almost total lack of attention paid to the wider macroeconomic and microeconomic effects of mergers and acquisitions, including questions of foreign ownership.

The third main phase in the evolution of UK merger policy has been imposed externally. As a member of the EU, the UK is subject to EU merger control procedures which require that all proposed deals with a 'Community dimension' have to be notified to the European Commission for approval before they are put into effect. Included in the definition of 'Community dimension' are mergers and acquisitions where the companies involved have worldwide sales of ECU 5000 mn (approximately US $6000mn); at least two of the groups to which the companies involved belong have sales in the EU of ECU 250 mn (approximately US $300m); and the companies involved do significant business in more than one EU member state. Companies achieving more than two thirds of their EU sales in one Member State are exempt from the legislation, since these cases are considered essentially national in character. The legislation covers both cross-border acquisitions within the EU and EU acquisitions by non-EU firms. More contentiously, the legislation also covers mergers and acquisitions between two non-EC firms. For example, a merger or acquisition between two US companies would have to be notified to the Commission if either had more than ECU 250 mn sales within the EU. As in the UK, the dominant criteria used by the EU in evaluating mergers and acquisitions is their effects on competition. A deal will be prohibited only when it 'strengthens a dominant position as a result of which effective competition in the market would be impeded'.

It can be concluded from the above review of UK and EU merger policy that the question of external acquisition of UK companies has not been a major concern of policy-makers and that existing merger control legislation is inadequate to deal with the issue. The concerns raised earlier in this chapter indicate that this is a serious weakness in current UK merger policy and that there may be a strong case for a more proactive approach – one which would lead to a more detailed evaluation of the economic impact of foreign acquisitions in the UK. At least four main arguments can be advanced for this approach: first, the scale of the phenomenon, with a total of 1278 British companies being externally acquired between 1985 and 1992 valued at £60 bn. Second, the fact that over 40 per cent of the total value of all crossborder acquisitions in Europe is accounted for by the foreign acquisition of UK companies, reflecting an 'unlevel playing field' which puts British companies at a major disadvantage in attempting to establish the scale necessary for competitiveness in the Single European Market. For a number of reasons (the importance of publicly listed companies, family ownership structures, more sophisticated financial markets and a more supportive regulatory structure) it is more difficult for UK companies to make large acquisitions in Continental Europe than the reverse, especially large hostile acquisitions. Third, the fact that foreign acquisitions may have certain detrimental effects on the UK economy, especially in the case of acquisitions by EU based firms. Finally, while the volume of foreign takeovers has declined significantly over the last year or so in line with the recession and the slump in the acquisition market generally, this is likely to be only a temporary interruption. The continuing globalisation of markets and competition and the trend towards further European integration are likely to lead to a further upsurge in activity over the next few years. As a consequence key British enterprises and sectors of the UK economy could pass into foreign ownership without any attempt to assess the net effects of such deals on the UK.

The need for a reassessment of current policy was clearly illustrated at the end of January 1994 with the announcement of BMW's £800 mn takeover of the UK's only remaining volume car producer, the Rover Group. The takeover was warmly welcomed by the UK Government as being evidence of the confidence of foreign investors in the UK economy. No account was taken of the fact that the economic impact of inward direct investment in the form of acquisitions may be radically different from that of greenfield FDI. Given the strategic importance of Rover to the UK engineering industry, it is surprising that no attempt was made to assess the long-term economic impact of the acquisition.

There is a strong case, therefore, for a change in UK government policy in relation to foreign acquisitions of British companies. As to the type of policy to be introduced, however, the government's room for manoeuvre is severely limited by policy at an EU-wide level. In addition, returning to the pre-1980 position (see earlier) is not a solution given the problems in defining 'public interest' criteria and the time involved in investigating proposed deals. Moreover, the introduction of tight controls might lead to retaliatory measures being imposed on British companies who have been major acquirers abroad. At a very minimum, the government should encourage foreign acquirers in the UK to make public their short- and long-term plans for the newly acquired subsidiary. This would at least lead to some degree of public debate and accountability in the post-acquisition period.

CONCLUSIONS

The argument advanced above should not be interpreted as one in favour of autarky or for imposing stringent controls on foreign ownership. Rather, it is based on a realistic assessment that a continuation of past trends in foreign acquisitions could have a profound effect on the future, long-term well-being of the British economy. This should be a legitimate area of concern for policy-makers.

The UK's relationship with EU partners has come under severe strain in recent years (e.g. the 'Social Chapter'; ERM; the election of a new European President) with British politicians and managers being seen as less committed to the pan-European 'ideal'. The policy recommendations outlined above could be interpreted as another example of UK ethnocentrism with the emphasis being on national self-interest rather than European efficiency. The recommendations made, however, are intended to contribute to a wider debate on the impact of crossborder acquisitions in Europe generally. One of the main objectives of the Single Market was to improve the global competitiveness of European industry *vis-à-vis* Japanese and US rivals. To achieve this, the European Commission has adopted a *'laissez-faire'* approach to cross-border mergers, acquisitions and strategic alliances (M&As) between European companies with such deals being seen as creating the 'critical mass' necessary to compete in global markets. In addition to the impact on industry concentration levels, policy-makers should be aware that M&As suffer from a very high failure rate (Hamill, 1993b) and are no guarantee of improved efficiency or competitiveness.

Taking all of these comments together, there is a very strong argument for a detailed research study to examine the impact of the recent wave of crossborder M&As in Europe, taking into account the impact both on national economies and industry competitiveness.

Note

The authors are extremely grateful to Philip Healey, Editor and Publisher of *Acquisitions Monthly*, for providing the acquisition data on which the first part of this chapter is based.

References

Ashcroft B. (1988) 'External takeovers in Scottish manufacturing: the effects on local linkages and corporate functions', *Scottish Journal of Political Economy*, 35 (2), pp. 129–48.

Ashcroft, B. and Love, J.H. (1988) 'The regional interest in UK mergers policy', *Regional Studies*, 22 (4), pp. 341–4.

Ashcroft, B. and Love, J.H. (1990) 'Corporate takeovers and the interests of regions and local communities', *Hume Occasional Paper*, 17 (Edinburgh: David Hume Institute).

Ashcroft, B. and Love, J.H. (1993) 'Takeovers, mergers and the regional economy', *Scottish Industrial Policy Series*, 5 (Edinburgh: Edinburgh University Press).

Ashcroft, B., Love, J.H. and Scouller, J. (1987) 'The economic effects of the inward acquisition of Scottish manufacturing companies 1965 to 1980', *ESU Research Paper*, 11 (Edinburgh: Industry Department for Scotland).

Brech, M. and Sharp, M. (1984) 'Inward investment: policy pptions for the UK', *Chatham House Papers*, 21 (London: Routledge & Kegan Paul).

Coppins, B. (1989) 'The spatial dimension of takeovers and geographical transfer of corporate control: evidence from the UK, 1968–85', Department of Economics and Financial Studies, Napier Polytechnic, mimeo.

Dunning, J.H. (1958) *American Investment in British Manufacturing Industry* (London: Allen & Unwin).

Dunning, J.H. (1976) *US Industry in Britain*, EAG Business Research Study (London: Wilton House).

Dunning, J.H. (1986) *Japanese Participation in British Industry* (London: Croom Helm).

Hamill, J. (1992) 'Crossborder mergers, acquisitions and alliances in Europe', Chapter 6 in S. Young and J. Hamill (eds), *Europe and the Multinationals: Issues and Responses for the 1990s* (Aldershot: Edward Elgar).

Hamill, J. (1993a) 'Crossborder mergers, acquisitions and strategic alliances', Chapter 4 in P. Bailey, A. Parisotto and G. Renshaw (eds). *Multinationals and Employment : The Global Economy of the 1990s* (Geneva: ILO).

Hamill, J. (1993b) 'Managing crossborder mergers and acquisitions in Europe', Chapter 1 in M.J. Baker (ed.) *Perspectives on Marketing Management*, vol. 3 (Chichester: John Wiley).

Hood, N. and Young, S. (1976) 'US investment in Scotland: aspects of the branch factory syndrome', *Scottish Journal of Political Economy*, 23 (3), pp. 279–94.

Hood, N. and Young, S. (1982) *Multinationals in Retreat: The Scottish Experience* (Edinburgh: Edinburgh University Press).

Hood, N. and Young, S. (1983) *Multinational Investment Strategies in the British Isles: A Study of MNEs in the Assisted Areas and in the Republic of Ireland* (London: HMSO).

Hood, N. and Young, S. (1984) *Industry Policy and the Scottish Economy* (Edinburgh: Edinburgh University Press).

Hughes, A. (1989) 'The impact of merger: a survey of empirical evidence for the UK', in J.A. Fairburn and J.A. Kay (eds), *Mergers and Merger Policy* (Oxford: Oxford University Press).

International Labour Office (1993) *Multinationals and Employment: The Global Economy of the 1990s*, P. Bailey, A. Parissoto and G. Renshaw (eds) (Geneva: ILO).

Leigh, R. and North, D.J. (1978) 'Regional aspects of acquisition activity in British manufacturing industry', *Regional Studies*, 12 (2). pp. 227–45.

Panić, M. and Joyce, P.L. (1980) 'UK manufacturing industry: international integration and trade performance', *Bank of England Quarterly Bulletin* (March).

Panić, M. (1991) 'The impact of multinationals on national economic policies', in B. Bürgenmier and J.L. Mucchielli (eds), *Multinationals and Europe 1992* (London: Routledge).

Smith, I.J. (1979) 'The effect of external takeovers on manufacturing employment change in Northern region between 1963 and 1973', *Regional Studies*, 13 (5), pp. 421–37.

Smith, I.J. (1982) 'Some implications of inward investment through takeover activity', *Northern Economic Review* (February). pp. 1–5.

Steuer, M.D. *et al.* (1973) *The Impact of Foreign Direct Investment on the UK* (London: HMSO).

Stopford, J. M. and Turner, L. (1985) *Britain and the Multinationals* (Chichester: John Wiley).

United Nations Conference on Trade and Development (UNCTAD) (1994) *World Investment Report, 1994; Transnational Corporations, Employment and the Workplace* (Geneva: UNCTAD).

Young, S., Hood, N. and Hamill, J. (1988) *Foreign Multinationals and the British Economy* (London: Croom Helm).

6 European Cooperative Ventures between Spanish and UK Firms

Fred Burton and Dorothea Noble

INTRODUCTION

Cooperative ventures between firms, in their best-known form of joint ventures, have attracted academic interest for many years, but much of the early work mostly addressed factors influencing their life-span and internal performance. Theorists, grappling to provide explanations for the emergence and spread of international firms and their strength and resilience, treated inter-firm cooperation – international joint ventures and other cross-border activities, such as licensing – as a second-best option entered into by firms when denied the opportunity to establish wholly owned subsidiaries. Only in the 1980s did circumstances begin to be evaluated when cooperative arrangements might be first-choice preferences of firms, for example when a local partner could contribute competencies which the foreign partner lacked, allowing both partners to gain through joint internalisation, or when there were government inspired barriers to foreign ownership (Dunning, 1981).

Transaction cost analyses, both the internalisation approach (Buckley and Casson, 1976) and the markets versus hierarchy model (Williamson, 1975), has been particularly fruitful in teasing out the potential benefits each partner can bring to a cross-border venture. But if the contemporary view is that partners can benefit by sharing competencies, a belief still prevails that western firms, particularly when doing business in developing countries, would prefer full ownership and control if there were no legal obstacles to foreign ownership. In any event, the management of cooperative ventures is likely to pose complex problems associated with the level of trust between the partners and their willingness to share information and decision-making. How well problems are handled will be influenced by the relative bargaining power of the partners and their ability to avoid an excessive reliance on forbearance (Buckley and Casson, 1988), the rewards being a potential reduction in long-term costs relative to pure hierarchical or market operations (Beamish and Banks, 1987). Economic analysis has since been complemented by organisational learning perspectives (Kogut, 1988), network analysis (Johanson and Mattson, 1988; Aoki et al, 1990), and by agency and game theories, to develop the notion further that cooperative ventures, in many situations, will be the preferred choice, both as an organisational asset and a strategic tool.

SPANISH–UK COOPERATIVE VENTURES

This chapter considers (1) the motives of a sample of Spanish and UK firms involved in cooperative ventures in, respectively, the UK and Spain, (2) the role played, if any, by these ventures in the strategies of the parent companies, and (3) whether the longevity and ownership and control structures of ventures are influenced by strategies of dominant partners or parent firms to integrate their European or global markets.

The ventures in the sample were formed during the post-war period to 1991, but the analysis relates mostly to those formed from the 1980s onwards when memories of the executives consulted about the characteristics of the ventures were still fresh. A surge in venture activity in the EU occurred in the 1980s when completion of the Single European Market took pride of place on the European corporate policy agenda.

The 1986 Single European Act accelerated the changes imposed on Spain by its membership of the EU and introduced a new urgency into government policy and the strategic thinking of businesses. Spanish firms were driven by an optimism that was tempered by a fear that foreign firms, attracted by the growth potential in newly opening Spanish markets, would become dominant by strengthening their physical presence in Spain. In the face of these competitive threats, Spanish firms embarked on various forms of cross-border expansion within the EU. For example, in 1985 the EU accounted for 30 per cent of Spain's outward flows of foreign direct investment, and for 54.0 per cent by 1990. Over the same period, flows to the UK increased from 7.0 per cent to 20.0 per cent of Spains's total outward flows. The fear in the UK was that UK firms were not doing enough to prepare for the closer integration of European markets that the 1992 programme signified. Nevertheless, UK firms increased their flow of foreign direct investment into the EU from 29.0 per cent of total outward flows in 1985 to 55.0 percent in 1990. Flows to Spain over the same period increased from less than 1.0 per cent to around 15.0 per cent (*Boletin Economico* and *Business Monitor*, various editions). An increase in cross-border cooperative ventures of various kinds also occurred in response to much the same threats and opportunities.

The Sample

The analysis draws on a study of 34 affiliated operations established in the UK by 16 Spanish parent firms and 56 operations established by 17 UK parents in Spain. Foreign direct investment (FDI) in wholly owned subsidiaries

Table 6.1 Ownership methods and types of cooperative Spanish–UK business ventures

| | Ownership type | | | |
	Joint ventures	Shared ventures	Equity alliances	Total
Child	13	3		16
Partner–child	6	2		8
Alliance			3	3
Majority venture		6		6
Merger		2		2
Total	19	13	3	35

Source: Authors' data.

was stated to be the preferred market entry mode of both sets of parent firms, but 35 of these 90 separate operations were cooperative ventures of one kind or another, seven of which were initiated before 1970. These 35 ventures are the ones to which the analysis relates. In broad terms, the Spanish firms claimed to be attracted to UK locations by the UK's open economy and tradition for hosting foreign firms, and by the opportunity a UK location gave them to gain experience applicable to international markets, not simply the UK market. The UK firms were attracted to Spain by the growth prospects Spain offered to products that had reached, or were approaching, life-cycle maturity elsewhere.

Information came from interviews with senior executives in the parent companies. Open-ended questions captured respondents' own ideas and perceptions, and closed questions produced a standardised data bank. The interview evidence was supported by published data and additional information supplied by the companies. Two brief case studies are used to specify some of the observations.

The cooperative arrangements in the sample, as shown in Table 6.1, comprise 'equity alliances', joint ventures and 'shared' ventures. An equity alliance is defined as an agreement to cooperate on specific activities backed by an exchange of shares or the participation of one partner in the equity of the other. A 'joint venture' is defined as a new business venture set up by two or more partners to achieve synergies and benefits not available to any one partner acting alone. In a shared venture, one partner takes up an equity interest in an established business, bringing to it attributes that may guarantee its survival, bring about a change of direction, or help it to expand, frequently with a view to eventual acquisition.

As seen in Table 6.1, most of the joint ventures were 'child' ventures set up as distinct operations. Five of the partner–child ventures were small first-entry distribution centres. The sixth was a group of small companies in which

Table 6.2   Industry distribution of the cooperative ventures

	Spain	UK	Both[1]	Total
Automotive	1	9	1	11
		(3)	(1)	(4)
Financial services	2	5	1	8
	(1)	(1)		(2)
Other manufacturers	5	5	1	11
	(3)	(3)	(1)	(7)
Energy	1	2		3
		(2)		(2)
Tourism	1		1	2
	(1)			(1)
Total	10	21	4	35
	(5)	(8)	(2)	(16)

Notes: 1. 'Both' denotes ventures where both partners are sample firms.
　　　 2. Figures in brackets indicate terminated ventures.

Source: Authors' data.

a lead partner contributed finance and technical and managerial expertise. Of the shared ventures, the partner–child operations were treated by the parents as joint ventures; six were stable majority owned ventures, each run by the dominant partners as though a wholly owned subsidiary; the two 'mergers' were allowed autonomy until such time as they were fully acquired by the dominant partner. In what follows, shared and joint ventures will be grouped together.

The industry distribution of the ventures is shown in Table 6.2. In the 1970s, four UK and Four Spanish parent firms were involved in ventures that related to traditional agricultural products, tourism or engineering (one of these being a venture between Spanish and UK parents represented in the sample). The ventures in financial services were established during the 1980s when Spain began to liberalise and open up its economy. The ventures in the energy sector also began in the 1980s when the oil monopoly began to break up in Spain and the privatisation programme for the energy sector began in the UK.

Of the 35 ventures, 19, involving 15 parent firms, were still active into the 1990s. All the rest had by then been disbanded in venture form: seven had been taken over by a parent; in four ventures, one partner had sold out to another; and the remaining five had been dissolved.

Table 6.3 shows when the ventures started up and their longevity. The early ones were set up at a time when regulatory regimes inhibited foreign ownership, whereas the surge in venture formation from 1980 testifies to the increased confidence of partners in their likely success. Many of the terminations represented successful ventures that had served their purpose

Table 6.3 The timing and duration of ventures, pre-1970 to 1990–2

	pre-1970	1970–9	1980–4	1985–9	1990–2	Total
Start-up	7	2	6	17	3	35
Surviving ventures	1	1	4	10	3	19
Duration (years)	< 2	3–6	7–10	> 10	Total	
Surviving ventures	5	8	2	4	19	
Duration (years)	1–5	6+				
Terminated ventures	9	7			16	

Source: Authors' data.

and had been acquired by a partner. Evidence of high mortality rates in the service sector, observed elsewhere (Kogut, 1988), also arose in this sample. The same explanation is offered here: service firms seek cross-border cooperative ventures to learn quickly about local market conditions and the suitability of their products or to gain an appreciation of how such ventures might serve as a tool of group strategies, following which the purpose of a particular venture will have been served.

MOTIVES FOR THE CHOICE OF COOPERATIVE VENTURES

Since the motives of the ventures set up prior to 1980 are obscured by time, the discussion will centre on those ventures established from 1980 onwards (Table 6.4). One of three motives largely accounted for the parent firms' choice of a cooperative venture rather than a wholly owned foreign subsidiary: the need to harness local experience and expertise; to secure resources and/or gain access to the local market at a lesser cost and risk than go-it-alone operations; to contribute to strategies to integrate a firm's international markets. To describe the orientation of many of the ventures as European, let alone global, would be an over-statement. Even some of the firms which had an international focus entered into ventures specifically to handle local issues. The third motive, therefore, applies to only to a small number of ventures.

The relative significance of these motives is influenced by the size and nationality of the parent firms and the industrial sector(s) to which they belong. Spanish firms, smaller than their UK counterparts, have typically used ventures to harness the market knowledge of the local partners. Most of the UK parents with this priority were mainly financial service firms newly liberated for foreign expansion but aware that local markets had distinctive characteristics that would have a bearing on the acceptance of their service provision. Strategies to integrate cross-border markets were confined to UK firms.

Table 6.4   Primary motives for the choice of a cooperative venture

	Spain	UK	Total
Harness local experience and expertise	6	5	11
Secure resources/access markets	2	7	9
Contribute to globalisation strategies	0	6	6
Total	8	18	26

Source: Authors' data.

Harness Local Experience

Of the 11 cases for whom this motive was dominant, 10 were service centres, four of which were ventures between manufacturers and local distributors. One of these represented a first step into the UK by a Spanish manufacturer, who set up separate production and distribution ventures. These ventures were merged once manufacturing started up, and the Spanish partner then took responsibility for relocating and restructuring the business. The other parent-company manufacturers used their ventures to gain control of distribution channels, which they considered to be the key to growth. Only one of the three was successful and was eventually taken over by the parent firm. The other two both had Spanish parents and were experiencing difficulties; in one case because a costly and unnecessary link was added to the distribution chain, and in the other because skills that were inappropriate to the local market were internalised in an attempt to replicate home market distribution systems.

Five of the ventures, in retail financial services, were set up to develop new activities following the easing of regulations across Europe. The need for local expertise is especially strong in this sector in consequence of the ability of national market regulations and consumer protection measures to favour local firms. The foreign partner is seeking access to local clients' networks, expertise in interpreting local regulations and customer needs, and local staff to deliver the service. Spanish firms in this group were attempting to integrate upstream and looking for local expertise in products and ideas and field support for downstream activities. UK partners were in pursuit of horizontal integration, taking existing products to new markets and looking to local expertise to establish the interface. A local partner was often selected to help to position the foreign partner in the market. That is to say, an association with a reliable and prestigious local partner was used to establish the credentials of the new entrant – a kind of 'bridging' internalisation. Attempts were made in all these cases to raise the market's awareness of the foreign partner's identity as a first step towards establishing a long-term presence. Since indivisibilities and barriers to merger are temporary

(Buckley and Casson, 1988), a wholly owned subsidiary, in time, is the likely outcome for cooperative ventures in financial services.

Secure Resources and/or Market Access at Reduced Cost and Risk

Three of four manufacturing ventures in this group are local sourcing operations in the automotive components sector in Spain with UK multinational parents. Although the ventures support the European strategies of their parents, their main role has been to serve subsidiaries operating in Spain.

In one case, the parent firm was able to source in the local market without having to absorb all the output of its joint venture. In exchange, the local partner gained access to process technology, which gave quality improvements across its product range, and retained a high degree of autonomy.

In the second case, a UK multinational bought into a Spanish firm which was a licensee of a European rival's technology. This secured access to that technology without calling forth the retaliatory action which would have occurred had a wholly owned subsidiary been set up.

The third case was a consortium of UK and Spanish interests, including financial institutions and the Spanish government, set up to rationalise production in the sector in the face of over-capacity and at the same time to sustain R&D expenditure. The sharing of technology and the desire of the private sector partners to achieve long-term return on investment objectives clashed heavily with the employment and industry-restructuring ambitions of the government. The interests of the various partners were so diverse and the venture, in consequence, was so unstable that after two troubled years the UK partners withdrew.

In the fourth case, a number of Spanish firms in associated businesses decided that a merger would be of mutual benefit if an experienced lead partner could be found. Within the group, there was no experience of large-firm management, no experience with mergers, limited financial resources and only a rudimentary knowledge of exporting. It was also recognised that technological improvements would have to be introduced to offer any chance of a successful merger. A business link between one of the group and a UK multinational led to an invitation to the UK firm to enter into a venture with the group and to act as the lead partner. A respected Spanish bank played a major role in policing the integrity of the negotiations between the parties. The Spanish partners successfully merged their activities into the venture, gained immediate access to the UK partner's export markets, and learned to compete abroad. The UK partner won the chance to expand rapidly in the Spanish market, and to distribute the partners' product range, which included high value added products that complemented its export portfolio. Despite the many parties to the venture, several factors, documented in other studies, were present that contributed to the success of the venture – clarity of the objectives, the skills of a mediator, and the early achievement of benefits for all the partners (Killing,1982; Kogut,1988; Harrigan, 1988).

Three of the remaining ventures with this main motive were in financial services. Two were equity alliances in which the partners were seeking access to each other's markets. In each case, there was at least one partner who hoped to avoid an unwanted takeover. Once this threat receded, the UK partner in the first alliance did little to promote joint activities causing the alliance to be disbanded and sold off, a risk that is always likely to be present when a 'white knight' motive is present. The second alliance is the subject of the second case study.

The third venture, in the Spanish financial sector, was initiated to allow the gradual takeover of an ailing Spanish firm by the UK partner. The investment input and experience of the UK partner was expected to turn the business round and allow phased action to establish the UK firm's name and reputation in the market. Expectations were realised and the UK partner gained fast entry to the market, a phased introduction of resources, a low risk learning period, and a guarantee that the venture could be purchased if desired. On acquisition, the venture adopted the parent's name and extensive expansion plans were announced. The final venture in this group, set up to acquire pioneer status in a new market segment, is the subject of the first case study.

Contribute to Market Integration

A cooperative venture can contribute to a partner's globalisation strategies when it is linked to the partner's desire to integrate its diverse national markets. Many of the ventures represented here were set up simply to add to or establish operational capabilities in either Spanish or UK markets. In other cases, even though the ventures supported European, even global, strategies of one or more partners, operations could just as readily have been located elsewhere.

Some ventures, successful in meeting the initial objectives in local markets, may be abandoned nevertheless in favour of new coalitions better able to support higher level strategies and objectives. Global networks, for example, have long been utilised by firms in the financial services sector to spread risk and to widen both the product and the customer base. Insurance firms in the sample were linked to reinsurance networks, sometimes accessed through ventures with stronger operators. One Spanish firm, a member of several ventures serving European markets, was also a member of a US reinsurance network headed by a much larger American partner. When the American firm expanded directly into Europe, the Spanish firm withdrew from its European ventures and formed a broader alliance with the American firm that greatly strengthened its ability to penetrate, compete in, and integrate its European markets.

A second example illustrates how successful ventures may be abandoned for strategic reasons. A UK multinational in the sample, producing a range of branded consumer goods, used its network of wholly owned subsidiaries and cooperative ventures, including a successful venture in Spain, to distribute its products throughout Europe. In the early 1980s, the firm redefined its mission and made a complete switch out of manufacturing into distribution. Its distribution network was strengthened by entering into more ventures with national distributors and negotiating exclusive agreements for the distribution of local and European branded products in various European territories. Compliance with performance standards and exclusivity clauses within the network was expected to be enforced by 'hostage' positions in which the quality of service each partner received within the network was dependent on the quality of service it delivered to the network. As the network grew, it began to enjoy oligopolistic advantages and yet avoid antitrust scrutiny. Despite the success of the national ventures in the group, they all became wholly owned subsidiaries to give the parent greater control over group standards and operating procedures. A particular benefit was the enhanced ability to adopt a differential pricing strategy across the group's markets.

The study threw up other examples of how strategic realignment of cross-border territorial expansion can cause cooperative ventures to outlive their usefulness and be abandoned or have their ownership and control structure changed.

CASE STUDY 1: THE INITIAL CONFIGURATION OF A JOINT VENTURE

The literature on cooperative ventures in the 1980s began to focus more sharply on their distinctive merits as preferred market entry and development modes, and to identify the likely influences on their ownership and control structures, their longevity and stability, and factors leading to subsequent changes in formal and informal agreements negotiated between the partners – the *modus operandi*, referred to by Harrigan (1984) as the 'configuration' of cooperative ventures.

The following case offers an appraisal of the likely success and stability of a joint venture based on Harrigan's model of joint venture configuration. The case is a 50:50 joint venture between Spanish and UK multinational firms, each leaders in their respective industries. The venture was set up to combine the respective competencies of the partners to create an opportunity to become the pioneeers in an unexploited market segment in Spain, namely, the provision of roadside services on trunk roads to travellers that would offer petrol, fast-food outlets and stop-over accommodation on single sites. The 'concept', already well-established in France, the UK and Germany, features low prices, consistent branded-quality products and services, and nation-wide availability.

Barriers to pan-European integration of the roadside services sector included the presence of dominant national firms in the UK, France and Germany, the neccesity to generate nation-wide market penetration to create brand image and high volume sales, the need to develop the market quickly to pre-empt pioneer-status challenges from competitors, and the probability of government antipathy to a foreign go-it-alone operation. On the other hand, some barriers were being lowered. Health and safety standards within the EU were being harmonised, financial markets were set to be deregulated, and many trade and cross-border investment barriers were being dismantled under the Single Market initiative.

Spain had no dominant national firm in the sector, but the UK firm was able to identify a potential (and eventual) Spanish partner with complementary attributes. Had the partners decided to act alone, the Spanish firm would have entered the market with a land bank, finance, local knowledge and influence in government circles, but no experience of the roadside service concept or of its management. The UK firm would start with ownership and experience of the concept, and marketing and design skills, but would be faced with a lack of sites and no means of testing the market without incurring high start-up costs. It was clear to both parties that, acting together, they had the range of competencies necessary to contemplate market entry.

A negotiated agreement to a long-term partnership, sharing equally the costs and risks, seemed set to experience few obstacles to cooperation because hostage positions were finely balanced, and mutual forbearance and a strong build-up of trust could be expected. The venture seemed able to guarantee quick market access to the partners, both of whom were strong competitors with sound performance records and at a similar stage in their strategies to expand in Europe. In consequence, the initial configuration promised a balanced, stable and successful cooperative venture (Bleeke and Ernst, 1991), subject to government support in assisting the venture to get quickly into its stride. However, the significance to each partner of the other's contributions to the venture can be expected to fade in time, implying that there may become a need for contracts to be renegotiated (Rugman *et al.*, 1986). Looking ahead, should asymmetric relationships develop, or the venture's role become strategically redundant, exit barriers would mostly relate to the disposal of assets and any loss to the reputations of the partners.

The reality of the venture is that its start-up was driven by the need to diversify and reduce dependencies on home markets, and the willingness of the partners to share the risks of seeking pioneer status in a new, untested, market in which a successful outcome promised a major advance towards the internationalisation of the sector and the standardisation of EU markets for these services.

CASE STUDY 2: STRENGTHENING STRATEGIC POSITIONS IN EU
MARKETS

This case is a representative of European alliances set up in the 1980s between financial services firms to strengthen their strategic posture in EU
markets by depriving competitors of potential allies (Kogut, 1988). This
particular alliance between two relatively small Spanish and UK firms was
considered likely to succeed by the partners without sacrificing their small-
firm ability to respond rapidly to regulatory and technology-based changes
in the markets for their products. An exchange of equity between the partners signalled to potential predators that the partners were determined to act
in unison. Some early and successful projects led to further exchanges of
equity and a number of joint acquisitions.

The coalition risks included the possibility that the staffing of specific
projects would be inadequate, that there would be haphazard dissemination
of information within the alliance on decisions that affected both firms, and
a lack of cultural affinity that would detract from a build-up of trust. Also,
one partner had ambitions, not shared by the other, to expand beyond Europe. However, these risks were considered to outweigh the higher costs
associated with a merger or the possibility of being taken over.

The alliance, which served its initial purpose of defending the partners
against predators and turned two competitors into allies (Contractor and
Lorange, 1988), offered horizontal integration opportunities to both firms
(Williamson, 1975), and opportunities to share market knowledge and distribution channels (Lyles, 1988) and reduce financial risk (Beamish, 1991).
In addition, the sharing and spreading of information technology costs across
many markets improved the quality and range of services to the parents'
client base. The creation of these benefits through the alliance represented a
major strategic response by relatively small players to the anticipated market integration and internationalisation dynamics of the Single European Act.

Despite the strategic success of the alliance, some of the potential risks
were realised. Staff were not kept fully informed of joint activities, and
strong personal relationships at senior management levels gave way to cul-
ture-bound suspicion and some inter-firm hostility lower down. External
perceptions of cultural problems inside the alliance likely to affect performance found expression in critical reports by market analysts, which exerted
downward pressure on the market value of the firms' assets. The alliance
needed to build up mutual trust, which the determination of senior managers
to make the alliance achieve its aims, and a string of successful joint operations, helped in time to create.

CONCLUSIONS

Foreign direct investment (FDI) by European firms in the EU, although often focused on the rationalisation of operations and minimum efficient scale, will contribute to the closer integration of European markets. Cross-border European cooperative ventures can also be seen to be playing an integrating role and to be adding further dimensions to firms' international business strategies: making access possible to otherwise difficult-to-penetrate new markets, allowing competencies to be shared which the other partner(s) lack, and offering a framework for organisational learning – these and other dimensions all contributing to a strengthening of a firm's competitive positioning in national, and sometimes Europe-wide, markets. Cooperative ventures were seen to ease the way into new markets even for experienced firms (mainly from the UK), and to allow less experienced firms (mainly Spanish) to phase in their commitment. In all cases, successful ventures allowed the partners to widen their product and market portfolios. Cooperation also gave firms safer access to new markets, for example by their name-association with a respected local partner.

UK energy companies, larger than their Spanish counterparts, used cooperative ventures to defuse competitor and government reaction in Spain. This gradual approach to merger assured them of a strong position in the Spanish market. Spanish energy companies were equally cautious in entering the UK as non-dominant players. Their aim was to learn of international competitive operations from their experiences in the UK.

Cooperation in financial services gave UK companies fast penetration of the Spanish market. Spanish companies, again, regarded a presence in the UK as strengthening their ability to compete in wider international markets. Both partners to the alliance in this sector were seeking expansion and market integration in Europe. The ventures established by UK automotive firms in Spain reflected the importance of controlling quality standards. Among the 'other' manufactures, Spanish firms gained the opportunity to learn about UK and other European products and markets. UK firms used cooperative ventures to replicate the competitive positions they held in other European markets.

Finally, whatever the international experience of venture partners or their motives, success will depend on how well cultural differences are managed, even between European partners in an integrated Europe.

References

Aoki, M. Gustafsson, B. and Williamson, O.E. (1990) *The Firm as a Nexus of Treaties* (London: Sage Publications).
Beamish, P. (1991) *International Management: Text and Cases* (New York: Irwin).

Beamish, P. and Banks, J.C. (1987) 'Equity joint ventures and the theory of the multinational enterprise', *Journal of International Business Studies*, 18 (2) (Summer), pp. 1–16.

Bleeke, J. and Ernst, D. (1991) 'The way to win in cross-border alliances', *Harvard Business Review*, 69 (6) (November–December), pp. 127–36.

Buckley, P.J. and Casson, M. (1976) 'Organisational forms and multinational companies', in Buckley P.J. (ed.), *Studies in International Business* (London: Basingstoke).

Buckley, P.J. and Casson, M. (1988) 'A theory of cooperation in international business', in F.J. Contractor and P. Lorange (eds), *Cooperative Strategies in International Business* (Lexington: Lexington Books).

Contractor, F.J. and Lorange, P. ((1988). 'Competition vs. cooperation: a benefit/cost framework for choosing between fully-owned investments and cooperative relationships', in P.J. Contractor and P. Lorange (eds), *Cooperative Strategies in International Business* (Lexington: Lexington Books).

Dunning, J.H. (1981) *International Production and the Multinational Enterprise* (London: Allen & Unwin).

Harrigan, K.R. (1984) 'Joint ventures and global strategies', *Columbia Journal of World Business*, 9 (2), pp. 7–14.

Harrigan, K.R. (1988) 'Strategic alliances and partner asymmetries' in P.J. Contractor and P. Lorange (eds), *Cooperative Strategies in International Business* (Lexington: Lexington Books).

Johanson, J. and Mattson, L-G. (1988) 'Internationalisation in industrial systems – a network approach', in N. Hood and J.-E. Vahlne (eds), *Strategies in Global Competition* (New York: Croom Helm).

Killing, J.P. (1982) 'How to make a global joint venture work', *Harvard Business Review*, 60 (3) (May–June) pp. 120–7.

Kogut, B. (1988) 'A study of the life cycle of joint ventures', in P.J. Contractor and P. Lorange (eds), *Cooperative Strategies in International Business* (Lexington: Lexington Books).

Lyles, M.A. (1988) 'Learning among joint venture sophisticated firms', *Management International Review* (Special Issue), pp. 85–98.

Rugman, A.M. Lecraw, D.J. and Booth, L.D. (1986) *International Business: Firm and Environment* (New York: McGraw-Hill).

Williamson, O.E. (1975) *Markets and Hierarchies: Analysis and Anti trust Implications* (New York: Free Press).

7 European Cross-border Acquisitions – The Impact of Management Style Differences on Performance

Richard Schoenberg

INTRODUCTION

Acquisitions have long been recognised as a means of increasing a firm's European competitiveness (Kitching, 1974). They allow rapid entry into new or expanding geographic markets as well as a means to diversify into new product markets (Norburn and Schoenberg, 1994). Indeed the promise of a single European market has seen a rapid increase in European cross-border acquisition activity. Since 1987, the number of cross-border acquisitions completed within the EU has risen four-fold. By 1992 over 800 cross-border deals a year were completed within the EU, with UK companies accounting for nearly a quarter of the total. Despite this level of activity, empirical studies continue to highlight the low success rates associated with such acquisitions. Research by McKinsey (Bleeke and Ernst, 1993) reveals the overall success rate for cross-border acquisitions to be as low as 57 per cent, a marginal improvement only over Kitching's 1973 finding. Increasing emphasis has focused upon the post-acquisition integration stage as being a key determinant of acquisition success (Haspeslagh and Jemison, 1991): even the best strategic logic can only bear fruit if properly implemented. Indeed, pathbreaking work on European acquisitions (Kitching, 1973) estimated that one third of all acquisition failures were due to ineffective integration. Continuing this direction, research on domestic intra-country acquisitions has converged upon the importance of cultural compatibility and associated management style compatibility.

The current chapter extends this research stream into the international context, investigating empirically the extent to which management style compatibility influences the performance of European cross-border acquisitions. Do management style differences originating in the cultural diversity of Europe hinder the use of acquisitions as an effective means of European expansion? What steps can corporate policy-makers take to optimise the success rate of the acquisitions they do choose to make? The sections that follow develop formal research hypotheses from the literature, describe testing of the hypotheses

122

using a sample of 124 cross-border acquisitions, and discuss the implications of the results for corporate policy.

PRIOR RESEARCH AND HYPOTHESES

Impact of Management Style Differences

Datta (1991) reviews the management style literature, highlighting that management groups can exhibit significant differences along dimensions such as risk-taking propensities, decision-making approach, and preferred control and communication pattens. It has been hypothesised (Buono and Bowditch, 1989; Datta, 1991; Cartwright and Cooper, 1992) that if such differences in management styles exist between the acquiring and acquired company in an acquisition the performance of that acquisition will be inferior to one in which there is a match between the styles of the two managements. Indeed, this hypothesis has been upheld in a study of 173 domestic US acquisitions (Datta, 1991), where the author concludes that

> acquisitions of firms with a different management style can result in conflicts, difficulties in achieving operational synergies, market share shrinkages and poor performance.

Although contemporary empirical study has been limited to domestic acquisitions, differences in management styles may be of even greater importance in cross-border acquisitions which are subject to national as well as corporate influences. Hofstede (1980) argues strongly that national culture influences the underlying values held by members of a firm, giving rise to associated national management style preferences. Indeed, it has been demonstrated that managers from different nations exhibit different behaviours and beliefs (Laurent, 1983; Schnieder and DeMeyer, 1991).

Thus the basic hypothesis underlying the research is:

> *H1* The extent to which there exist differences between the management styles of the acquiring UK organisation and the acquired European organisation is negatively correlated to the performance of the cross-border acquisition.

Form of Integration

However, the extent to which the management styles of the acquirer and acquired need to come into contact and the extent to which one management style is imposed on the other is governed to a large degree by the form of post-acquisition integration adopted towards the acquired company.

Haspeslagh and Jemison (1991) identify three common forms of acquisition integration:

Preservation Where the acquired organisation is granted a high degree of autonomy, typically positioned within the acquiring organisation as a stand-alone subsidiary.

Symbiosis Where the acquiring company attempts to achieve a balance between preserving the organisational autonomy of the acquired company while transferring strategic capability between the two organisations.

Absorption Where the aim is to achieve full consolidation of the operations, organisation and culture of both organisations, ultimately dissolving all boundaries between the acquired and acquiring firms.

Preservation integration involves little, if any, contact between operating managements (Nahavandi and Malekzadeh, 1988); differences in management styles can be expected to have a low impact in such circumstances. Conversely, differences in management styles are likely to assume a higher level of importance in absorption integration where the degree of strategic interdependence is high, and close collaboration between the two sets of managers and the adoption of common policies and procedures is argued to be essential (Nahavandi and Malekzadeh, 1988; Cartwright and Cooper, 1992).

Closely allied to this, the extent to which the acquired company comes under pressure to accept the management style of its new parent is set to increase as the degree of autonomy granted by the integration process decreases. Where absorption integration is adopted, the acquired organisation gives up all autonomy and typically relinquishes its own management style in favour of that of the acquiring organisation (Sales and Mirvis, 1984; Cartwright and Cooper, 1992). Differences in management styles under such circumstances may cause significant internal conflict and a deterioration in business performance (Chatterjee *et al.*, 1992; Buono and Bowditch, 1989).

However, in acquisitions where the acquired company is established as an autonomous subsidiary, as in preservation integration, it has been argued that the acquired firm should be relatively unaffected by the acquirer's organisational climate (Shrivastava, 1986; Chatterjee *et al.*, 1992), suggesting that differences in management style should have little adverse impact on performance.

These arguments are summarised in the hypothesis that:

H2: Differences in the management styles between the acquiring and the acquired organisation will adversely impact acquisition performance to a greater extent in cross-border acquisitions characterised by 'absorption integration', than in those characterised by 'symbiotic integration', and in turn those characterised by 'preservation integration'.

Source of Competitive Advantage: Manufacturing versus Service Industry Acquisitions

The final hypothesis of the study relates to the influence an acquisition's source of competitive advantage can have on the performance–management style difference relationship.

Haspeslagh and Jemison (1991) and Cartwright and Cooper (1992) have argued that where the source of an acquired firm's competitive advantage is based primarily in its human assets, as for example in service sector businesses (Normann, 1984), maintenance of the organisational climate can be key to the satisfactory performance of the acquisition. Where employees' 'psychic value' is reduced as a result of perceived changes in the organisational climate the potential of the acquisition to create value can be destroyed as the primary value-creating assets become unwilling to work toward the acquisition's success (Haspeslagh and Jemison, 1991) or leave the organisation (Walsh, 1988). In contrast, where the competitive advantage of the acquired firm is derived primarily from capital assets, any value created by the acquisition will tend to come from restructuring of the assets or economies of scale (Porter, 1987). Differences in management style are likely to be of only secondary importance under these conditions.

The above arguments lead to the hypotheses that:

H3a: In acquisitions where the competitive advantage of the acquired firm is based primarily in human assets, the extent to which there exist differences between the management styles of the acquiring UK organisation and the acquired European organisation will be negatively correlated to the performance of the cross-border acquisition.

H3b: In acquisitions where the competitive advantage of the acquired firm is based primarily in capital assets, the extent to which there exist differences between the management styles of the acquiring UK organisation and the acquired European organisation will not be correlated to the performance of the cross-border acquisition.

Other Factors

Previous research by acquisitions scholars has highlighted factors additional to those discussed above which may affect acquisition performance. In particular, relative organisational size (Kitching, 1967; Kusewitt, 1985), the degree of strategic fit or 'relatedness' (Chatterjee, 1986; Lubatkin, 1987; Singh and Montgomery, 1987), the previous acquisition experience of the acquirer (Channon, 1976) and the pre-acquisition profitability of the acquired company (Kitching, 1973) have all been shown to influence acquisition performance, although authors do not agree in every case on the direction of the influence.

Accordingly, each of these factors was taken into account in the present work. Only acquisitions meeting the criteria of relatedness were included in the study's sample, as defined by the businesses of the merging firms being in the same two digit Standard Industrial Classification, (following Chatterjee et al, 1992). Relative organisational size, previous acquisition experience and prior target profitability were included as control variables in the empirical study (see the section on Methodology below).

METHODOLOGY

The hypotheses presented above were tested using data collected by a postal questionnaire survey, following methodology established in the strategic management literature (see, for example, Datta, 1991; Chatterjee *et al.*, 1992). This section describes the survey sample, the choice of measures for the independent and dependent variables, and the method of data analysis.

Sample

The study's sample consists of cross-border acquisitions made in the EU countries of continental Europe by UK firms during the period January 1988 to December 1990.

Acquisitions of minority holdings (here defined as less than 50.01 per cent) were excluded from the sample, as were those acquisitions which had been made through an overseas subsidiary and were therefore potentially not cross-border. This gave an initial listing of 534 cross-border acquisitions, compiled from the data base of *Acquisitions Monthly* magazine.

Several acquiring companies were responsible for more than one acquisition within this listing, with 312 firms accounting for the 534 acquisitions. In order to avoid several questionnaires being sent to the executives of multiple acquirers, the single largest acquisition in terms of bid value for each acquirer was selected for inclusion in the survey sample.

Potential respondents were current executive directors of the acquiring firms who were also serving as directors at the time of the acquisition. This ensured that questionnaires were mailed only to those directors who were in a position to be knowledgeable about the complete history of the acquisition. The names and corporate addresses of the current acquiring firm directors were identified using the FAME data base (CD-ROM Publishing Company, February 1993, London) and compared with those listed for the year of the acquisition in Key British Enterprises (Dun & Bradstreet International, 1988, 1989, 1990). This resulted in a further 65 acquisitions having to be excluded from the sample: 25 where the acquiring firm was found to have subsequently gone into receivership, 19 where no current directors were also serving at the time of the acquisition, and a further 21 where the directors or address of the acquiring firm could not be identified.

This brought the total number of acquisitions in the starting sample to 247, and a total of 886 questionnaires were sent out to an average of four acquiring firm directors per acquisition. The mail-out implementation was adapted from Dillman (1978), with an initial follow-up letter being sent after one week and a second follow-up with replacement questionnaire materials after one month.

Completed questionnaires were received from 132 of the 247 acquiring UK firms mailed, representing a response rate of 53 per cent. Subsequently, one response was discarded as it referred to an unrelated acquisition, and a further seven of the responses were discarded due to incomplete data. This left 124 acquiring firms providing usable responses. Seventy-one firms replied declining to participate, the most common reasons given being due to the number of survey requests received (sixteen firms), company policy towards questionnaire completion (nine firms), or confidentiality concerns (four firms). The total response rate to the survey was thus 50 per cent.

Potential non-response bias was checked by comparing respondent and non-respondent companies along the dimension of acquisition size, selected for its potential influence on both the objectivity of responses and the variables under investigation (Kitching, 1967). The t-statistic value indicated no evidence of non-response bias.

Measurement of Study Variables

Difference in Management Styles
Khandwalla (1977) presents a comprehensive review of the management style literature, proposing a series of dimensions along which a company's management style should be characterised. Datta (1991) develops these dimensions into a questionnaire instrument to measure differences in management styles between two companies.

The present study uses an adapted version of Datta's (1991) instrument. The scale comprised 17 items measuring risk-taking propensity, decision-making approach, levels of participation and emphasis on formality. Respondents were asked to indicate their perceptions of the management style of the acquiring and acquired companies at the time of acquisition along each item, using five-point Likert-type scales. The scores of management style difference along each of the 17 items then were calculated. The Cronbach Alpha value of the resulting scale was 0.76, indicating a reasonable degree of internal consistency. The 17 items were aggregated to produce a single index of the overall difference in management styles between the acquiring and acquired companies.

Form of Acquisition Integration
The typology of acquisition integration put forward by Haspeslagh and Jemison (1991) is adopted in the present study, following its widespread acceptance

amongst acquisition scholars (Chatterjee *et al.*, 1992). Haspeslagh and Jemison (1991) state that the form of acquisition integration adopted by a company is characterised by two dimensions: first, the degree of strategic interdependence achieved between the two companies and, second, the level of autonomy that is granted to the acquired company. Each of these dimensions is measured separately here.

Strategic Interdependence

The degree of strategic interdependence established between the acquiring and acquired firms is dependent upon the extent of skills transfer and resource sharing built up between the two firms post-acquisition, at either the functional or general management level (Haspeslagh and Jemison, 1991).

Thus, in the present study 'strategic interdependence' was assessed by asking respondents to indicate the extent to which skills had been transferred or activities shared for seven functional and four general management areas, using five-point Likert-type scales. The functional areas were adapted from Porter's (1985) value chain activities, while the general management items were derived from Haspeslagh and Jemison's (1991) description of general management skills transfer.

Principal component analysis with varimax rotation on the 11 skills transfer items extracted three factors, with general management skills loading on the first and the two functional categories of operations skills and marketing/sales skills loading on the second and third factors respectively. The 11 items relating to activity sharing loaded onto two factors, one for the general management activities and one for the functional activities. The individual scores relating to each of these five principal components of skills transfer and activity sharing were then averaged and the averages used to compile a composite index of strategic interdependence. Acquisitions were classed as exhibiting high strategic interdependence where this composite index was greater than 3.0 (mid-point value of the index), and as low strategic interdependence where this index was less than 3.0.

Degree of Autonomy

This variable seeks to measure the degree of organisational autonomy granted to the acquired company in the post-acquisition period.

Respondents were asked to indicate the current decision making process for 18 separate operational and strategic decisions within the acquired firm using a five-point Likert-type scale (1 = decision made by acquiring firm, 5 = decision made by acquired firm). The instrument was synthesised from one previously developed and used with reported high levels of reliability and validity by Weber (1988).

The data obtained were reduced to two aggregate measures, relating separately to autonomy granted for operating and strategic decisions. This distinction between operational and strategic autonomy is important when considering the form of integration adopted towards the acquired company. For example, in discussing successful preservation acquisitions, Haspeslagh and Jemison (1991, p. 215) state,

> although these acquisitions were operationally autonomous, the strategic choices that led to their development were arrived at in a highly interactive fashion between the parent and the subsidiary.

Classification of Integration Type

Following these arguments, those acquisitions exhibiting high degrees of operating autonomy (defined by inspection as those scoring 3.0 or above on this dimension) were classified as being subject to preservation or symbiotic integration dependant on whether they also displayed low or high strategic interdependence scores respectively. Absorption integration was said to be present where an acquisition exhibited low degrees of both operating and strategic autonomy (scores of less than 3 along both dimensions) together with a high degree of strategic interdependence between the two companies.

Acquisition Performance

The choice of performance measure has long been a difficult issue facing acquisitions researchers (Kitching, 1967; Burgman, 1983; Hall and Norburn, 1987; Shanley and Correa, 1992). Two broad categories of methodology can be identified from previous studies. First, there are those studies that focus on objective measures of performance, either in terms of accounting variables (Cowling *et al.*, 1980; McKinsey & Co., 1988), the acquirer's stockmarket performance (Chatterjee, 1986; Lubatkin, 1987; Singh and Montgomery, 1987; Seth, 1990; Chatterjee *et al.*, 1992), or subsequent divestment rates (Montgomery and Wilson, 1986; Scherer, 1986; Porter, 1987). Secondly, there are those that focus on perceptual measures of overall performance, typically the extent to which managers believe the acquisition has met their original objectives (Kitching, 1967; Burgman, 1983; Hunt, 1990; Datta, 1991).

A perceptual measure was adopted in this study in view of the established limitations associated with the alternative 'objective' methodologies (Kitching, 1967; Burgman, 1983; Hall and Norburn, 1987; Porter, 1987). Accounting measures of performance for individual cross-border acquisitions are typically not available due to national differences in accounting standards (Walton, 1992) and difficulties in disaggregating the performance of individual operating units from consolidated accounts (Burgman, 1983). Similarly, stock market measures of acquisition performance based on abnormal returns methodology are available only in cases where the acquiring firm is publicly quoted and, further, give information only on expected *ex ante* acquisition performance rather than that actually achieved *ex post* (Montgomery and Wilson, 1986; Hall and Norburn, 1987). Finally, those who advocate the use of divestment rates as a measure of acquisition outcome themselves admit that subsequent divestment can only suggest poor performance of the acquisition (Montgomery and Wilson, 1986). It may, of course, indicate that a successful restructuring of the acquired company has been implemented, enabling sale at a premium price (Porter, 1987).

These limitations render the objective measures inappropriate for the present study, suggesting (after Dess and Robinson, 1984) the use of a manager's subjective assessment as a more appropriate measure of acquisition outcome. Indeed, there is empirical support for the validity of such subjective performance measures. In the related field of cross-border joint ventures Geringer and Hebert (1991) found a strong and statistically significant positive correlation between managers' subjective assessments of overall joint venture performance and each of three separate objective performance measures. Similarly, Dess and Robinson (1984) reported that subjective and objective measures correlated in their investigation of business unit performance.

Acquisition performance was thus measured here using the acquiring management's assessment of the extent to which the original performance expectations for the acquisition have been met. The instrument comprised nine financial performance criteria and six non-financial performance criteria synthesised from recent theoretical and empirical studies of acquisition objectives (Walter and Barney, 1990; Trautwein, 1990). For each criterion, respondents are asked to indicate using five-point Likert-type scales first, the performance of the acquisition relative to their initial expectations and, second, the importance assigned to the particular performance measure. The Cronbach Alpha value for the performance scale was 0.84, demonstrating good scale reliability and internal consistency. The data thus allowed a single weighted average performance index to be established for each acquisition (after Datta, 1991).

Control Variables
Relative organisational size was operationalised as the ratio of the sales turnover of the acquired firm to that of the acquiring firm at the time of the acquisition, following Kitching (1974).
Pre-acquisition profitability of the acquired company was operationalised using an instrument adapted from Kitching (1967). Respondents were asked to indicate their perception of the acquired company's return on capital employed relative to its major competitors at the time of the acquisition, using a scale of 1 (very poor) to 5 (very good).
The degree of relatedness was derived from the Standard Industrial Classification (SIC) codes of the acquiring and acquired firms, as reported in *Acquisitions Monthly*. Acquisitions were classed as related if the businesses of the merging firms were in the same two-digit SIC, following Chatterjee et al (1992). All acquisitions in the sample satisfied this criteria of relatedness.

The measure of *Previous acquisition experience* follows Burgman (1983) in asking respondents to indicate the number of cross-border European acquisitions made in the five years prior to the acquisition under investigation. This variable therefore focuses specifically on the acquiring firm's experience of planning and integrating acquisitions of the type under investigation.

Method of Analysis

The above procedures provided single indices representing acquisition performance, management style difference, and control variables. The study's hypotheses were therefore tested using the following regression model:

Acquisition performance = Constant + $B1$ (Management style difference) + $B2$ (Relative size) + $B3$ (Prior profitability of acquired firm) + $B4$ (Experience of acquirer)

Hypothesis H1 was tested using the entire sample of 124 acquisitions. Hypothesis H2 was tested by estimating the regression equation separately for those acquisitions characterised by preservation, symbiotic or absorption integration. Similarly, in order to test Hypothesis H3 the regression equation was run separately for those acquisitions in the service sector and for those in the capital-intensive manufacturing sector.

RESULTS

Table 7.1 presents the regression results for the complete sample of 124 cross-border European acquisitions. The results show strong statistical support for Hypothesis H1, which predicts an inverse relationship between acquisition performance and differences in the management style of the acquiring and acquired firms. This is evidenced by the negative and significant t-statistic associated with the style difference variable ($t = -3.32$; $p<0.001$). Intercorrelations for the independent variables used in the regression equation were calculated and the results suggested no problems with collinearity (Pearson correlation coefficients -0.17 to $+0.04$; not significant.)

The procedures outlined in the section on Methodology above characterised 50 of the acquisitions in the complete sample as subject to preservation integration, 33 as subject to symbiotic integration and 10 as subject to absorption integration. Although the low incidence of absorption integration is interesting in itself (only 10 per cent of cases where data were available), the very small absolute number of cases meant that any regression results would have been of limited reliability. This class of integration was therefore excluded from further analysis. Accordingly two separate subsamples were compiled, one comprising the 'preservation' acquisitions and one the

Table 7.1 Regression results showing relationship between management style differences and performance for complete sample of cross-border acquisitions

Independent variables	Regression coefficient	
Style differences	−0.34***	(-3.32)
Relative size	0.58	(1.21)
Prior profitability	0.33**	(3.23)
Experience	0.01	(0.39)
(Constant)	3.23***	(6.39)
The Model		
No. of cases	124	
F-statistic	6.10***	
R^2	0.18	

Notes:
* $p < 0.05$.
** $p < 0.01$.
*** $p < 0.001$.
Figures in parentheses represent *t*-statistics.

'symbiotic' acquisitions. The regression equation was then estimated separately for each of these subsamples in order to test Hypothesis H2 as far as the data allowed.

Table 7.2 reveals that no statistical support was found for the Hypothesis: the similar regression coefficients (−0.41 and −0.40 respectively and both significant at the 0.05 level) provide evidence suggesting that differences in management style have broadly the same negative influence on acquisition performance in both 'preservation' and 'symbiotic' acquisitions. The integration strategy adopted towards the newly acquired company does not appear to moderate the performance–management style compatibility relationship.

The impact of differing bases of competitive advantage, human assets in service sector acquisitions and capital assets in manufacturing acquisitions, was tested for in a similar manner. The complete sample contained 21 acquisitions involving companies from the service sector, defined as those where the business of the acquired firm carried an SIC code of 80-99 (Banking, Finance, Insurance, Business Services, Leasing and Other Services). In contrast, 51 acquisitions were identified in the capital-intensive manufacturing sector, defined following Geringer and Hebert (1991) as SIC codes 20-39 (Engineering, Automotive, Chemicals and Mining). Again, Hypothesis H3 was tested by running the regression equation separately using subsamples of the service acquisitions and the manufacturing acquisitions.

The results in Table 7.3 show statistical support for Hypothesis H3: the presence of management style differences had a clear negative influence on

Table 7.2 Regression results showing relationship between management style differences and performance for acquisitions characteristics, by preservation or symbiotic integration

Independent variables	Preservation acquisitions		Symbiotic acquisitions	
	Regression coefficient		Regression coefficient	
Style differences	−0.41*	(−2.02)	−0.40*	(−2.40)
Relative size	−0.87	(−0.55)	0.98	(1.67)
Prior profitability	0.18	(0.98)	0.35*	(2.14)
Experience	−0.01	(−0.28)	0.05	(0.89)
(Constant)	4.10***	(3.80)	3.27)***	(4.50)
The Model				
No. of cases	50		33	
F-statistic	1.51		2.83*	
R^2	0.13		0.29	

Notes:
* $p > 0.05$.
** $p > 0.01$.
*** $p > 0.001$.
Figures in parentheses represent *t*-statistics.

Source: Authors' data.

Table 7.3 Regression results showing relationship between management style differences and performance for manufacturing and service industry acquisitions

Independent variables	Manufacturing acquisitions		Service acquisitions	
	Regression coefficient		Regression coefficient	
Style differences	−0.23	(−1.51)	−0.52*	(−2.12)
Relative size	0.56	(0.31)	−0.22	(−0.21)
Prior profitability	0.35	(1.87)	0.70*	(2.82)
Experience	0.00	(0.10)	0.07	(0.78)
(Constant)	2.94*	(2.99)	2.69*	(2.10)
The Model				
No. of cases	51		21	
F-statistic	1.20		5.65**	
R^2	0.10		0.61	

Notes:
* $p > 0.05$.
** $p > 0.01$.

Source: Authors' data.

the subsequent performance of cross-border acquisitions in the service industry sector (t 5 -2.14; $p<0.05$), but exhibited no statistically significant influence on the performance of acquisitions in the manufacturing sector ($t = -1.15$ but insignificant at even the 0.1 level). Management styles do indeed appear to be of particular and central importance in acquisitions where competitive advantage is derived primarily from the human capital of the firm.

The regression model statistics for the service sector acquisitions ($R^2 = 0.61$ and F-statistic significant at the 0.01 level) indicate that the model was excellent at explaining the performance variance of these takeovers, evidencing the robustness of these results even given the small sample size ($n=21$).

DISCUSSION

The overall results of this study show that differences in the management styles of acquiring British firms and their continental European targets do have a negative impact on the subsequent performance of such cross-border acquisitions. This supports similar findings obtained with samples of domestic US–US acquisitions (Datta, 1991; Chatterjee *et al.*, 1992). The findings also provide empirical support for the numerous articles in the financial press highlighting the potential for clashes of management styles in European cross-border acquisitions (see, for example, *Financial Times*, 12 September 1991; *Acquisitions Monthly*, November 1991).

The incidence of management style differences and their subsequent impact should be of no surprise when one considers the typical nature of these acquisitions. Our sample of British firms buying in Continental Europe revealed that two thirds of the acquirers were buying in countries new to them, raising the possibility of potentially limited knowledge of local management style preferences (Hofstede, 1980) or local political, economic, and social environments (Shore, 1990). Further, while 95 per cent of acquiring firms were ultimately publically quoted, 67 per cent of the Continental European firms taken over were owner-managed businesses prior to acquisition. This implies that the majority of acquirers must manage the transition from family to professional management in the acquired firm, with all the management style implications it raises (Greiner, 1972). For example, previous studies have highlighted the anxiety and uncertainty acquired firm personnel frequently experience post-acquisition as they anticipate more performance orientated control and reward systems and new attitudes towards investment and decision-making (Cartwright and Cooper, 1992). Given these issues, the potential for inferior performance due to different managerial approaches is easy to appreciate. This was reinforced by our findings that differences in management style reduced performance regardless of the form of integration adopted towards the newly acquired business.

Contrary to what had been hypothesised, the performance of acquisitions characterised by 'preservation integration' appears to be adversely impacted by differences in management style to broadly the same extent as in those acquisitions characterised by 'symbiotic integration'. The use of preservation integration does not therefore appear to be an option for avoiding the consequences of management style incompatibilities in cross-border acquisitions.

While unexpected, this result is not perhaps counter-intuitive when one considers Haspeslagh and Jemison's (1991) definition of preservation integration used in the study. In defining preservation acquisitions they state,

> although these acquisitions were operationally autonomous, the strategic choices that led to their development were arrived at in a highly interactive fashion between the parent and the subsidiary.
> (Haspeslagh and Jemison 1991, p. 215).

Thus, while any differences in management styles between the two companies should not be exposed during the day-to-day running of operations, they are likely to come to the surface during the strategy-setting process. In this latter respect, preservation integration is therefore similar to symbiotic integration. These results suggest that it is not operating autonomy but the degree of strategic autonomy granted to the newly acquired firm that may be a critical factor in determining whether differing management philosophies have an impact on acquisition performance.

A further interesting finding of this study was that the industry sector in which an acquisition is based does appear to affect the relationship between management style compatibility and acquisition performance. Management style differences were found to have an unfavourable influence on the performance of service sector acquisitions, but not on those in the manufacturing sector. Our empirical results are in line with trends observable in case study research on the human aspects of acquisition performance: the vast majority of host acquisitions described as exhibiting negative performance outcomes as a result of clashes of managerial philosophies have been in service industries (see, for example, Sales and Mirvis, 1984; Buono and Bowditch, 1989; Cartwright and Cooper, 1992).

These findings were expected given the differing nature of service and manufacturing industries. In services, consumption is simultaneous to delivery, and customer value is created to a large extent by the actions of a firm's personnel (its human assets) at the point of delivery (Normann, 1984). Under these conditions any anxiety and uncertainty felt by employees as the result of perceived management style changes following an acquisition can translate directly to inferior service delivery and so to reduced customer satisfaction and performance. Ultimately, management styles are lived out through individuals, and it is individuals that directly determine the performance of a service industry.

In manufacturing industries customer value is created to a much greater extent through the tangible product produced, and hence the firm's physical production processes (its capital assets) (Normann, 1984). Here, employee concern following an acquisition will be distanced from having a direct impact on performance as the prime determinants of customer satisfaction remain unchanged.

A potential methodological limitation to this result is recognised as being the use of SIC codes to classify the industry sector of an acquisition. The general shortcomings of the SIC classification system for this type of research have been well documented, and will not be repeated here (see for example Gort, 1967). However, an additional implicit assumption in the discussion above is that those industries here defined as services by SIC codes 80-99 derive their primary source of competitive advantage from human rather than capital assets. This is unlikely to hold true in all cases; for example, in retail banking (SIC 8140) considerable competitive advantage can be gained from capital assets in the form of high street branch networks (Channon, 1986). It would be interesting therefore to see if the results obtained in this study are repeated when a direct capital intensity measure is used rather than SIC codes.

CONCLUSIONS – CORPORATE POLICY IMPLICATIONS

This study has shown the strong impact that differences in the management styles of the acquiring and acquired firms can have on the subsequent performance of a cross-border acquisition.

Europe may be moving towards a genuinely single market in some areas, but cultural diversity and the associated national preferences for particular management styles remain much in evidence. The current research has shown that the presence of management style diversity does impact on the choice of the most effective route for corporate growth within Europe. Cross-border acquisitions provide companies with a means of rapid European expansion, but carry with them the risk that the marriage of two different management styles will lead to difficulties in the post-acquisition period, so hindering the attainment of corporate goals. However establishing definitive corporate policy guidelines in this area is a difficult, if not impossible, task. Of the alternatives to acquisition, strategic alliances share similar susceptibility to divergent national cultures and corporate management styles (Schoenberg et al, 1995). Organic growth alleviates the need to bring together established and previously independent management styles, but the research evidence warns of the considerable time-scales involved in meeting strategic and financial objectives via this route (Biggadike, 1979). Realistically, cross-border acquisitions are likely to retain a key role for those companies wishing to build or strengthen a pan-European presence.

On a positive note, the study provides clear messages for those implementing an acquisitions policy. An evaluation of management style compatibility must be included in the planning stage of a cross-border acquisition if the chances of success are to be maximised. Our results show that this holds regardless of the form of integration the purchaser plans to adopt. Managing acquired European companies at arm's length (preservation integration) will not soften the impact of any management style differences on the subsequent performance of an acquisition. Further, our findings suggest that an evaluation of management styles is particularly warranted if the acquisition is one of a service sector business: any differences in management style do appear to have a greater impact when competitive advantage is based directly in the human assets of the firm.

This study has also extended the work of previous scholars by beginning to link the importance of management style differences with the acquisition strategy pursued. The work now needs extending to investigate the impact of elements other than the form of integration and source of competitive advantage. For example, are particular acquisition rationales more susceptible to the impact of management style differences? Are differences along particular dimensions of management style more critical than others? Does a high rate of executive turnover in the acquired firm post-acquisition have a moderating effect on the impact of initial management style differences? Continuing answers to questions such as these will allow fuller frameworks to be developed, assisting the corporate policy maker in identifying and managing the potential impact of management style differences when undertaking cross-border acquisitions.

References

Adler, N.J. (1986) *International Dimensions of Organisational Behaviour* (Boston: Kent Publishing).

Biggadike, R. (1979) 'The risky business of diversification', *Harvard Business Review* (May–June), pp. 103–11.

Bleeke, J. and Ernst, D. (1993) *Collaborating to Compete: Using Strategic Alliances and Acquisitions in the Global Marketplace* (New York: John Wiley).

Buono, A. and Bowditch, J. (1989) *The Human Side of Mergers and Acquisitions* (San Francisco: Jossey-Bass).

Burgman, R. (1983) *A Strategic explanation of Corporate Acquisition Success*, unpublished dissertation, Purdue University.

Cartwright, S. and Cooper, C. (1992) *Mergers and Acquisitions: The Human Factor* (Oxford: Butterworth-Heinemann).

Channon, D. (1976) *The Service Industries Strategy, Structure and Financial Performance* (London: Macmillan).

Channon, D. (1986) *Bank Strategic Management and Marketing* (London: John Wiley).

Chatterjee, S. (1986) 'Type of synergy and economic value: the impact of acquisitions on merging and rival firms', *Strategic Management Journal*, 7, pp. 119–39.

Chatterjee, S., Lubatkin, M., Schweiger, D. and Weber, Y. (1992) 'Cultural differences and shareholder value in related mergers: linking equity and human capital', *Strategic Management Journal*, 13 (5), pp. 319–34.

Cowling, K., Stoneman, P., Cubbin, J., Cable, J., Hall, G., Domberger, S. and Dutton, P. (1980) *Mergers and Economic Performance* (New York: Cambridge University Press).

Datta, D. (1991) 'Organisational fit and acquisition performance: effects of post-acquisition integration', *Strategic Management Journal*, 12, pp. 281–97.

Dess, G. and Robinson, R. (1984) 'Measuring organisational performance in the absence of objective measures', *Strategic Management Journal*, 5, pp. 265–73.

Dillman, D. (1978) *Mail and Telephone Surveys: The Total Design Method* (New York: John Wiley).

Geringer, M. and Hebert, L. (1991) 'Measuring performance of international joint ventures', *Journal of International Business Studies*, 22 (2), pp. 249–63.

Gort, M. (1967) *Diversification and Integration in American Industry* (Princeton: Princeton University Press).

Greiner, L. (1972 'Evolution and revolution as organisations grow', *Harvard Business Review* (July–August) pp. 37–46.

Hall, P. and Norburn, D. (1987) 'The management factor in acquisition performance', *Leadership and Organisational Development Journal*, 8 (4), pp. 23–30.

Haspeslagh, P. and Jemison, D. (1991) *Managing Acquisitions* (New York: Free Press).

Hofstede, G. (1980) *Culture's Consequences* (London: Sage).

Hunt, J. (1990) 'Changing pattern of acquisition behaviour In takeovers and the consequences for acquisition processes', *Strategic Management Journal*, 11, pp. 69–77.

Khandwalla, P. (1977) *The Design of Organisations* (New York: Harcourt, Brace, Jovanovich).

Kitching, J. (1967) 'Why do mergers miscarry?', *Harvard Business Review* (November–Dececember), pp. 84–101.

Kitching, J. (1973) *Acquisition in Europe: Causes of Corporate Success and Failure* (Geneva: Business International).

Kitching, J. (1974) 'Winning and losing with European acquisitions', *Harvard Business Review* (March–April) pp. 124–136.

Kusewitt, J. (1985) 'An exploratory study of strategic acquisition factors relating to performance', *Strategic Management Journal*, 6 (2), pp. 151–69.

Laurent, A. (1983) 'The cultural diversity of Western conceptions of management', *International Studies of Management and Organisation*, 13 (1–2), pp. 75–96.

Lubatkin, M. (1987) 'Merger strategies and stockholder value', *Strategic Management Journal*, 8 (1), pp. 39–53.

McKinsey & Co (1988) *Shareholder Value Creation in Major Acquisition Programmes* (London: McKinsey & Co.).

Montgomery, C. and Wilson, V. (1986) 'Mergers that last: a predictable pattern?', *Strategic Management Journal*, 7, pp. 91–6.

Nahavandi, A. and Malekzadeh, A. (1988) 'Acculturation in mergers and acquisition', *Academy of Management Review*, 13 (1), pp. 79–90.

Norburn, D. and Schoenberg, R. (1994) 'European cross-border acquisition: how was it for you?', *Long Range Planning*, 27 (4), pp. 25–34.

Normann, R (1984) *Service Management: Strategy and Leadership in Service Businesses*, (London: John Wiley).

Porter, M. (1985) *Competitive Advantage: Creating and Sustaining Superior Performance* (New York: Free Press).

Porter, M. (1987) 'From competitive advantage to corporate strategy', *Harvard Business Review* (May–June), pp. 43–59.

Sales, A. and Mirvis, P. (1984) 'When cultures collide: issues in acquisition' in J. Kimberly and R. Quinn (eds), *New Futures: The Challenge of Managing Corporate Transitions* (New York: Dow-Jones Irwin), pp. 107–33.

Scherer, F.M. (1986) 'Mergers, sell-offs, and managerial behaviour' in L.G. Thomas (ed.), *The Economics of Strategic Planning* (Lexington: Lexington Books), pp. 143–70.

Schneider, S. and De Meyer, A. (1991) 'Interpreting and responding to strategic issues: the impact of national culture', *Strategic Management Journal*, 12, pp. 307–20.

Schoenberg, R., Denuelle, N. and Norburn, D. (1995) 'National conflicts in European alliances', *European Business Journal*, 7 (1) (forthcoming).

Seth, A. (1990) 'Value creation in acquisitions: a reexamination of performance issues', *Strategic Management Journal*, 11 (2), pp. 99–116.

Shanley, M. (1987) *Post-Acquisition Management Approaches: An Exploratory Study*, unpublished dissertation, University of Pennsylvania.

Shanley, M. and Correa, M. (1992) 'Agreement between top management teams and expectations for post acquisition performance', *Strategic Management Journal*, 13, pp. 245–66.

Shleifer, A. and Vishny, R. (1991) 'Takeovers in the 60s and the 80s: evidence and implications', *Strategic Management Journal*, 12 (Special Issue), pp. 51–9.

Shore, G. (1990) 'Continental mergers: differences and deal making,' in G. Shore. (ed.), *Continental Mergers are Different* (London: London Business School).

Shrivastava, P. (1986) 'Postmerger integration', *Journal of Business Strategy*, 7 (2), pp. 65–76.

Singh, H. and Montgomery, C. (1987) 'Corporate acquisition strategies and economic performance', *Strategic Management Journal*, 8, pp. 377–86.

Trautwein, F. (1990) 'Merger motives and merger prescriptions', *Strategic Management Journal*, 11 (4), pp. 283–96.

Walsh, J.P. (1988) 'Top management turnover following mergers and acquisitions', *Strategic Management Journal*, 9, pp. 173–83.

Walter, G. and Barney, J. (1990) 'Management objectives in mergers and acquisitions', *Strategic Mangement Journal*, 11 (1), pp. 79–86.

Walton, P. (1992) 'Differential reporting and the European community – a suitable case for treatment', *European Business Journal*, 4 (3), pp. 43–50.

Weber, J. (1988) *The Effects of Top Management Culture Clash on the Implementation of Mergers and Acquisitions*, unpublished dissertation, University of South Carolina.

Part Three

The Transition Process in Eastern Europe

Mo Yamin

The dismantling of the 'iron curtain' and the opening up of East European economies is at least as significant as the process of economic and political integration in Western Europe. Both East and West Europe are in a process of transition and face, in different ways, a fundamental and difficult set of transformations. Western Europe is grappling with the problems of fully integrating already functioning market economies, the problems arising from economic, political and institutional differences between member countries and from a deep-seated resistance to trading-off national for transnational sovereignty.

Eastern Europe's problems are a mirror image of those encountered in western Europe, namely, how to break up a regional 'union' or at least a political and economic block. As a consequence of this break-up, individual countries are facing the twin tasks of economic restructuring and marketisation. Following the collapse of COMECON, restructuring involves, *inter alia*, the switching of military to civilian production in many economies and the establishment of new trading links with West Europe and beyond. Marketisation involves not only the privatisation of state owned assets, a task that has proved more difficult than expected, but also more fundamental organisational and institutional changes. These two problems are closely related. Restructuring is only necessary now because in the former command economies of eastern Europe much economic activity responded not to to buyer needs, whether domestic or foreign, but to the dictates of central planning which created a highly autarchic regional trading structure. It is also evident that the 'backlash' provoked by the consequences of restructuring, for example, rising unemployment coupled with inadequate welfare provisions, undermines the privatisation programme.

Although the two chapters in Part Three focus on privatisation, the importance of broader institutional and socio–political issues is also stressed, both directly and indirectly. Chapter 8, by Buck, Filatotchev and Wright, considers the rationale for and possible consequences of one form of privatisation in Russia, namely, management buyouts. In Chapter 9, Cook and Kirkpatrick highlight the interplay between marketisation and structural issues across individual countries.

Arguably, the central question *vis-à-vis* privatisation in East European economies is how to affect the privatisation of state owned assets in economies where supporting institutions and structures, including capital and equity markets and an effective banking system, do not exist or are developing only slowly. UK privatisation, for example, was significantly eased in many ways by the fact that the UK is already a market economy. Buck *et al.* face this issue directly by stressing that although there are a variety of possible forms of privatisation, many of these require a complex set of institutional backgrounds and are effectively ruled out in the Russian context. Buyouts are the least demanding institutionally and thus can be advocated for kick-starting the privatisation process. In fact, the buyout has been virtually the only instrument for 'large' privatisation in the Russian Federation. The downside, as Buck *et al.* show, however, is that the 'insider control' that buyouts imply can have negative efficiency and governance consequences, especially as product markets are not sufficiently competitive. As others have also noted, it is unlikely that such privatised entities will prove a major change agent in the transition process. Buck *et al.* also point to the transitory nature of buyouts in the west. It remains to be seen whether this will also prove to be the case in Russia. However, buyouts in the west compete with other organisational forms, whereas in Russia they have the field to themselves. The evolution of organisational form in Russia may thus be subject to 'path-dependency'.

In the rest of East and Central Europe, too, as Cook and Kirkpatrick show in Chapter 9, the privatisation programme has progressed less smoothly than expected. Difficulties encountered include lack of buyers for large conglomerate enterprises saddled with debts and in need of major restructuring, and the reluctance of governments to face the fiscal and labour market consequences of such restructuring. The most successful programme has been in East Germany, which is perhaps not surprising. Here, privatisation has been part of the German unification process and has benefited from financial and administrative support that has been lacking elsewhere. In some respects, therefore, East German privatisation could be treated as if taking place in an existing market economy.

As Cook and Kirkpatrick point out, the relative failure of the privatisation programme has not prevented private sector development, although both the rate of growth and the size of the sector vary significantly from country to country being, as might be expected, higher in Hungary, the Czech Republic and Poland compared to the Russian Federation. Foreign business participation shows a similar pattern. Thus, with the exception of Hungary, East European privatisation programmes have not proved attractive to western firms and direct investment in them is either absent, as in Russia, or modest. On the other hand, there is extensive international business interest in these economies and the number of joint ventures, in particular, has increased very rapidly. This is perhaps not surprising: market entry analysis advises some sort of alliance with domestic entities for markets that are unfamiliar and risky and where local knowledge and contacts of their partner may thus prove valuable. This certainly fits East Europe rather well and, as might be expected, business leaders regard joint ventures as the most sensible mode for doing business there (Quelch *et al.*, 1993).

Few would argue that foreign business participation is unlikely to have a positive influence on the transition process in Eastern Europe. The most important contribution of international business will not necessarily be the transfer of advanced technology or investment funds but the transplanting of attitudes and behaviour appropriate to a market economy (Casson, 1994). In this respect, joint venture may turn out to be the most useful vehicle for 'learning' by East European partners. Links with Western firms, for example, will enable them to appreciate the importance of customer satisfaction for business viability. The overall conclusion, as Cook and Kirkpatrick suggest, is that an undue concentration on the privatisation issue may miss out other significant developments taking place in Eastern Europe with respect to private sector growth and foreign participation in these economies.

References

Casson, M. (1994) 'Enterprise culture and institutional change in Eastern Europe', in P.J. Buckley and P.N. Ghauri (eds), *The Economics of Change in East and Central Europe* (London: Academic Press).

Quelch, J., Joachimisthaler, E. and Nueno, J. (1993) 'After the wall – marketing guides for Eastern Europe', in C. Halliburton and R. Hunerberg (eds), *European Marketing: Readings and Cases* (Wokingham: Addison-Wesley).

8 Buyouts and the Transformation of Russian Industry

Trevor Buck, Igor Filatotchev and Mike Wright

INTRODUCTION

The 1990s have seen the collapse of the political and economic systems of the former Soviet Union (FSU) and its former satellites in the rest of Central and Eastern Europe (CEE). Progress has been made towards the political vision of democracy, but the economic vision of a market economy has proved more elusive. Citizens associated a market economy with consumer sovereignty, high living standards, rapid innovation and economic growth, but the reality has produced falling living standards and economic growth (as officially measured, at least), and high rates of unemployment and inflation. In reality, the full transition to a market economy must involve deregulation, price liberalisation, privatisation and the development of legal and financial institutions to underpin market processes. Many governments decided to privatise first and concentrate on other reforms later, in an attempt to achieve an irreversible reform of the centrally planned economy.

This chapter does not question the vision of the market economy or the sequence of reforms. Rather, the analysis concentrates on practical issues concerning the actual process of privatisation in Russia and its implications for would-be western investors. It takes Russian privatisation as given and considers the fact that privatisation has many forms which have short-term implications for enterprise efficiency and arguably more important long-term consequences for corporate governance, i.e. the means by which enterprise decision-makers are controlled by owners and other stakeholders. It concludes that western investors have been quite rational to virtually ignore privatised firms as targets for active or portfolio investment. The dominant privatisation vehicle, the employee–management buyout, is not yet a safe haven for western funds which have therefore preferred joint ventures and greenfield developments to investment in privatised firms. Nevertheless, if privatised firms do embark on a buyout life-cycle that has been observed in the West, privatised firms in Russia may soon become realistic investment targets.

The analysis is in five stages:

First, the issue of the *speed of the privatisation process* is addressed. Although economic reform in the FSU is generally seen to have been slow, the privatisation of large industrial firms in Russia was proceeding in 1993 and early 1994 at the rate of about 800 per month. The administration of these sales is organised locally and the process can be described as rapid and decentralised compared with the centralised case-by-case approach adopted elsewhere in CEE (see European Bank, 1993, p. 32).

Second, the choice in Russia of a rapid pace of privatisation implicitly rules out the Anglo–American flotation on a capital market or privatisation based loosely on German–Japanese corporate governance, with shares in the hands of financial institutions. It is argued that a Russian preference for a rapid pace explains the *dominance of the employee buyout (EBO)* in the process of Russian industrial privatisation. Given the low incomes of most employees, however, the inevitability of the 'giveaway' nature of both enterprise valuation and the financing of employees' share purchases is demonstrated.

Third, the importance of EBOs in Russian privatisation has short-term implications for enterprise efficiency, but their long-term significance will lie in the area of corporate governance. The corporate governance properties of EBOs are first analysed in the context of *employees as enterprise controllers.*

Fourth, the significance of EBOs as governance structures can be further analysed by considering *employees as owners* of their privatised companies.

Finally, the full governance implications of *employees as combined owners and controllers* are drawn out in the fifth section. It is argued that although EBOs have great shortcomings in relation to corporate governance, they at least facilitate rapid privatisation and start the process of market reform, probably irreversibly. On the basis of the theory of employees as owners and controllers and the empirical experience with EBOs in the West, it is predicted that EBOs will be a transitional stage in the life-cycle of Russian enterprise. EBOs can offer flexibility in the evolution of more stable governance structures in the longer term.

THE SPEED OF PRIVATISATION AND CORPORATE GOVERNANCE

Privatisation has been seen to be necessary in CEE to the promotion of consumer sovereignty and profit tests, to raise enterprise efficiency through effective corporate governance and to facilitate the provision of finance for investment according to its expected productivity. Privatisation can, however, take many practical forms that depend crucially on its desired speed. Table 8.1 shows the main economic issues involved at the (macroeconomic) systemic level, in the individual enterprise (microeconomic) and in between at the intermediate level of the State budget. With a *slow* rate of privatisation (see European Bank, 1993, p. 32), a State privatisation agency can give

Table 8.1   The speed of privatisation

Level	Privatisation objectives
1. Economic system as a whole	*Transformation of an entire economic system* from one which politicians, planners and other bureaucrats make most resource allocations to one in which markets assume the role Such transformation has to be politically and socially acceptable and feasible In this respect the rate of transformation is crucial, with an over-riding concern that transformation should be *rapid* so that market reforms *quickly* overcome resistance from the old system and its beneficiaries to achieve a 'critical mass' that proves irreversible Rapid privatisation, however, may take place without the usual legal and institutional prerequisites in place
2. State budget	*Transformation of government finances* from conditions of *chronic financial deficit* where State agencies impose 'soft' budget constraints on enterprises, acting as a 'last resort' source of grants and loans to enterprises over-demanding resources to reach (ratcheted) output targets set by State Ministries Note that there is a *trade-off* between the rate of systemic transformation (see 1 above) and the reform of the State budget: with rapid privatisation, the proceeds from privatisation are lower and rapidly-assembled enterprise governance structures (see 3 below) are likely to yield low enterprise efficiency and hence low taxes payable to the State
3. Enterprise	*Transformation of enterprise governance* from a reliance on State orders and the resources that accompany them to survival in competitive product, labour and capital markets Enterprises must trade profitably to satisfy shareholders, in the case of capital markets Given the importance of management employees, such a transformation has to be acceptable to them Note that although enterprise efficiency and the balancing of State budgets are *complementary* privatisation objectives, since successful enterprises contribute taxes to the State and do not clamour for grants and loans, there is again a *trade-off* between the speed of systematic transformation and the effectiveness of reforms to enterprise governance

Source: Authors' data.

careful attention to both short-term sale proceeds and long-term governance on a case-by-case basis. This contrasts with *rapid* privatisation, where the State issues standard procedures which are then supervised locally by branches of the privatisation agency. Rapid privatisation can quickly render irreversible the process of market reform, but it will not maximise sale proceeds and may put in place unsustainable governance structures.

Unfortunately, privatisation has often been advocated without an appreciation of the variety of possible forms. The main options are shown in Table 8.2 in relation to the pace of privatisation and to Hirschman's (1958) distinction between a shareholder's ability to impose a discipline on management directly through the internal communication of opinion and recommendations for action in relation to performance ('voice') and/or indirectly through the sale and purchase of shares ('exit').

Although 'slow' forms of privatisation are shown at the top of Table 8.2, the term should not be interpreted in a negative sense. As Kornai observes (1992, p. 174) 'No one would call himself an advocate of slowness', though Murrell and Wang (1993) explicitly favour delays in CEE privatisation. Nevertheless, privatisation with flotation or financial institutions does have a number of preconditions that can only be satisfied in the long term in CEE.

In the case of *Anglo–American flotations* on the capital market, these preconditions would include developed capital markets, laws defining property rights, taxation laws, insolvency laws and company law covering the form of company accounts. With these preconditions in place, the central privatisation agency could carefully consider business plans, prepare an enterprise for sale, advertise the flotation widely and use sophisticated combinations of auctions, invitations to tender and placements to maximise the sale proceeds. Even if all this were achieved, together with product and capital market competition, the governance properties of the resulting conventional, Anglo–American firm have been widely criticised. 'Exit' by owners may be dominated by short-term imperatives (Miles, 1993) and shareholders' 'voice' is subject to free-rider abuse.

On western experience, the vast majority of *outside* shareholders (individuals and institutions) are subject to severe free-rider problems and have a negligible interest in monitoring managerial performance and voicing their opinions. Most shareholders rely on the 'exit' sanction and rarely even vote in proxy contests. Institutional investors (owning around half of all industrial shares in the USA and two thirds in the UK) have always been notoriously reluctant to get involved in the internal affairs of companies and have only recently begun to act collectively and voice their opinions on corporate managers and policies (see Drucker, 1991).

There is assumed, however, to be a subset of would-be 'core' investors who buy a company's shares for the direct financial return *and* for the indirect improvement in that return that they expect can be achieved by their

Table 8.2 Corporate governance and the rate of privatisation

	Means of control		
	'Voice' by individual shareholders	*'Voice' by institutional shareholders*	*'Exit'*
Slow privatisation			
(Anglo–American) Capital market flotation	Low, unless a 'core' investor establishes effective control	Low to medium	High
(German–Japanese) Ownership by financial institutions	–	High	Low
Rapid privatisation			
Trade sale	Medium	Medium	Quite high
Voucher scheme			
– Individual bases	Insignificant	–	
– Withholding companies / Investment trusts	Low	High, depending on the abilities and incentives for institutional managers	High, depending on the development of markets in shares and an absence of trading restrictions
Management buyouts (MBOs)	Potentially high, depending on the 'hardness' of loans for share purchases	Potentially high, depending on the 'hardness' of budget constraints on institutional investors	Low
Employee buyouts (EBOs)	Potentially high (see above) Decision control by employees becomes more problematical with the size of firms	Potentially high (see above)	Low

Source: Authors' data.

monitoring of managerial performance (i.e. voice). According to Shleifer and Vishny (1986, p. 461):

> In a corporation with many small owners, it may not pay any one of them to monitor the performance of management [but (p. 461)] the presence of a large minority shareholder provides a partial solution to this free-rider problem.

The size of such a controlling, core stake cannot be exactly determined, but Shleifer and Vishny (1986, p. 462) find that a typical large industrial firm in the USA has 15.4 per cent of shares in the hands of the largest shareholder, with the five largest shareholders holding 28.8 per cent. These results are broadly confirmed by Demsetz (1993).

The minimum size of such a core stake which will justify the costs of monitoring managers is determined by the amount of firm-specific uncertainty (Demsetz and Lehn, 1985, p. 1159), with 'noisier' environments requiring larger core stakes. This point has obvious implications for diffuse share ownership in CEE: outside investors must seek larger stakes in very uncertain CEE company environments in order to justify the costs of monitoring managers. The development of core stakes is dependent upon the accumulation of sufficient wealth on the part of a core shareholder (or core group). Since larger cores seem necessary in the context of CEE where shareholders' costs of monitoring managers are higher, and the existence of potential core investors is determined by inequalities in the distribution of income (Demsetz, 1993), it follows that if the effective governance of Anglo–American privatised firms depends upon effective voice by core investors, this can only be feasible in the long term with the development of income inequalities. Again, the slowness of Anglo–American privatisation is emphasised.

The other slow form of privatisation with demanding preconditions is shown in Table 8.2 as *institutional ownership*. This could include ownership and control by banks on either a German or Japanese model (see Corbett and Mayer, 1991; Bös, 1993) or by investment trusts, mutual funds and other financial intermediaries, favoured for CEE by Demsetz (1993), and by Frydman *et al.* (1993). In addition to the preconditions for flotation listed above, privatisation with financial intermediaries assumes the existence of sophisticated financial institutions with appropriate incentives mechanisms in place for their managers who constitute another layer of agency problems, and it should be remembered that in the case of Japan (Gilson and Roe, 1993) bank shareholdings are supplemented by ownership and voice by other stakeholders, including suppliers, customers and in the form of interlocking shareholdings with associated firms. Although mutual fund managers can be disciplined by the fear of withdrawals by depositors (Demsetz, 1993), the case of the Czech Republic makes it clear that without product market competition, sophisticated governance devices (as in Japan) and without effective competition between financial intermediaries with experienced and motivated managers, privatisation through financial institutions can be a process giving excessive emphasis on the short term, e.g. in the form of one-year reimbursement promises to investors (see Bös, 1993, p. 99).

If slow privatisation is ruled out for any of these reasons, a number of candidates are shown in Table 8.2 if there is a perceived need for *rapid* privatisation. These include *trade sales* of State businesses to other enterprises. This can generally be disregarded in CEE, however, since the vicious circle of State ownership dominating industry precludes this option in the short term.

As a rapid alternative to trade sales, privatisation *with vouchers* may be used on an individual basis, with financial intermediaries or in conjunction with EBOs, see Table 8.2. Voucher schemes, like buyouts, at least allow privatisation to proceed quickly and without significant opposition from citizens as a whole (see p. 154 below). However, their governance properties depend crucially on the price that is paid for vouchers on an individual basis and whether competing investment trusts can provide responsible voice. Individual shareholders are unlikely to provide any effective governance, having little information about company decisions and using voices which are subject to the usual free-rider problems, i.e. small stakes provide insufficient motivation for active monitoring and voice by individual shareholders that bring benefits for all shareholders. Vouchers obtained on 'giveaway' terms will further discourage voice in relation to loss-avoiding decisions, since shares obtained through giveaway voucher schemes have nothing to lose (Ben-Ner, 1993, p. 340). Individual voucher schemes are also likely to reproduce the 'short-termist' exit properties associated with Anglo–American capital markets discussed above.

Vouchers deposited with financial intermediaries can reduce the diffuseness of shareholdings together with the information requirements of investors, but the 'Nirvana Fallacy' of assuming perfectly-functioning institutions should be avoided, and the motivations and governance of institutional managers is a key issue in this respect. Even if such institutions could perform responsibly, it would bring the problems of large institutional shareholders already encountered in the West – see Drucker (1991), where financial institutions already own more than 60 per cent of UK and over 40 per cent of US industrial equities. For example, institutions with 'inside' information on a company may be inhibited from trading by insider dealing laws. In any case, their large blocks of shares are difficult to exit without damaging the market for their remaining holdings of shares.

This leaves *buyouts* (BOs; see Table 8.2) as the only remaining form of privatisation, albeit the most common form in the West's largest privatisation programme (i.e. in the UK, see Filatotchev *et al.*, 1992, p. 266). As a governance structure featuring insider control, BOs replicate the high voice characteristics of German/Japanese insider control by banks, but in the case of BOs the quality of voice by managers or other employees depends cru-cially upon the price that is paid for shares and the way in which share purchases are financed. In the case of BOs in the West, managers and other employees are subject to hard and extensive monitoring by outside lenders, including a detailed consideration of business plans, equity ratchets and reg-ular performance reviews (see Filatotchev *et al.*, 1992, p. 269). Without a significant supply of venture capital (Stiglitz, 1985, p. 140) 'to the extent that control is exercised, it is by banks, by lenders and not by the owners of equity'. In the case of CEE there is a danger that banks may not be in-volved in lending to employees to buy shares or they may remain the politi-cised institutions they were under Communism (Kornai, 1992, p. 166). With enterprise governance already weakened by share transfer restrictions that obstruct the exit route, any damage to voice within BOs is particularly im-portant. This can happen where enterprises receive soft State credit through the banking system, some of which is passed on to employees to finance share purchases (see p. 156 below).

Besides soft loans for employees' share purchases, BO governance may be damaged by any tendency for employees (especially managers) to use their shares as a means of blocking the transfer of ownership, especially to outsiders. Managers may be able to control employee ownership in the face of perceived threats to the enterprise, and according to Frydman *et al.* (1993, p. 183)

> worker ownership in the United States is widely regarded as a mechanism for entrenching the control rights of the managers against those of outside shareholders. As a potential 'poison pill' to discourage takeover raiders, employee shares designed to reduce managerial power may ironically have the effect of reinforcing managerial power by offering takeover protection.

Although this chapter does not argue the case for privatisation BOs, the BO at least gets the practical process of privatisation moving and has few preconditions: a vital attribute when political barriers block much legisla-tion. These preconditions include only the ability to enforce contracts so that parties to a BO can agree to an acquisition, and clear definitions as to who grants the authority to transfer State property to the BO. In some CEE countries even these minimal preconditions are still not in place, but when they are BOs can proceed in a rapid, decentralised manner supervised by local privatisation agencies applying a standard set of rules supplemented by sample checks. Of course, BOs may involve asset under-valuation and other opportunism in an environment where local monopoly power is preva-lent in product markets, raising trade-offs which may need to be dealt with (Valentiny *et al.*, 1992).

In the section that follows, it is explained that despite these potential costs, Russia has nevertheless chosen the EBO as the dominant privatisation vehicle, presumably in the hope that product market competition will develop, together with an active market for corporate control. Although product competition may emerge rapidly in service industries and small firms, large-scale manufacturing is likely to develop competitive markets only slowly. By opting for rapid privatisation without extensive regulation (except in the banking sector), the Russian government has implicitly adopted a neo-Austrian preference for spontaneous market development (Kornai, 1992, p. 160) as opposed to the promotion of competition by government regulation. On this neo-Austrian view, 'temporary' excess profits through monopoly power are the signal for entrepreneurs to overcome barriers and enter the industry. The privatisation EBO may at least allow these market processes to begin, though there may be major entry barriers for new firms and other competitors.

This chapter now abstracts from these controversies concerning the desirability of BOs, however. The next section describes the particular form of privatisation vehicle (EBO) chosen by Russia with a view to analysing its governance properties in subsequent sections.

PRIVATISATION IN RUSSIA

Although Russia and the rest of the FSU has been slow to start the process of privatisation for large firms, legislation in July 1992 opted for rapid privatisation, with 7000 large and medium firms due for privatisation by the end of 1993. Late in 1993, large privatisations were being carried out at a rate of 800 per month, supervised by State Property Committees and Funds on a decentralised (usually city) basis. In December 1993 it was announced (*Financial Times*, 6 December 1993, p. 2) that by the deadline (1 July 1994) for the use of vouchers, 80 per cent of Russia's industrial capacity should be in private hands.

The choice of a rapid pace meant that only privatisation vehicles in the lower half of Table 8.2 could be employed. Fearing worker and citizen opposition to privatisation, the Russian government opted for privatisation through EBOs supplemented by the sale of vouchers available to all citizens, regardless of age.

It has been argued above that the commitment given by the Russian government to rapid privatisation placed an emphasis on BOs, without any grand notions of workplace democracy. Legislation in July 1992 allowed for privatisation in the form of three 'variants', although in practice Variant 2 has been dominant. Under each variant, employees are given every encouragement to obtain shares, and further encouragement was provided by hyperinflation and the availability of enterprise grants and loans to employees to finance share purchases. If employees did not buy shares or subsequently sold them on to managers or outside investors, the government could at least claim that either they had the opportunity for employee control or were compensated for giving it up.

Under each of the variants shown in Table 8.3, employees and other local citizens were each entitled to claim free of charge one privatisation voucher nominally worth Rbl 10 000 (US$22 at the time, see *The Economist*, 28 November 1992, p. 93). Arrangements in each city varied with the attitudes of the local soviet, but generally these vouchers could be sold for cash, used together with cash in exchange for shares or, as in St Petersburg, deposited with a mutual fund on the Czech model. Privatisations began after July 1992, set up by regional agencies of the Russian State Property Office (State Property 'Committees') and with the actual sales conducted by local bodies variously set up by the regional parliaments and city soviets (State Property 'Funds')

The most significant feature of Table 8.3 is the insider control that is guaranteed before public auction for collectives choosing Variant 2, while with Variants 1 and 3, at least 60 per cent of shares must go to auction, with the risk of outsiders gaining control. It is therefore no surprise that in the first eight months of 1993, over 80 per cent of all medium and large industrial privatisations in Russia were EBOs using Variant 2 (authors' own estimates). It should be noted that although Variant 2 is usually more expensive for employees, it is the only variant that guarantees majority employee control before the auction stage, if they want it. Managers' shares are generally restricted to 10 per cent of employees' shares at the pre-auction stage and in the case of Variant 1, no share transfers are permitted for three years, thus safeguarding employee control from managers and outside investors. In practice, however, powerful managers have ways of preserving their position.

Before making testable predictions about the performance of such BOs in Russia as a result of their governance properties (p. 160 below), two observations can be made concerning under-valuation and the governance implications of 'giveaway' BOs.

First, it is clear that if market reform is designed to put investment decisions ultimately into the hands of profit-motivated entrepreneurs (or groups of entrepreneurs in the case of EBOs) and privatisation is rapid, entrepreneurs can be expected to behave opportunistically during the privatisation process itself, acquiring assets as cheaply as possible.

Rapid privatisation weakens competitive forces at auction, and the early evidence from Russian privatisations is not inconsistent with systematic under-valuation, though the usual caveats regarding arbitrary book valuations are even more relevant in a period of rapid inflation. In many cases, a single year's rouble profits often exceed the purchase price, e.g. by a factor of 3.5 in the case of the Gidroprivod enterprise (CMBOR Privatisation Database). Western experience with BOs suggests many safeguards to prevent excessive undervaluation (e.g. privatisations without land sales, clawback clauses

Table 8.3 Privatisation 'variants', Russia, 1992–3

	(%) Variant 1	(%) Variant 2	(%) Variant 3
Employees	25 (non-voting, free) 10 (voting, vouchers or cash 30 discount)	51 (4/5 vouchers, 1/5 cash) for managers and other employees via a 'closed tender' bidding process	40 (employee group, up to 4/5 vouchers)
Managers	5 (cash)		
Managers can bid for shares at auction (below) or in subsequent share markets			
For auction, State Property Agency	60	49	60
	100	100	100

Notes: With all variants, firms (managers) tend to lend cash to employees to buy shares.

Variant 2: a two thirds majority of employees is needed to support Variant 2. Assets of the firm are valued at 1.7 times the book value at January 1992.

Variant 3, announced November 1992. The employee group who acquires shares must be supported by a majority of all employees. The group must undertake to maintain the volume of output after privatisation. One half of the employee group's shares can be bought at a 30% discount.

Source: 'State privatisation programme for state and municipal enterprises in the Russian Federation, 1992', *Economika i Zhizn*, no. 29 (1992), pp. 15–17.

and equity retention by the State and the taxation of capital gains), but any such device must run the risk of driving away potential buyers, including employees (see Valentiny *et al.*, 1992).

Second, however, even if enterprises are acquired cheaply, employees investing significant amounts of their own savings or borrowings in shares can be expected to monitor actively company decisions (i.e. provide high levels of 'voice' according to Table 8.2) to secure capital gains and avoid losses on their shares. Western BOs have usually been highly leveraged, with lenders offering 'hard' repayment terms and monitoring their loans closely (see European Bank, 1993).

In Russia, however, it seems likely that the financing of BOs has been on such 'soft' terms that privatisation BOs can be described as 'giveaway' sales, regardless of any undervaluation of the acquisition price. There are three grounds for this assertion:

- The free distribution of vouchers to every citizen including infants and pensioners. The authors' own calculations suggest that if all employees contributed three vouchers from their family's entitlement, this could secure for employees a majority share of the average large industrial privatised enterprise in 1992. (After 1992, however, a series of coefficients were used to inflate estimates of statutory capital, supposedly to take account of inflation. For example, in February 1993, a multiplier of 19 was applied to asset values as at 1 January 1992 for the purposes of privatisation.)
- Legislation that permits enterprises to make Development Fund (FARP) grants to employees out of enterprise profits to buy shares up to a maximum of 10 per cent of the acquisition price (Variant 1) and 5 per cent (Variant 2).
- In a period of rapid inflation, enterprises to be privatised are able to make soft loans to employees to buy shares. There are no reliable statistics on the use of company profits to promote employee ownership, but the personal experience of the authors in a few actual privatisations suggest that they are common. For example, the authors monitored the 'Bolshevik' bakery in Moscow closely, including three separate visits to the plant itself. At 'Bolshevik' the employees were given grants and subsidised loans to buy shares, and were given paid leave to attend the share auction with free transport provided.

With 'giveaway' financing, the governance properties of the EBO shown in Table 8.2 will be changed as employees have less incentive to express 'voice', especially in relation to the avoidance of losses, since employees in 'giveaway' EBOs have no downside risk. 'Giveaway' EBOs should ultimately be outcompeted in product markets if companies with more conventional governance structures win market share.

The full governance properties of EBOs (conventional and 'giveaway') are analysed in more detail in the next three sections, which build on the theory of private property rights, summarised in Alchian (1987). This theory explains that there are potential gains at least to be obtained from specialisation in *control* (decisions about the use of assets) and *ownership* (the right of shareholders to any residual income resulting from control and the right to transfer ownership to others). The governance properties of *employees* as, first, controllers and then owners are therefore considered. Finally, since the EBO reunites ownership and control, the final section considers the governance properties of firms where decision authority (control) and the market value of the consequences of decisions (ownership) are *combined* in employees. This final section considers the EBO with combined employee ownership and control and provides testable propositions in relation to its governance properties.

EMPLOYEES AS CONTROLLERS

Managers and other employees in EBOs combine the roles of decision-maker and owner, and in practice it is impossible to distinguish the quality of decisions (control) from the bearing of their consequences (ownership). For the purposes of analysis, however, it is useful to keep these roles separate for the time being. In the discussion on p. 160 below, ownership and control are reunited (as in the EBO itself) and testable predictions derived in relation to the EBO's governance properties.

Employee control has a long tradition and in the economic literature. Actual employee control exists in cooperative firms, partnerships (see Hansmann, 1990) and in the participative structures within capitalist firms, though such decision-sharing may be restricted to fairly minor issues. In the economic literature, employee control appears under the guises of 'worker participation', 'self-management', and in the 'teamwork' literature on firms with a 'Japanese' philosophy (see Aoki, 1990).

The great potential strength of *employees* as decision-makers is that, given an appropriate incentive structure (see p. 159), employees may be prepared to offer voice in the form of *mutual monitoring* (Ben-Ner, 1993, p. 346) in relation to the decisions and behaviour of themselves and each other. Such self-monitoring and horizontal monitoring can in theory replace the vertical structures within companies and foster a workplace climate that is less authoritarian (Ben-Ner, 1993, p. 391) and more cooperative than in a conventional firm, eliminating many conflicts. Indeed, employee control can be seen as turning employees from agents into principals, eliminating hierarchical managers and thus a whole tier of potential agency problems. Such mutual monitoring can be particularly effective in terms of transaction costs in industries where the nature of processes and products determines that all employees must make a high proportion of non-routine decisions that are expensive to monitor within a vertical hierarchy. In other words, the viability of employee control is contingent upon

> the nature of the product and the market, firm size, and the availability of financial resources. (Ben-Ner, 1993, p. 350)

Perhaps for this reason, employee control in practice in the West has been restricted to certain industrial niches, and Hansmann (1990, p. 163) cites the dominance of employee control in professional partnerships and some service industries. In addition, groups of employees can improve the quality of decisions within otherwise conventional firms, where they can be effective in avoiding and resolving crises, in improving the design of products and processes and in raising the quality (reliability) of products (see Aoki, 1990).

At the same time, however, employee control has potential weaknesses. In particular, if it is assumed that the individual employee has bounded rationality and limited time resources to monitor others, it follows that the horizontal monitoring in teams that can replace the vertical monitoring of conventional hierarchies is likely to be less efficient in transactions cost terms, the larger is the workforce. In Williamson's (1975, p. 46) language, 'all channel' communications between any pair of employees in a large firm will be very costly without a 'peak coordinator' as a focus for communications. In other words, *the relative effectiveness of employee control is expected to decline with firm size*. This result has particular significance in the context of Russia's large EBOs, with a minimum size of 500 employees and some very large privatisations indeed.

Of course, horizontal monitoring can be partitioned into groups and an element of (perhaps elected) vertical hierarchy may be able to economise on transactions costs. This proposal is also relevant to the potential weakness of employee control in relation to the cumbersome nature of its decision-making. Frequent meetings of workers' councils are infeasible in large firms and employee control of strategic decisions will risk the leakage of commercially-sensitive information to competitiors.

Each of these weaknesses is likely to increase with the size and complexity of the firm, but all these problems can be reduced by the introduction of some element of vertical hierarchy as a supplement to mutual monitoring. The question then arises whether such vertical relationships still constitute employee control. The important point for the purposes of this chapter, however, is that, as with mutual monitoring itself, vertical relationships superimposed on horizontal monitoring can be expected to be less effective, the larger the workforce. Since other aspects of the impact of mutual monitoring are bound up with the rewards it brings, these are left until after the next section on employee ownership.

EMPLOYEES AS OWNERS

Besides the right to control, property rights within a firm are defined in terms of the right to a share of residual income and a right to transfer (alienate) this right to other owners (Alchian, 1987). In other words, ownership rights constitute the rewards and penalties for decision control. Although the next section is concerned with ownership and control united in an EBO, the typical western corporation separates the two functions and it is possible to isolate the characteristics of employee ownership from control issues at this stage. With the exception of possible informational advantages, it will be argued that employee owners have certain disadvantages that will be seen to impinge upon the quality of decisions discussed in the next in section.

The typical, non-'core' shareholder in an Anglo–American company (see Table 8.2) has *little access to information* about a firm that is not already in the public domain and therefore reflected in the share price. As a result of the usual free-rider problems, this shareholder has little incentive to invest time in monitoring the company's activities, and will simply exit the share if the return is unsatisfactory in terms of dividend or capital gain. In contrast, the employee as shareholder will be acquainted with internal, company-specific information without any significant personal effort, and can thus be expected to improve corporate governance through internal voice. Unfortunately, however, the significance of this inside information and voice opportunities are likely to decline with the size of firm, and exit may also be inhibited for employees in countries with laws against insider trading, where they would not be free to trade on the basis of inside, price-sensitive information.

Apart from this potential informational strength, employee ownership introduces potential weaknesses in relation to the incentives for effective governance and the suitability of employees as sources of investable funds for the enterprise.

In terms of *incentives*, it is assumed that the objective function of outside shareholders comprises the maximisation of their share's value, since this comprises the present value of all future expected dividends. An employee owner, however, is likely to have value maximisation as only one argument in a utility function that is assumed to include labour income, job security and the preservation of a local community (Putterman, 1993, p. 259). Putting a value on such non-value components means that employees will be prepared to pay a premium to keep shares away from outside investors, or they will vote for the imposition of restrictions on the alienability of shares. For example, privatised firms in Russia under Variant 1 are forbidden by law to allow the sale of shares for three years, and in practice many firms have voted to restrict shares to insiders. Indeed, Ben-Ner (1993) advocates a law that only permits share sales to new employees, and

> The ownership of tradable shares gives members correct investment incentives, because they can recover their investment when they leave the firm. (p. 356)

Unfortunately, however, restrictions on tradability to new employees only has the effect of excluding willing outside investors and thus raising the effective cost of capital to the firm, with implications for the quality of control (see below).

Employees also have shortcomings that further reduce their value as *suppliers of investable funds* to the firm. With relatively low incomes, and unable to borrow significantly, employees are unlikely to provide large injections of funds for investment. Furthermore, any capital they do provide will have a high cost. On the assumption that risk-averse employees have only one full-time job, with few financial savings other than their investment in the firm's shares, it follows that the employee shareholder is relatively undiversified compared with any outsiders (usually investment funds in Russia) able to enjoy a significant degree of portfolio diversification (Putterman, 1993, p. 253). As long as the returns on different securities are not perfectly correlated, the outsider can achieve a level of portfolio risk that is lower than the weighted average of the risks associated with the individual securities comprising the portfolio. In the limit, a perfectly diversified outside investor can achieve risk-neutrality in relation to firm-specific risks, thus reducing the effective cost of capital to a firm owned by outsiders who are less risk-averse than employees. By way of contrast, employees of Russian enterprises may be considered *super-undiversified and therefore risk-averse*, since their incomes are relatively low and employment with a firm brings wages plus various infrastructural support in the form of homes, sanatoria, schools, kindergartens, holidays, etc.

Of course, the shortcomings of employees as a source of investable funds would be weakened if they could borrow to buy shares. In practice, however, lenders will be more willing to lend to diversified outside investors than to encourage employees offering no significant collateral to make their portfolios of human and financial capital even more dependent on the fortunes of one firm by acquiring more shares. This unwillingness to lend to employees further explains the 'giveaway' nature of Russian privatisations (see above).

With these shortcomings as owners in mind, the next section considers the interaction between employee ownership and control in order to produce testable propositions concerning the performance of EBOs in Russia.

RUSSIAN EBOs – EMPLOYEES AS OWNERS AND CONTROLLERS

This final main section builds on the last two and compares the EBO as a governance structure with combined employee ownership and control with the alternative of a conventional Anglo–American firm with a core shareholder or group having the incentive to monitor incumbent managers. This removes the problem of free-rider abuse associated with the voice of disinterested, individual shareholders, but the comparison does have the effect of biasing the analysis against EBOs. On the other hand, it is a realistic comparison in the sense that it is the would-be core investor who threatens the control of the Russian employee shareholder.

Furthermore, it is assumed that employee shareholders do *not* offer more effective voice than conventional core investors. This position is justified for a number of reasons:

- Any mutual monitoring by employees is liable to free-rider abuse when employee control is combined with a share of residual income: an individual employee with $(1/n)$th of total equity will only enjoy $(1/n)$th of the benefit of any monitoring supplied by the individual. Any coalition of employees that agrees to provide collective mutual monitoring (Nuti, 1987) is also liable to abuse, since an individual free-rider can leave mutual monitoring to the rest of the coalition.

- Very large privatisations in Russia raise the transactions costs of mutual monitoring and make (n) a very large number indeed (see above). Communications costs within large enterprises can be further increased by the great distances between plants.
- The 'giveaway' nature of Russian enterprise valuation and of the finance of employees' share acquisitions attenuates the incentive for employees to monitor effectively.
- Employee ownership and control has succeeded in certain niche industries where vertical monitoring invokes high transactions costs. There is no evidence that it causes any general harm, but nor is there evidence that it offers a general improvement in voice, efficiency and profits.

With this explicit assumption that employee ownership and control offers no voice advantages in general compared with conventional core investors, five testable propositions are derived. In each case it is demonstrated that decision control is weakened by ownership and control being combined in employees, but it must be remembered that despite such negative propositions, EBOs are a *versatile* governance structure in a life-cycle of firms (Green and Berry, 1991). Each individual proposition contributes in a complementary way to the prediction of EBOs being a transitional enterprise form.

Proposition 1 follows from the inclusion of arguments in the objective function of an employee owner besides share values (Putterman, 1993, p. 259, and above). If employees *as owners* seek high wages, job security and community infrastructure provision in addition to share value enhancement, this has implications for employee decisions *as controllers* (see p. 157 above).

Proposition 1

Employee owners will in the short term voice for *higher wages, infrastructural provision and lower levels of restructuring and redundancy* than in conventional firms. In the longer term these decisions result in lower labour productivity which threatens the ability of EBOs to compete in labour and product markets.

Although product market competition for Russian EBOs can only come from imports and new private firms, evidence on Proposition 1 should emerge soon, and the proposition is at least consistent with the following two examples. Investigations by the authors into the privatised electrical company 'Elex' in Vladimir (Moscow Region) in 1993 has revealed that senior managers estimated that new products and 1500 redundancies were needed to make their products competitive on world markets. Employees (with 80 per cent of shares) have so far blocked restructuring.

In the case of 'Bolshevik' privatised bakery in Moscow, monitored by the authors in 1993, employees with 70 per cent of shares persuaded the Board to acquire a social club and sports centre that represent significant liabilities for the new firm.

Proposition 2 is concerned with the formal and informal restrictions that are placed on the actions of employees *as owners* (advocated by Ben-Ner, 1993, p. 356; see p. 158) that also have implications on employees' *control* (see p. 157 above). With competitive capital markets, a conventional shareholder can exit a share and receive a price that reflects the present value of all expected future dividends. In comparison, BOs often put formal restrictions on share transfers, (for example, transfers are forbidden under Variant 1 privatisations in Russia). In addition there may be informal pressures on employees to retain their shares. Since current wages and dividends are now worth more than illiquid future dividends, it is proposed that this produces a special kind of 'short-termism' among employee shareholders.

Proposition 2

Employee owners will in the short term voice for *higher levels of dividends* than core investors in conventional firms. In the longer term, lower levels of investment out of ploughed-back profits will inhibit EBOs' ability to compete in product markets.

Again, evidence is starting to emerge which does nothing to refute Proposition 2. In the case of 'Bolshevik' (see above) the threat during 1993 of a potential core investor ('Alfa Kapital') from outside the enterprise caused the General Director to protect his position by promising higher current dividends to employees with 70 per cent of shares. Early results from a survey of privatised firms in St Petersburg suggest that firms are even borrowing to pay higher dividends.

Proposition 3 follows from the decision of EBO firms to raise the majority of equity capital from individual employees *as owners* to the exclusion of would-be core investors from outside the firm. Unfortunately, individuals are relatively more undiversified in their portfolios of human and financial capital than external investors (Jensen and Meckling, 1979, p. 486) and at lower levels of average income and wealth (Putterman, 1993, p. 247). Low wealth and less diversification implies greater risk-aversion from employees *as controllers*, and therefore a higher cost of capital. Indeed, in the case of Russia, it can be argued that employees are super-undiversified, with much local infrastructure that is provided by local authorities in the West being the responsibility of local firms.

Proposition 3

With the higher cost of capital, employee shareholders will voice for *lower investment levels* out of plough-back than conventional firms in the short term. In the long term, lower investment will threaten the ability of EBOs to compete in capital and product markets.

Propositions 4 and 5 constitute further development of the general point that undiversified owners can be expected to make different decisions as controllers. Employee controllers who are relatively risk-averse as a result of their jobs and shares will produce biased *strategic* as well as operational decisions.

Proposition 4

Relatively undiversified employee shareholders as controllers will voice for *higher levels of product diversification* than in conventional firms, and this tendency will be stronger in firms where there are restrictions on the freedom of employees to exit from shares in favour of outsiders. In the long run, such over-diversification of products will threaten EBOs' ability to compete on product markets. It may even prompt a "second wave" of BOs from over-diversified companies.

Proposition 5 again depends upon the implications of relatively undiversified employee owners. Building on empirical experience with western privatisation BOs (Filatotchev *et al.*, 1992), it assumes that as soon as employees are free to sell shares without exit restrictions, they will sell to buyers offering the highest price. Given that external, would-be core investors and employees both seek shares for the income and voice they offer, the highest bids are likely to come from the more highly diversified potential owner, i.e. the outsider (Jensen and Meckling, 1979, p. 486). This has implications for control passing out of the firm.

Proposition 5

Relatively undiversified employee shareholders wishing to exit from their shares will ultimately sell to would-be core investors from outside the firm who seek control and voice within the firm and who are already well-diversified in their asset portfolios.

Preliminary research by the authors from primary sources in Russia confirms that outside control is starting to emerge. In the case of the 'Uralmash' association in Ekaterinburg, an outsider ('Bioprocessor', controlled by one of Russia's wealthiest individuals) secured 18.5 per cent of shares at auction and has already won a place on the Board. Similarly at 'Bolshevik' (see above), 'Alfa Kapital' is building up a controlling stake by acquiring shares from employees.

At the Vladimir Tractor Works (privatised under Variant 2 in 1993) a former senior manager is bidding for control with the backing of a Russian–American joint venture, 'Renova', of which he is a director. He has already secured a place on the Tractor Works Board. In fact, the involvement of former and current senior managers with outside backers is becoming quite common in the battle for enterprise control. In the case of 'Elex' (see above), managers are seeking to establish a core holding of employees' shares, but outside backers are likely to demand voice and control in enterprises.

In the long term, income inequalities may evolve and managers may be able to finance their own bids for control, but their relatively undiversified positions will encourage them to borrow from outsiders and buy shares in other companies besides their own, and lenders are likely to impose vertical monitoring on managers who borrow. Again, there is the expectation of the emergence of a life-cycle of firms as BOs succeed in achieving systemic transformation, but then give way to enterprise forms offering superior corporate governance in the long term.

CONCLUSIONS

The emergence of the EBO as the predominant form of privatisation for large industrial firms has attracted much criticism from Russian citizens and western academics, (see, for example, Frydman *et al.*, 1993; Blanchard *et al.*, 1991). Indeed, this chapter has also drawn attention to evidence of asset under-valuation and the giveaway nature of the financing of employees' share purchases. The impression is given that the EBO is a primitive structure chosen hurriedly by a Russian government in crisis.

Yet it can be argued that the emphasis on EBOs has been sensible and pragmatic. The preconditions for EBOs are modest compared with the demands of privatisation by flotation, ownership by financial institutions and trade sales: these options were simply not available in July 1992 and seem unlikely for a number of years yet. Citizens' vouchers and privatisation variants biased in favour of employees were necessary to push through a privatisation programme that had to be rapid in order to achieve irreversible market reform.

Whether by design or accident, and probably a mixture of the two, the government chose an enterprise governance structure in the EBO which still has severe limitations, especially given the giveaway nature of the privatisation process and the damage this does to employees' willingness to voice effectively within the firm. Yet in the West the BO has proved a vital and sophisticated means of dealing with over-centralisation in firms in the public and private sectors. It is well known that the BO is often a transitional phase in a life-cycle of firms (Green and Berry, 1991). For example, in UK privatisations, the average life of a privatisation BO in this form has been 3.5 years (Filatotchev *et al.*, 1992, p. 268).

The testing of the propositions in this chapter must await the emergence of conventional Anglo–American firms with managers or external core investors holding controlling stakes, so that their performance may be compared with EBOs. Early evidence suggests that testing should not have long to wait, and if conventional firms do emerge without excessive social disruption this will have been a very real achievement for a privatisation programme whose emphasis on EBOs was so criticised at the time.

Meanwhile, the preference shown by western investors in Russia for joint ventures and new, greenfield projects seems understandable in the light of the government's promotion of EBOs as the dominant privatisation vehicle. As EBOs evolve into structures with more stable governance properties, western investors may find privatised enterprises more appealing.

Note

Financial support for CMBOR from the Economic and Social Research Council (grant no. R000221142), Barclays Development Capital Ltd and Touche Ross Corporate Finance is gratefully acknowledged, together with the comments of Mo Yamin.

References

Alchian, A.A., (1987) 'Property rights', in J. Eatwell, M. Milgate and P. Newman (eds), *The New Palgrave Dictionary of Economics*, vol. 3 (London: Macmillan), pp. 1031–4.

Aoki, M. (1990) 'Toward an economic model of the Japanese firm', *Journal of Economic Literature*, 28(1), pp. 1–27.

Ben-Ner, A. (1993) 'Organizational reform in Central and Eastern Europe. A comparative perspective', *Annals of Public and Co-operative Economy*, 64(3), pp. 329–65.

Ben-Ner, A., Montias, J.M. and Neuberger, E. (1993) 'Basic issues in organization', *Journal of Comparative Economics*, 17(2), pp. 207–242.

Blanchard O., Dornbusch, R., Krugman, P., Layard R. and Summers, L. (1991) *Reform in Eastern Europe* (Cambridge, Mass. MIT Press).

Bös, D., (1993) 'Privatization in Europe: a comparison of approaches', *Oxford Review of Economic Policy*, 9(1), pp. 95–111.

Buck, T.W., (1988) 'Soft budgets and administration', *Comparative Economic Studies*, 30(3), pp. 51–70.

Chandler, A.D. Jr., (1993) 'Organizational capabilities and industrial restructuring: a historical analysis', *Journal of Comparative Economics*, 17(2), pp. 309–37.

Corbett, J. and Mayer, C., (1991) 'Financial reform in Eastern Europe: progress with the wrong model', *Oxford Review of Economic Policy*, 7(4), pp. 57–75.

Demsetz, H. (1993) 'Putting wealth and enterprise control in the production function', University of California, mimeo quoted with the permission of author.

Demsetz, H. and Lehn. K. (1985) 'The structure of corporate ownership: causes and consequences', *Journal of Political Economy*, 93(6), pp. 1155–77.

Drucker, P.F., (1991) 'Reckoning with the pension fund revolution', *Harvard Business Review*, 69(2), pp. 106–14.

European Bank for Reconstruction and Development, (1993) *Management and Employee Buyouts in Central and Eastern Europe: an Introduction*, M. Wright, I. Filatotchev, T. Buck and K. Robbie (eds) (London: EBRD).

Filatotchev I., Buck T and Wright, M. (1992) 'Privatisation and buyouts in the USSR', *Soviet Studies*, 44(2), pp. 265–82.

Frydman, R., Phelps, E.S., Rapaczynski, A. and Shleifer, A., (1993) 'Needed mechanisms of corporate governance and finance in Eastern Europe', *Economics of Transition* 1(2), pp. 171–207.

Gilson, R.J. and Roe, M.J., (1993) 'Understanding the Japanese Keiretsu: overlaps between corporate governance and industrial organization', *The Yale Law Review* 102(4), pp. 871–906.

Green, S. and Berry, D.F. (1991) *Cultural, Structural and Strategic Change in Management Buy-Outs* (London: Macmillan).

Hansmann, H., (1990) 'The viability of worker ownership: an economic perspective on the political structure of the firm', Chapter 8 in M. Aoki, B. Gustatson and O.E. Williamson (eds), *The Firm as a Nexus of Contracts* (London: Sage).

Hirschman, A., (1958) *The Strategy of Economic Development* (New Haven: Yale University Press).

Jensen, M.C. (1989) 'The eclipse of the public corporation', *Harvard Business Review*, 67(5), pp. 61–74.

Jensen, M.C. and Meckling, W.H. (1979) 'Rights and production functions: an application to labor-managed firms and codetermination', *Journal of Business*, 52(4), pp. 469–506.

Kornai, J. (1992) 'The principles of privatization in Eastern Europe', *De Economist*, 140(2), pp. 153–76.

Miles, D. (1993) 'Testing for short-termism on the UK stock market', *Economic Journal*, 103(121), pp. 1379–96.

Murrell, P. and Wang, Y. (1993) 'When privatization should be delayed', *Journal of Comparative Economics*, 17(2), pp. 385–406.

Nuti, D. (1987) 'Co-determination and profit-sharing', in J. Eatwell, M. Milgate and P. Newman (eds), *The New Palgrave Dictionary of Economics*, vol 1 (London: Macmillan), pp. 465–9.

Putterman, L. (1993) 'Ownership and the nature of the firm', *Journal of Comparative Economics*, 17(2), pp. 243–63.

Shleifer, A. and Vishny, R.W. (1986) 'Large shareholders and corporate control', *Journal of Political Economy*, 94(3), pp. 461–88.

Stiglitz, J.E. (1985) 'Credit markets and the control of capital', *Journal of Money, Credit and Banking*, 17(2), pp. 133–52.

Thompson, R.S. and Wright, M. (1991) 'UK management buyouts: debt, equity and agency cost implications', *Managerial and Decision Economics*, 12(1), pp. 15–26.

Valentiny, P., Buck, T. and Wright, M., (1992) 'The pricing and valuation of public assets: experiences in the UK and Hungary', *Annals of Public and Co-operative Economy*, 63(4), pp. 601–19.

Weitzman, M. (1993) 'How not to privatize', in M. Baldassain, L. Paganetto and E. Phelps (eds) *Privatization Processes in Eastern Europe* (New York: St Martin's Press).

Williamson, O.E. (1975) *Markets and Hierarchies: Analysis and Anti trust* Implications (New York: Free Press).

Wright, M., Thompson, S., Chiplin, B. and Robbie, K. (1991) *BuyOuts and Buy-Ins: New Strategies in Corporate Management* (London: Graham & Trotman).

9 Privatisation in Transitional Economies – East and Central European Experience

Paul Cook and Colin Kirkpatrick

INTRODUCTION

The role of privatisation in the European transitional economies in creating a market structure and fostering the development of a private sector immediately distinguishes it from the privatisation model followed in the UK and other western industrialised countries. The non-transferability of the western model has meant that the approach to privatisation that has evolved in the European transitional economies has reflected the particular historical, institutional and economic characteristics of these countries. However, while most economies began the transition to the market with broadly similar objectives and have gone through similar phases in progressing the privatisation process, nevertheless each has developed its own privatisation programme, which have differed in the timing, sequencing and outcome of the policy measures taken.

The object of this chapter is to examine the privatisation experience so far in the European transitional economies. In so doing, we focus on both the similarities and the differences among the transitional economies, and identify the major constraints and problems that have been encountered in pursuing privatisation. We review the changes that have taken place and the extent to which privatisation has occurred, and discuss the contribution of enterprise reform and foreign capital to the process of private sector development. Finally, a number of lessons for future policy are drawn from the analysis of the experience of the years 1990–5.

THE SCALE OF PRIVATISATION

The experience of the transitional economies with privatisation has been mixed, with respect to both the speed and scale of implementation. With the exception of the former East Germany, progress in implementing privatisation programmes has been much slower than early expectations, and a sizeable proportion of economic activity remains to be transferred to private ownership.

In the immediate aftermath of the fall of communism, the rapid transfer of enterprises from state to private ownership was seen as offering the quickest route to the market economy. Advocates of the 'big bang' approach envisaged government concentrating on achieving a stable macroeconomic environment, if necessary by severe demand constraint and monetary contraction. A programme of deregulation and liberalisation, accompanied by the construction of a legal and institutional framework which would protect private property rights, would provide the 'enabling environment' for private enterprises to flourish. The improvement in the business environment would in turn attract foreign capital and technology to the privatisation programmes.

The early approach to privatisation, therefore, was to transfer the ownership of state owned enterprises to the private sector as quickly as possible and to have a minimum degree of state involvement in enterprise restructuring or rehabilitation (ECE, 1994, p. 9). With the exception of Bulgaria, all the countries of eastern Europe proceeded with small-scale privatisation at the outset of the reform process. In most countries, the size of the enterprise in terms of employment or value of assets has been used as a yardstick. In Russia, for example, the first wave of privatisation concentrated on enterprises employing less than 200 persons. Shops, restaurants, housing, hotels and workshops were often the first enterprises to be privatised. Progress with small-scale agricultural enterprises has been slower, due to complexities of land ownership rights following the end of collectivisation.

The scale of small privatisation appears to be significant in a number of the central European economies. The Czech Republic, Hungary, Poland and the Slovak Republic are close to completing their programmes. In the Russian Federation and Lithuania more than two thirds of small firms have been privatised. The pace of small-scale privatisation has been slower, however, in most of the former Soviet republics (EBRD, 1993, p. 39). Table 9.1 summarises the progress with small-scale privatisation in each of the transitional economies.

The information contained in Table 9.1 may, however, over-state the extent of ownership transfer that has occurred. Much of the 'privatisation' in the retail sector has not involved a transfer of ownership rights. Instead, it has often involved short-term leasing arrangements for retail trade and service sector outlets from the state (Frydman and Rapaczynski, 1993). Where the restitution issue has not been addressed, it has become a major barrier to rapid privatisation. Bulgaria, for example, has encountered severe difficulties in small-scale privatisation because it deferred dealing with restitution claims, without denying them, until after it began privatisation (EBRD, 1993, p. 40). In contrast, in the former Czechoslovakia, restitution was carried out simultaneously with small-scale privatisation. As van Brabant (1995) emphasises, the commitment to restitution, which has been justified on moral or ethical grounds, has proved to be a major complication for the transfer into private entities. The identification of former owners, and the valuation of assets which were substantially modified during the period of central

Table 9.1 Small-scale and large-scale privatisations, 1990–3

Country	Small-scale privatisation (1)	Large-scale privatisation (2)
Albania	Trade and started 1991, stalled April 1992 Agriculture, 80% of cooperatives privatised	None as of summer 1993
Armenia	90% of agriculture, some housing and small businesses	No large-scale programme as of summer 1993
Azerbaijan	Law adopted January 1993	Large-scale programme to start in 1995
Belarus	New law adopted January 1993 Less than 10% of all eligible units privatised	By the end of 1993, 535 enterprises targeted for privatisation, equivalent to 15% of total fixed assets
Bulgaria	Just begun, but encountering problems with restitution	83 companies being prepared for privatisation in 1993
Croatia	70% of small enterprises privatised	20% of all firms identified for privatisation, but no comprehensive programme has been adopted due to the war
Czech Republic	Completed 26 000 unit sold	First wave completed 2300 firms book value CSK 700bn = 100% of annual GDP Multiple methods used including voucher privatisation
Estonia	40% of total complete	Less than 10% of eligible firms privatised
Georgia	10% of small enterprises privatised	No large-scale programme as of summer 1993
Hungary	Completed for 70% of small firms identified for privatisation	Large firms accounting for 18% of the book value have been privatised
Kazakhstan	First programme 1991–3 Small-scale privatisation about 6% completed	1% of all large-scale privatisation completed Voucher privatisation programme launched 1 July 1993
Kyrgyzstan	No clear distinction between small and large privatisation Various methods planned Voucher including 5% of state assets book value privatised at end 1992	
Latvia	30% of small firms by summer 1993	Fewer than 10% of large firms eligible for privatisation
Lithuania	Over 80% of all small firms by summer 1993 Nearly completed in the housing sector	1506 out of 1934 eligible enterprises privatised by share subscription, four firms have been sold for hard currency at a value of USD 650 000
FYR Macedonia	70% of small firms	Bill in Parliament will cover privatisation of large firms
Moldova	No clear distinction between small- and large-scale privatisation Programme approved March 1993 10% of agriculture land privatisation	

	Mass privatisation start in the second half of 1993, 1993–4 target: privatise over 1000 enterprises, about one third of state assets earmarked for privatisation	
Poland	Rate of small privatisation high Most assets of the few SOEs liquidated in 1992 were leased	600 firms had been identified for privatisation as of summer 1993 Current plan calls for 200 large firms to be transferred to 5–8 investment funds Shares will be distributed to pensioners and public sector employees The remaining 400 firms will be privatised more slowly through 15 additional funds, the shares of which will be sold of the general public
Romania	2300 SEMs to be privatised in 1993 This accounts for 90% of retail outlets and 45% of retail trade	70% of farm land privatised 15.5 million Certificates of Ownership (COs) distributed as of December 1992 (estimated value for a CO is Lei 150 000) The plan calls for establishment of five funds to assume ownership of 6280 identified firms
Russian Federation	By May 1993 about two thirds of small-scale businesses had been privatised Small privatisation is planned to be completed in 1994	Mass privatisation programme underway Distribution of vouchers completed by the end of January 1993 About 1260 large and medium industrial firms privatised in voucher auctions by May 1993 in 554 regions of Russia The 1993 programme covered 6000 enterprises For medium-sized enterprises, a new mass privatisation scheme will be launched in 1994 Sales of shares of the largest enterprises also started in March 1993
Slovak Republic	Completed 9000 units sold	First wave completed, 711 firms (book value CSK 166bn = 40% of annual GDP) via voucher privatisation Multiple methods used including voucher privatisation

Source: EBRD (1993, pp. 35–7).

planning, places large demands on a legal infrastructure which is itself undergoing radical change.

Small-scale privatisation proceeded rapidly in former East Germany, with more than 20 000 retail outlets, restaurants and hotels being privatised within two years of reunification, and about 90 per cent of the more than 12 000 industrial enterprises were either closed or transferred to the private sector (IMF, 1993a, p. 96). It is important to recognise, however, that the process of privatisation in East Germany has been fundamentally different to that in the other economies in transition (Schwartz, 1995). The West German economy was able to provide considerable financial support to enable a rapid transformation of the state sector. The mandate of the Treuhandanstalt, the trust fund agency responsible for privatising enterprises in East Germany, was to restructure and transfer most state owned assets to the private sector by 1995. This mandate has been largely fulfilled, although as Bös and Kayser (1995) emphasise, the longer-run viability of the privatised enterprises will depend upon their capacity to develop their management skills and market competitiveness.

'Large' privatisation refers to the divestment of the vast bulk of the state owned enterprises that tend to be large, often organised in conglomerates, and typically highly monopolistic. A significant share of employment is provided by these large enterprises. The methods of privatisation for large enterprises are therefore considerably more complex than is the case for assets that have been subjected to 'small' privatisation.

The implementation of large-scale privatisation programmes has been slow in most transition economies, due to the complexity of the task. First, it has proved difficult to find buyers for large enterprises, many of which are conglomerates, with high levels of debt and structural problems. In many instances, governments were unwilling to accept the budgetary and political implications of a massive rise in unemployment that would occur as private owners restructured the enterprises. Governments have therefore been forced to give consideration to the restructuring and rehabilitation of enterprises prior to divestment. But simply imposing a 'hard' budget constraint, as advocated by some observers (Bleaney, 1994), may encourage resistance to change on the part of management and labour. A hardening of budget constraints needs, therefore, to be combined with other policies for strengthening the enterprise sector, including financial restructuring and debt reduction. The success of the Treuhandanstalt suggests,

> the need for a co-ordinated strategy incorporating: a clear, de-politicized policy towards enterprise and industrial restructuring, including specific measures to reduce the burden of accumulated enterprise debt; a programme to re-capitalize the banks and to privatize them; and a significant increase in infrastructure spending on transport and communications. (ECE, 1994, p. 11)

The dilemma which the transitional economies have faced is that such a programme of massive restructuring requires a level of financial support which exceeds their current fiscal capabilities. The transformation of the huge state owned enterprise sector into privately owned and efficiently operated firms has, therefore, been more difficult than anticipated:

> Both the expertise and financial capital required to manage the transition properly have been underestimated in most cases, and privatization, including the resolution of property rights, has been politically charged and thus prone to delay. (IMF, 1993, p. 91)

The slow progress with implementing large-scale privatisation is shown in Table 9.1, column (2). The most significant privatisation has occurred in the Czech Republic, where a variety of standard and non-standard methods has been used. Standard methods have included: restitution of property to the original owners or their heirs, the sale of property to domestic or foreign investors through public auctions and tenders, direct sales to designated owners, transformation into joint stock companies, and the free transfer of property to municipalities, pension funds and similar institutions (ECE, 1994, p. 165). The non-standard method has been voucher privatisation, which has been used as the main instrument for mass privatisation. Between 50 and 60 per cent of Czech national assets have been distributed through the voucher scheme. More than 400 investment privatisation funds, which invest voucher points on behalf of individuals, have been established, and some 72 per cent of the total investment points issued by the voucher scheme have been invested by the funds (EBRD, 1993, p. 40).

The use of the voucher scheme enabled the Czech authorities to proceed with privatisation without prior restructuring so that the existing management and workforce could be retained in the transferred enterprises. Instead, the change in ownership is expected to induce changes in the internal structure of enterprises. However, it remains to be seen how much pressure the new owners will be able to exert for effective restructuring through the investment privatisation funds which hold a large proportion of the shares.

Poland has used two main methods of privatisation: liquidation and capitalisation. Liquidation refers to the dissolution of the state enterprises by the sale or lease of assets directly to a private firm. Capitalisation refers to the conversion of state owned enterprises into joint stock or limited liability companies prior to their privatisation by share sales (Hychak and King, 1994). Liquidation was intended for small and medium firms, and most privatisations have been of this type. About 500 larger enterprises have been capitalised but most have remained wholly owned by the state.

In Hungary, the approach to privatisation has been piecemeal, with state owned enterprises being privatised on a case-by-case basis. In Russia, the voucher scheme was adopted, and by mid-1993 the distribution of vouchers had been completed and the government was progressing with enterprise auctions (see Chapter 8 in this volume). But in the majority of former Soviet Union (FSU) countries, large privatisation programmes have yet to be implemented, and in most cases less than 10 per cent of eligible units have been privatised.

The route to privatisation has therefore been less direct than initially anticipated, and the deviations have paralleled the changes in thinking that have marked the transition process in general since 1989:

> An initial euphoria and expectations of rapid change based on an over-simplified analysis of the likely obstacles, followed by disappointment and disillusion when progress proved to be much slower than expected and the costs of adjustment more painful, leading gradually to a more pragmatic approach to highly complex and interdependent problems. (ECE, 1994, p. 9)

PRIVATE SECTOR DEVELOPMENT

The problems of implementing large-scale privatisations have been described as

> The most stubbornly resistant roadblock jutting up in the path of almost every Eastern European country on the road to market. (IMF, 1993b, p. 248)

Nevertheless, it is important not to lose sight of the fact that privatisation is an instrument for establishing a market economy, rather than an objective in itself. There has in fact been significant private sector development and market expansion occurring independently of the privatisation process.

The growth of new private enterprise activity has been encouraged by the broader programmes of economic liberalisation and reform adopted by the transition economies. These measures have ranged from legalising private ownership and enacting bankruptcy laws, to reform of the banking system, to relaxation of controls on the current and capital accounts of the balance of payments (EBRD, 1993, Chapter 3; Schwartz and Lopes, 1993). A number of central European countries – Croatia, Hungary, Poland and Slovenia – already had significant private sectors before 1989, since they had introduced liberalisation measures prior to the collapse of communism. Indeed, in Poland a substantial part of agriculture remained in private ownership throughout the central planning period. Other countries – Bulgaria, the Czech Republic and Romania – began with smaller private sectors.

The share and growth of the private sector are shown in Table 9.2. The figures indicate that the private sector has grown rapidly, increasing its share

Table 9.2 Average growth rate of GDP and private sector output and employment, 1989–92

Country	Annual growth of GDP (1989–92)	Private share in GDP (1992)	Annual growth of private share in GDP (1989–92)	Private share in total employment (1992)	Annual growth of private sector share in total (1989–92)
Central Europe					
Bulgaria	−9.0	15.6	21.3	14.1	33.7
Croatia	−16.5	19.0	30.8	12.3	16.0
Czechoslovakia	−5.8	20.0	48.6	16.4	139.1
Hungary	−4.8	34.0	11.0	56.7 (1990)	−
Poland	−4.6	47.5	13.5	57.0	6.5
Romania	−10.6	25.6	18.5	21.5	53.9
Slovenia	−5.0	19.5	23.8	22.5	13.8
Former Soviet Union					
Armenia	−14.1	36.7	45.9	37.1	33.2
Belarus	−3.1	8.1	12.3	3.5	30.7
Estonia	−13.0	22.0	11.5 (1991–2)	15.0	19.5 (199–2)
Georgia	−19.4	23.4	10.0	−	−
Kazakhstan	−0.6	12.2	−6.7	4.4 (1991)	10.1
Latvia	−1.4	−	−	5.9	40.8
Lithuania	−14.1	20.0	17.8	25.4	80.4
Russia	−7.2	10.1	24.0	4.8	44.2
Ukraine	−5.7	9.6	2.9	−	−
Uzbekistan	−4.2	6.6	−17.9 (1991–2)	23.9	3.1 (1991–2)

Source: EBRD (1993), Tables 3.1 and 3.2.

in total GDP, even in those economies where GDP growth has declined.

The capacity of the market economy to grow independently of privatisation through ownership transfer reintroduces the role of enterprise restructuring policy in the transition to the market process. There is considerable evidence on the comparative economic performance of private and public enterprises in advanced market economies to suggest that ownership *per se* is not a critical determinant of performance. Internal managerial incentives and external competitive market conditions are more significant influences on economic efficiency (EBRD, 1993, pp. 113–29). Attention has therefore switched to the role of enterprise restructuring and reform in moving the public enterprise sector in the transitional economies into the market. In particular, it is argued that a hardening of the enterprise budget constraint will promote management-led restructuring and improved economic performance. A 1993 World Bank study of 75 large state owned enterprises in Poland provides convincing empirical evidence of the enterprises' capacity to respond to a tightening budget constraint resulting from the government's adherence to macro-stabilisation goals, and to import competition resulting from trade liberalisation (Hume and Pinto, 1993).

The impact of a hard budget constraint in inducing enterprise restructuring may be significantly reduced by labour market conditions. If employees (and in some instances, managers) expect to lose from the restructuring process, they will act as a barrier to efficiency-oriented enterprise reform. This suggests that government will need to assist the restructuring process, while maintaining the hard budget constraint on enterprises, by making provision for the 'safety-netting' of labour that is adversely affected by restructuring.

LABOUR AND SOCIAL SECURITY UNDER PRIVATISATION

With the initiation of privatisation programmes, all transitional economy governments stressed the importance of a comprehensive social safety net and agreed to protect vulnerable groups of the population by providing a minimum level of income. Most governments introduced comparatively generous unemployment benefit schemes but, as unemployment increased, the fiscal burden of maintaining a comprehensive social safety net increased dramatically (ECE, 1994, p. 89).

The consequences of transition in general, and privatisation in particular, for employment and social security are complex (Cook and Kirkpatrick, 1994a). Prior to 1989, the state provided benefits for the employed labour force in the form of old-age and disability pensions, free medical care, maternity benefits and child allowances. In addition, the state provided guarantees for life-time employment and for the basic social goods, including housing and education. The process of economic reforms to assist transition to a market economy has posed major challenges to this type of social protection. In the first instance, life-time guarantees of employment are inconsistent with the requirements for flexibility in labour markets demanded by a decentralised market system (Burgess *et al.*, 1993). Second, the process of transition has had an adverse impact on output growth (Table 9.2), and employment (Table 9.3).

In most cases of transition, output has fallen faster than employment. Enterprises in some countries have preferred wage cuts to employment cuts as stabilisation has reduced public expenditures. Enterprises that have continued to operate with soft budgets have been able to hold on to redundant workers in the hope that the market will improve in the future. In some cases, work practices have changed and shorter working hours have been introduced. Some workers have been placed on unpaid leave.

The policy responses to unemployment during transition can be categorised as unemployment benefit systems, active labour market policies and social welfare programmes, even if the latter are relatively rudimentary. The initial reaction to the decline in output and the rise in unemployment was to erect a social safety net, including a component for paying unemployment compensation. As the cases of the Czech Republic and Hungary show, these were initially quite generous, with benefits to the unemployed lasting for one year or more. With the rise in unemployment, above 10 per cent in

Table 9.3 Unemployment in transitional economies, % labour force, 1990–3

Country	1990	1991	1992	1993
Albania	9.8	9.4	26.7	
Bulgaria	1.8	11.5	15.6	16.4
Croatia	8.0	14.1	17.8	16.9
Czech Republic	0.7	4.1	2.6	3.5
Hungary	1.7	7.4	12.3	12.1
Poland	6.1	11.8	13.6	15.7
Romania	1.3	3.1	8.2	10.1
Slovakia	1.6	11.8	10.4	14.4
Slovenia	5.3	10.1	13.3	15.4
Macedonia	17.1	24.5	26.8	29.6
Yugoslavia FR	14.7	15.7	24.6	24.6

Source: ECE (1994), Table 3.4.4.

most cases, and the pressure on public finances as the tax base shrinks and the numbers in need of social protection continue to grow, other components beyond temporary unemployment compensation have to be introduced. Labour market policies, designed to alleviate skill shortages, improve labour mobility and promote growth of job opportunities in the private sector are beginning to emerge.

More recently, benefit regimes are tightening and the relative amounts of benefits appear to be falling. Indeed, the average level of unemployment benefits relative to the average wages fell between 1991 and 1992. In Bulgaria, the benefit–wage ratio nearly halved, to 34 per cent in 1992. In Poland, entitlements were reduced by the Employment Act introduced in December 1991, which cut the level of benefits from 50 per cent to 36 per cent of the average wage. In Russia the benefit–wage ratio was only 10 per cent. Besides providing low social protection, such rates are likely to discourage people registering as unemployed. Besides these rate reductions, the duration of benefits has been shortened and the criteria for eligibility increased. In the Czech Republic, for example, the eligibility for benefits declined from 80 per cent of the total number registered as unemployed in 1991, to less than 40 per cent in 1992. Similar reductions occurred in Bulgaria, Hungary and Poland between 1991 and 1993.

Benefits for the unemployed were also introduced on the basis of social insurance rather than social assistance. As such, they were related to previous earnings, and have been eroded by high inflation and only partial indexing of benefits. Initially, the benefits system offered replacement rates of between 50 to 60 per cent but rapidly converged to minimum income support, as for example in the Czech and Slovak Republics.

In many cases, workers in the transitional economies are able to influence the process of privatisation and the distribution of benefits. In Poland, workers are given considerable power of influence over privatisation. The 1990 Law on Privatisation of State Owned Enterprises stipulates that a public enterprise may be privatised at the initiative of its own management and the workers' council. It also grants employees substantial rights over the choice of process for reform; whether enterprises should be corporatised or liquidated and over the prospective buyers.

In Russia, despite large shortfalls in output, firms have been able, with easy access to banks' credit and workers' resistance to change, to delay restructuring. This is in marked contrast to the situation in Hungary, where unemployment is higher, the system of social security better and the influence of workers within firms weaker. Firms in Hungary have been more willing to shed labour to reduce operating costs and, therefore, adopt adjustment strategies favouring profit than firms in Russia (Hare, 1994).

Many layoffs have also involved the use of invalidity pensions to cope with the extent of redundancies. This had the consequence that not only did the level of unemployment rise but also the number of beneficiaries of early retirement and invalidity pensions increased. This has aggravated the social situation by putting strains on the budget for pensions and social security expenditures.

The shedding of labour in transitional economies has also had a differential impact on the various social strata that used to be employed, including older workers, minorities, women and the disabled. Old prejudices and stereotypes are re-emerging in relation to hiring women and some minorities. Since many of the major layoffs involved workers close to retirement age, these persons have found it difficult to reintegrate back into the workforce. Further, in Eastern and Central Europe, as opposed to OECD countries, there has been a tendency to provide wage subsidies to employers rather than spend money on developing training activities that would assist re-entry into employment (Scarpetta *et al.*, 1993).

FOREIGN DIRECT INVESTMENT

Foreign direct investment (FDI) can make an important contribution to the privatisation process, and to the development of the private sector. As is well known, FDI not only provides capital resources to augment domestic savings, but also acts as a conduit for the transfer of technology, skills and market access.

The flow of FDI into Eastern and Central Europe has been rising steadily, although the distribution between countries, as shown in Table 9.4, is highly uneven with the Czech Republic, Hungary and the Slovak Republic attracting two thirds of the total during 1990–3. The rest of the region, with approximately 90 per cent of the population, received only 32 per cent of the cumulative total (EBRD, 1994, p. 122). Hungary is the largest recipient

Table 9.4 FDI in transitional countries, US$ mn, 1990–3

	1990	1991	1992	1993
Albania			19	30
Bulgaria	4	56	52	48
Croatia			−1	75
Czech Republic	135	510	983	409
Hungary	311	1249	1471	2328
Poland	88	117	284	380
Romania	−18	37	73	48
Slovakia	53	82	71	120
Slovenia	−2	41	113	110
Total	573	2302	3055	3548

Source: ECE (1994, p. 136).

Table 9.5 FDI, by sector, eastern Europe and the former Soviet Union, 1991–March 1994

Sector	No of projects	% of total no.of projects
Electricals, electronics, computers, telecommunications	472	11.4
Food and beverage production, agribusiness	426	10.3
Oil and gas, mining and metals	389	9.4
Automotive, aircraft, railway manufacture, shipbuilding	373	9.0
Financial services	340	8.2
Chemicals, plastics, glass	188	4.5
Engineering, heavy machinery	180	4.4
Building materials, construction	165	4.0
Textiles, fashion, footwear	157	3.8
Miscellaneous services	901	21.8
Miscellaneous manufacturing	544	13.2
Total	4135	100.0

Source: EBRD (1994, p. 123).

of private investment, and foreign owned companies now account for almost 10 per cent of value added and 4.5 per cent of employment in Hungary (EBRD, 1993, p. 84).

Privatisation sales to foreign buyers have accounted for a significant share of the FDI inflows, and have been estimated to account for almost 67 per cent of all FDI receipts (UNCTAD, 1994). For example, Hungary received a net inflow of $2300 mn in 1993, of which $875 mn involved a single investment in MATAN telecommunications (ECE, 1994, p. 135).

The level of FDI inflows under-states the growth in foreign involvement by firms that have entered into joint venture agreements, while maintaining a low capital exposure. The number of joint venture agreements in eastern Europe and the former Soviet economies rose from almost 67 000 in 1992 to 94 000 in 1993 (Table 9.6).

The majority of countries of Eastern Europe and the former Soviet Union have passed legislation designed to make the environment for foreign investment more attractive, and 10 countries have established 'one-stop-shop' agencies to facilitate and promote FDI (EBRD, 1994, p. 124). Most sectors and forms of economic activities are open to foreign capital, with complete foreign ownership permitted. However, special registration of foreign joint ventures is required in two thirds of the transition economies, and licence and authorisation are also frequently required. Investment incentives for FDI are offered by most countries, and mainly take the form of tax holidays and lower rates of profit taxation.

The amount of FDI flowing to the transitional economies has, nevertheless, been below expectations, and can be attributed in part to the uncertainties in the business environment. The inadequacies of the legal and contractual framework for investors, the difficulties in establishing legal property rights, complex and arbitrary tax regimes, and the instability in the macro-environment have all contributed to the reluctance of foreign investors to become heavily committed.

Investor surveys have confirmed that economic and political uncertainty was a major constraint on FDI in the early years of the transition process (for a useful summary of the results of the foreign investor surveys undertaken in transition economies, see EBRD, 1994, pp. 130–1). However, more recent results have tended to give more weight to enterprise-level operating difficulties.

The experience of developing countries suggests that the restoration of a stable macro environment exerts a major influence in attracting foreign investment inflows. The international institutions, in particular the International Monetary Fund, play an important role in this regard. Agreement between the Fund and a host country on a stand-by stabilisation agreement, which will require the recipient to fulfil macro-policy reform conditions, is interpreted by foreign investors as a signal of greater stability in the future and acts as a catalyst for the release of additional foreign investment inflows.

In 1993, nine European transition economies (Albania, the Czech Republic, Estonia, Hungary, Latvia, Lithuania, Moldova, Poland and Kyrgyzstan) concluded full stand-by agreements with the IMF (ECE, 1994, p. 193). However, actual disbursements in 1993 were lower than in previous years, reflecting the difficulties many countries had in complying with IMF conditions (Table 9.7).

Trade policy represents an important area of potential conflict between the conditionality of the international finance institutions and domestic pol-

Table 9.6 Joint venture agreements in transitional countries, 1992–3

	1992	*1993*
Bulgaria	1200	2300
Czech Republic	3120	5000
Hungary	1 7182	2 1500
Poland	5740	6800
Romania	2 0684	2 9115
Slovakia	2875	4350
Slovenia	2815	3300
Belarus	714	1250
Russia	3252	7989
Ukraine	2000	2800
Estonia	2662	4150
Latvia	2621	2850
Lithuania	200	3000
Total	6 6865	9 4404

Table 9.7 Gross disbursements by IMF and development institutions to transitional economies, US$mn, 1991–3

	1991	*1992*	*1993*
To Eastern Europe			
IMF	3716	1266	314
Development institutions[1]	1304	1457	1383
To Former USSR			
IMF		1061	1985
Development institutions		3	506
Total			
IMF	3716	2327	2299
Development institutions	1304	1460	1889
Grand total	5020	3787	4188

Notes:
1. World Bank, European Investment Bank, European Bank for Reconstruction and Development.
2. World Bank.

Source: ECE (1994, p. 140).

icy towards FDI. A significant number of transitional economies have adopted an import protection strategy, aimed at attracting FDI into import-substituting production for the domestic market. A variety of trade related policies have been used, ranging from changes in effective rates of protection to the introduction of product-specific import quotas (EBRD, 1994, p. 137). In some cases, this has been as a result of lobbying by FDI interests and has been a precondition for the foreign investment to take place.

CONCLUSIONS

The experience of the East and Central European countries shows clearly that privatisation in itself will ensure neither a rapid nor smooth economic transition to a market based economy. The application of enterprise budget constraints, and the provision of adequate safety-netting to cover areas of social provision previously the responsibility of the state enterprises, are necessary conditions for the transformation of state enterprises into viable, market based enterprises. Equally, the development of a legal framework covering property and commercial matters, and the maintenance of a stable macroeconomic environment are prerequisites for the sustained growth and development of the private sector.

Where governments have sought to address these issues, FDI has responded and contributed to the marketisation process through the inflow of capital and other components of the FDI 'bundle'. At the same time, there is evidence that protectionist trade measures have been used to encourage the inflow of FDI. It is too early to quantify the economic benefits and costs of protectionist measures, but evidence from developing countries which pursued a similar policy of import-substitution and domestic market protection suggests that the longer-term result is likely to be the emergence of an uncompetitive and largely inefficient industrial structure. The creation of improved opportunities for the involvement of international capital in the transition economies may therefore run counter to the broader objectives of economic efficiency and international competitiveness.

If privatisation is regarded as a means to an end, rather than as an end in itself, then the method by which privatisation is achieved becomes a key concern. The world-wide movement towards trade liberalisation and globalisation (Cook and Kirkpatrick, 1994b; Kirkpatrick, 1995) has highlighted the role that international competition plays in determining national economic progress, and suggests that the extent to which economies succeed in integrating into the world economy, with the associated widening of international business linkages, will be a crucial factor in progressing the transition process.

References

Bleaney M. (1994) 'Economic liberalisation in Eastern Europe: problems and prospects', *The World Economy* 17 (4), pp. 497–507

Bös, D. and Kayser, G. (1995) 'The last days of the Treuhandanstalt', in P. Cook and C. Kirkpatrick (eds), *Privatisation Policy and Performance: International Perspectives* (Hemel Hempstead: Harvester-Wheatsheaf).

Burgess, R., Drèze, J., Ferreira F., Hussain, A. and Thomas, T. (1993) 'Social protection and structural adjustment' (London: London School of Economics) mimeo.

Cook, P. and Kirkpatrick, C. (1994a) 'Social protection in the context of privatisation', report submitted to the Social Security Department (Geneva, ILO) (July).

Cook, P. and Kirkpatrick, C. (1994b) 'Employment and growth policies in a period of increasing globalisation', report submitted to the ILO (Geneva: ILO) (September).

Economic Commission for Europe (ECE) (1994) *Economic Survey of Europe in 1993-1994* (New York and Geneva: UN).

European Bank for Reconstruction and Development (EBRD) (1993) *Annual Economic Outlook* (London: EBRD).

European Bank for Reconstruction and Development (EBRD) (1994) *Transition Report* (London: EBRD).

Frydman, R. and Rapaczynski, A. (1993) 'Privatization in Eastern Europe: is the state withering away?', *Finance and Development*, 30 (2), pp. 10–13.

Hare, P. (1994) 'Social protection and its implications for enterprise restructuring', paper prepared for the CEPR (London) and *IAS Vienna* conference, 'Enterprise as a Source of Protection in Transitional Economies' (25–26 March) (Vienna).

Hume, I. and Pinto, B. (1993) 'Prejudice and fact in Poland's industrial transformation', *Finance and Development*, 30 (2), pp. 18–20.

Hychak, T.J. and King, A.E. (1994) 'The privatisation experience in Eastern Europe', *The World Economy*, 17 (4), pp. 529–50.

International Monetary Fund IMF (1993a) *Economic Outlook* (Washington, DC. IMF) (October).

International Monetary Fund (1993b) *IMF Survey* (Washington, DC: IMF) (9 August).

Kirkpatrick, C. (1995) 'Does trade liberalisation assist third world industrial development? Experience and lessons of the 1980s', *International Review of Applied Economics*, 9 (1), pp. 22–41

Sader, F. (1993) 'Privatizations and foreign investment in the developing world 1988–92', World Bank, *PRE Working Paper* 1202 (October).

Scarpetta, S., Boeri, T. and Reutersward, A. (1993) 'Unemployment benefit systems and active labour market policies in central and eastern Europe: an overview', paper presented to OECD Workshop, 'The Persistence of Unemployment in Central and Eastern European Countries' (Paris) (September).

Schwartz, G. (1995) 'Privatisation in Eastern Europe: experience and preliminary policy lessons', in P. Cook and C. Kirkpatrick (eds) *Privatisation Policy and Performance: International Perspectives* (Hemel Hempstead: Harvester-Wheatsheaf).

Schwartz, G. and Lopes, P.S. (1993) 'Privatization: expectations, trade-offs and results', *Finance and Development*, 30 (2), pp. 14–17.

United Nations Conference on Trade and Development (UNCTAD) (1994) *World Investment Report 1994* Division on Transnational Corporations and Investment (New York and Geneva: UN).

van Brabant, J.M. 1995 'On the economics of property rights and privatization in transitional economies', in P. Cook and C. Kirkpatrick (eds), *Privatisation Policy and Performance: International Perspectives* (Hemel Hempstead: Harvester-Wheatsheaf)

Part Four

MNE Operations – Strategic and Regulatory Aspects

Stephen Young

Part. Four of the book focuses upon foreign direct investment (FDI) and multinational-enterprise (MNE) operations in Europe, with contributions relating to explanations for aggregate US FDI patterns, the technology characteristics of MNE subsidiaries in a number of European countries, and comparisons of the economic and political impact of MNEs in the EU and USA and the regulatory response.

A number of the chapters in this book have commented upon the gap between vision and reality in European integration. From an FDI perspective, however, all the authors in Part Four agree that foreign MNEs have enhanced EU market integration: Clegg (Chapter 10) notes that US firms were not encumbered by entrenched positions in national markets, unlike their EU competitors (and the comment would apply even more forcefully to the more recent entrant, the Japanese), and took a pan-European perspective from the outset; while Papanastassiou and Pearce (Chapter 11) contrast the optimising approach of US and Japanese MNEs in establishing a limited number of specialised, export-oriented production sites with the satisficing view of European multinationals. In support of their case, the authors show that one-half of subsidiaries of European MNEs operating in countries other than their parent perceived their host country as being their only market. It is, of course, the case (and hopefully always will be) that national markets retain idiosyncratic taste characteristics, and hence MNE subsidiaries in Europe have a role not only in global and European but also national strategies. According to Young, Hood and Hood (Chapter 12), FDI policies are still primarily national and have lagged behind MNE integration strategies. MNEs have proved efficient at overcoming policy imperfections, but their activities – both initial investments and restructuring in response to the Single Market – have undoubtedly been divisive, both in pitting EU member states against one another and potentially exacerbating centripetal tendencies in the Union. An EU FDI policy is viewed as an important means of harnessing the potential of multinational firms to promote European integration. This, moreover, is a requirement if progress is to be made in multilateral FDI policy harmonisation and liberalisation.

Clegg's Chapter 10 reviews US FDI into the EU over a 40-year period, confirming the critical importance of market size and growth in explaining long-term trends. An interesting observation is that 'the propensity of the EC to redraw its boundary has enabled it to maintain its grip on inward FDI' into manufacturing industry. The further enlargement of the EU in 1995 to include most of the former EFTA nations and the likely entry of some Eastern and Central European countries early in the next millenium should have a similar effect. Without this stimulus the Asia–Pacific region will be a more attractive target for US FDI in years to come. Clegg also hints at the potential for extensive FDI flows into the EU in services if and when internal market liberalisation takes place and external trade policy non-tariff barriers fall. Yet banking and financial services and real estate already make up 28 per cent of US FDI in the EU (Table 12.2, p. 233) and 49 per cent of Japanese FDI into Europe (Table 12.3, p. 234). Several of the earlier chapters of this book reveal the progress still to be made, however, in liberalising services' sectors.

Clegg's thorough review and evaluation of the statistical evidence on US FDI flows into the EU indicates that researchers have had only limited success in identifying important explanatory variables except market size and growth. The author does suggest that the role of oligopolistic rivalry might be more important than existing research indicates, linking this to trade policy uncertainty (the 'fortress Europe' fallacy, etc.). Although answering different questions, survey evidence has proved to be much richer in terms of explanation, and while at EU level market size and growth consistently top the list as locational determinants in manufacturing, at national level advanced telecommunications and transport infrastructure and other investments of a public goods nature (see Papanastassiou and Pearce on the role of local scientific inputs in Chapter 11 in this volume) are proving to be important attraction variables (Netherlands Economic Institute, 1992).

Moving from aggregate stocks and flows of FDI to multinational subsidiary behaviour, Papanastassiou and Pearce provide some fascinating and very revealing data on technology creation and application by MNEs' subsidiaries in Europe. What is confirmed is the growing importance of technology creation by MNE subsidiaries, especially in established R & D labs. While technology imported from elsewhere in the group was still the main source of technology for the sample subsidiaries, there was evidence in sectors such as chemicals and autos of above-average use of subsidiary R & D and established local technology and below-average use of imported MNE group technology. There were also country differences, with the subsidiary R & D labs of US and Japanese MNEs focusing more on development and less on adaptation than those of European MNEs. Generally, the authors conclude, technology imported from elsewhere in the group still played a pervasive role in the subsidiaries of European based MNEs.

Papanastassiou and Pearce in Chapter 11 pay particular attention to MNE subsidiaries in the UK, showing that multinationals in that country were more likely to use their R & D units for development than those located in the other three European nations surveyed. UK subsidiaries, moreover, were less likely to use imported technology and more likely to use established host country technology and their own R & D as sources of technology; this was even the case for European MNE subsidiaries in the UK, where the authors argue that in some cases UK operations may have a fairly unique role as integrated components of group European R & D programmes or may operate R & D labs in support of regional product mandates. A note of caution is perhaps, however, necessary in the sense that the UK is being compared with Belgium, Greece and Portugal. Work by Amin *et al.* (1994), for example, suggested a form of hierarchy of MNE subsidiaries, with Portugal and Brandenburg (former East Germany) at the lowest level of development, Scotland and the Republic of Ireland in an intermediate position with some illustrations of subsidiaries playing a relatively strategic role, and Rhône-Alpes subsidiaries in the most advanced position reflecting, *inter alia*, the quality of supply-side resources. In fairness, some similar points emerge from the case study at the end of Chapter 11.

Some of the most interesting observations of Papanastassiou and Pearce concern the linkages between technological development, subsidiary strategy and overall corporate strategy. The conclusion is that the more advanced MNE subsidiaries may have a twofold role, first, generating technology as part of global corporate innovation strategies and in support of regional or world product mandate (RPM and WPM) roles; and, secondly, adapting products and technology to cater for the distinctive taste characteristics of national markets within Europe.

The significance of RPMs and WPMs in the context of host country economic development is alluded to in both Chapters 11 and 12 (see also Young, Hood and Peters, 1994); and Young *et al.* follow through a discussion on the impact of multinationals in Europe and the USA with a review of policy and policy prospects. The approach taken in this chapter is to evaluate prospects for transatlantic policy as a component of multilateral policy through the WTO and the OECD. A critical observation is that there is no FDI policy in the EU. There has been a fairly fundamental shift of attitudes since the publication of the Cecchini Report (Cecchini *et al.*, 1989) in which virtually no reference was made to MNEs; the assumption was apparently that international production and trade were undertaken by uninational firms. In *An Industrial Competitiveness Policy for the European Union* (CEC, 1994), external constraints and opportunities are recognised; but the discussion is still couched very largely in trade trade as per as opposed to FDI, and solutions are perceived in terms of international rules on competition rather than FDI policy *per se*. The view of Young *et al.* is that the FDI implications of a range of existing policies in areas such as regional development, research and technology, trade and industry as well as competition require full consideration. At the same time a forum or mechanism for resolving problems of national government versus EU competence requires to be established. The objective would be to improve the environment for both new and expansionary FDI and to encourage technological upgrading and hence the economic contribution of multinational activity. An FDI policy framework at EU level and ultimately globally would provide a more certain environment which would reassure investors and hence produce welfare gains.

References

Amin, A. *et al.* (1994) 'Regional incentives and the quality of mobile investment in the less favoured regions of the EU', *Progress in Planning*, 41 (1).

Cecchini, P. *et al.* (1989) – *1992: The Benefits of a Single Market* (Aldershot: Wildwood House).

Commission of the European Communities (CEU) (1994) *An Industrial Competitiveness Policy for the European Union*, COM (94) 319 final (Brussels: CEU) 14 September.

Netherlands Economic Institute (NEI) (in cooperation with Ernst & Young) (1992) *New Location Factors for Mobile Investment in Europe* (Rotterdam/London: NEI/ Ernst & Young).

Young, S., Hood, N. and Peters, E. (1994) 'Multinational enterprises and regional economic development', *Regional Studies*, 28 (7), pp. 657–77.

10 US Foreign Direct Investment in the EU – The Effects of Market Integration in Perspective

Jeremy Clegg

INTRODUCTION

This chapter aims to re-examine the facts, the hypotheses, and the back catalogue of empirical findings on US foreign direct investment (FDI) in the EU over an era in which US multinational enterprises (MNEs) enjoyed undisputed precedence. It considers how this body of studies relates to current research on the prospects for EU market integration and the likely behaviour of multinational firms. It also reflects on the changing nature of FDI, particularly the supplanting of old investment patterns within the EU, which were orientated towards individual national markets.

The justification for the present focus on US FDI in the EU is not simply the ready availability of statistical data, it is also the fact that the USA has been the single largest foreign investor. In absolute terms, by 1991 the US stock of FDI in the EU had reached a figure of US$bn 223. Statistics on new capital outflows (excluding reinvested earnings) for 1984–91, however, suggest that the relative importance of US FDI has been diminishing. The level of intra-EU flows climbed by 624 per cent over the period, while flows from the USA rose by just 84 per cent. There has been an overall decline in the US share from 28 per cent of EU inflows to an eventual 10 per cent in 1991, passing through a low of just 3 per cent in 1988. Some caution is necessary in interpreting these data, as it is likely that the longer-established US affiliates in the EU have been growing through reinvested earnings, i.e. new capital flows are only part of the picture. Even so, it seems clear that intra-EU FDI has become the leading component of new FDI capital flows, reaching 60 per cent by 1991 (*Eurostat*, 1994).

THE IMPACT OF EU TRADE POLICY AND INTEGRATION ON FDI

The trade policy of the EU over the period covered by empirical research on US FDI in the EU is summarised in Table 10.1. Both the trade-weighted

Table 10.1 Tariff averages on total imports of finished and semi-finished manufactures, before and after the implementation of the Tokyo Round

Country or country group	Pre-Tokyo (%)	Post-Tokyo (%)	% change
EU			
Weighted	8.3	6.0	˙28
Simple	9.4	6.6	30
Japan			
Weighted	10.0	5.4	46
Simple	10.8	6.4	41
USA			
Weighted	7.0	4.9	30
Simple	11.6	6.6	43

Sources: World Bank (1987) data; GATT (1980), p. 37.

and simple average tariff rates on manufactures imposed by the EU actually exceeded those of the USA and Japan after the Tokyo Round (concluded in 1979), and the EU made the least sizeable reductions. The EU tariff wall will have undoubtedly stimulated import-substituting FDI. However, as tariff rates were already low in historical terms during most of the post-war period, the compelling percentage cuts in tariff rates gives a misleading impression of the extent to which import-substituting FDI will have been curtailed (Hine, 1985). The Uruguay Round (concluded in 1993) extended this pattern of tariff reduction.

Many non-tariff barriers (NTBs) are inherited from Member States' protectionism prior to the formation of the EU. Such barriers segment EU markets and discriminate against imports from the EU and non-EU alike. It is on these that the Cecchini Report (Cecchini *et al.*, 1989; CEU, 1989) focused in justifying the programme to integrate the EU market. As the EU has matured it has cultivated its own EU-wide discrimination against foreign imports through the use of novel NTBs. In effect, this new form of discriminatory trade policy has superseded the old scheme based on tariffs. Like earlier policy, it exerts an incentive to produce within the EU, for instance, to gain a government contract where there is favouritism towards local producers (Buckley *et al.*, 1983). Hard-core NTBs constitute the subgroup of NTBs that is the most likely to have significant restrictive effects (World Bank, 1987).[1] Table 10.2 reveals that, while tariff barriers (on manufactures) have fallen, the most persistent forms of NTB on EU imports from the rest of the world have increased, in effect to replace the protective effect lost through tariff reduction.

The main achievements of the Uruguay Round of present importance have been in respect of the planned phasing out of key import controls, and increased market access in services (Evans and Walsh, 1994). The arrange-

Table 10.2 Industrial country imports from industrial countries subject to 'hard-core' NTBs, per cent 1981 and 1986

Importing country	1981	1986
EU	10	13
Japan	29	29
USA	9	15
All industrial countries	13	16

Sources: World Bank data; World Bank (1987), Table 8.3.

ments in particular cover the multinational provision of services, where trade barrier reduction does not (as it does for manufactures) connote a pressure against import-substituting FDI. On the contrary, barrier reduction is likely to favour market-seeking FDI in service industries, where local production is often the preferred option, and in many industries it is the only option (Clegg, 1993). If such NTBs on services industries continue to fall (for instance, following market liberalisation through privatisation and deregulation), the prospects for extensive FDI flows into the EU in this sector would become greatly enhanced.

Market Integration and the FDI Strategies of Firms

The differences in strategy pursued by firms in response to the single market are largely attributable to the ownership of the firm, the length of time it has been established in the EU, its industry and its competitive position within the EU and globally (UNCTC, 1990). The period commonly known as Mark I integration began in 1957 and extended until the mid-1980s. The '1992' programme is often known as EC92 or Mark II integration (UNTCMD, 1993), and is reckoned from 1985 onwards. Mark I integration concerned the establishment of the Common Market by the six European founding nations, and its subsequent enlargements to a total of 12 members in 1986. It was based upon the eradication of tariff barriers and quotas affecting manufactures trade, with only limited attention to the growth of non-tariff distortions. Mark II integration concerns the programmed removal of non-tariff distortions.

US firms' business strategies under Mark I integration initially involved defensive import-substituting FDI to protect market shares built up through trade servicing of EU markets. Dunning and Robson (1988) point to two reasons why US (and other non-EU) MNEs have been in a better position to promote EU market integration, and to benefit from it subsequent to Mark I, compared with native EU firms. First, US firms were not encumbered by entrenched market positions prior to Mark I integration, and so were able to choose the most efficient production locations that became available. Secondly, US MNEs were typically larger than their EU counterparts, rendering the potential gains from corporate integration commensurately greater. In addition, such US firms enjoyed greater organisational flexibility. Consequently, Mark I integration allowed US MNEs to attain scale economies in production at the pan-European level, on account of the absence of intra-EU tariff barriers. However, all firms have tended to treat EU markets as separate on account of non-tariff distortions, particularly in marketing and service activities.

Most US affiliates in the EU are indeed well-established. This can be gauged by the fact that 85 per cent of the market for US goods and services is catered for by affiliate sales, and just 15 per cent by exports (UNCTC, 1990). Should the affiliates of US MNEs now believe that the single market is to be a reality, notwithstanding its slow progress, the characteristic US response would not be defensive, but would be based on reorganisation and offensive investment strategies. This reorganisation might be expected to be most apparent in the service sector activities of multinational firms, and in the behaviour of firms classified to the service sector. This points to the restructuring of marketing and distribution activities during the Mark II integration of the Single Market programme. Surveys suggested that by 1988 most EU firms (including US affiliates) had assumed a single market in their strategic plans, resulting in extensive corporate restructuring (UNCTC, 1990; KPMG Peat Marwick, 1989). Furthermore, cross-border restructuring by large firms preceded that by small and medium sized manufacturing and by service firms.

The Statistical Evidence

The tariff discrimination hypothesis features prominently in the literature on the effects of the formation and enlargement of the EU (e.g. Scaperlanda 1967, 1968). There are two variants of this hypothesis. The first is neoclassical in origin: that the existence (and raising) of tariffs induces inflows of internationally mobile capital (Mundell, 1957; Caves, 1971; Lunn, 1980). Here, impediments (such as tariffs) normally raise the prices of importable goods, so increasing returns in the import-competing sectors, eventually driving up the price of the scarce factor in the host country (assumed to be capital) and resulting in an inflow of capital. This argument clearly conjures up the idea of a 'tariff wall', and has been expressly invoked by several authors, for example, Lunn (1980). In the world of imperfect markets envisaged in the theory of the MNE, such discrimination will encourage firms to circumvent tariff barriers by relocating one or more stages of production within the customs union. The comparative efficiency of FDI (and that of contractual arrangements) relative to exporting will rise for firms outside the union. Therefore, although early analysis on the impact of tariffs was couched in terms of portfolio capital flows, these are easily re-scripted as FDI.

The combined statistical evidence for the EU suggests a net substitution of FDI inflows for imports at the aggregate (all industries) level. This is likely to be the result of the dominance of import-substituting FDI of the type that is typical between trade blocs (Goldberg, 1972; Cantwell, 1988) and of the period studied. The results for the first variant of the tariff discrimination hypothesis have been unsatisfactory, mainly because of shortcomings in the measure of the common external tariff (e.g., Lunn, 1980). The overall findings appear strongest for the second, or 'relative', variant of the tariff discrimination hypothesis. Scaperlanda and Balough (1983) and Culem (1988) found that the reduction of internal EU tariff barriers did promote inward US FDI. However, this is likely to be capturing the effect not only of pure discrimination, but also the impact of market integration. It has also been pointed out by Mayes (1985) that the decrease in the common external tariff (CET) of the EU from its 1956 starting point under successive GATT reductions is also entangled in the measure, i.e. the effect is not simply that of the relative movements of extra- and intra-EU tariffs.

The findings plainly reflect the empirical mix of theoretical influences, that is, the combination of different motives for FDI. This is not the result simply of the categorical aggregation of industries, but also of the fact that import-substituting FDI cannot be distinguished from new FDI aimed at catering for the wider European market. The continual decline in the EU common customs tariff (CCT) has had a relaxing effect on EU inward FDI, but it is likely to be a waning determinant of the direction taken by US FDI in the EU.

LEADING HYPOTHESES AND FINDINGS ON FDI FLOWS INTO THE EU

Market Related Variables

The role of demand conditions in determining the location of production is investigated in a wide range of studies. The absolute size of foreign markets is one of the leading locational factors employed in applied work to explain FDI inflows. It has been shown to lead to transaction cost reduction in conjunction with foreign location (internalisation abroad), and therefore to be theoretically positively related to the level of FDI (Buckley and Casson, 1981). This is used to explain FDI by new investors, together with the transition from sales to production affiliates, and on to vertically integrated or rationalised FDI (Scaperlanda and Mauer, 1972). According to the market growth hypothesis, increases in market size are viewed as a continuing outcome of integration. Rationalised FDI is expected to follow market integration, on account of the opportunity to service a larger area via specialised production (in those locations with the greatest comparative advantage) to exploit economies of scale. Rationalised FDI is, therefore, by its nature, directly linked to market growth.

There is a contrast between the findings of studies of early US FDI in the EU and their later counterparts. Culem (1988) discovered that EU market size did not attract US inward FDI, while US market size (but not growth) is important for EU FDI into the USA. This is a manifestation of the fact that the growth of EU MNEs in the USA (between 1969 and 1982) was primarily by new entry rather than expansion and vice versa for recent US FDI into the EU. One of the earliest quantitative studies, by Bandera and White (1968), found significance for EU market size alone (on data for the period 1953–62), as did Scaperlanda and Mauer (1969, 1972), again on data for the 1950s and 1960s, during which new establishments dominated FDI flows into the EU. Apart from these two early studies, the hypothesis on market growth overall receives qualified support. The majority of later work finds more consistently in its favour (Goldberg, 1972; Lunn, 1980; Scaperlanda and Balough, 1983; Culem, 1988), even extending it to intra-EU FDI (Culem, 1988). The fact that US market size (but not growth) appears more important for EU FDI in the USA also probably reflects the diversification benefits for growing EU MNEs.

Wage and Other Cost Factors

Theory suggests that wage costs should exert a discernible effect on the location of production. Many studies specify wage costs, though few record significance for this variable. At least between developed countries, other factors can dominate in the location decision. For example, Swedenborg (1979) reported only inconsistent evidence that Swedish FDI sales were directly related to the ratio of parent to affiliate wage rates. A general problem is that relative cost variables, as here, are often based on the invalid assumption that industrial cost structures are comparable across countries – even within firms this need not hold at all, particularly for vertically-specialised FDI.

Within integrated economic areas, a hallmark of rationalised production should be the sensitivity of investment to specific immobile factors, such as professional, scientific, technical and research manpower. This is exemplified in Culem (1988), who found that intra-EU FDI is attracted to locations with higher unit labour costs than the home country. Nevertheless, investors sought out foreign locations with labour costs at the lower end of the distribution. In this same study, both the absolute and differential (host–home) labour cost variables were insignificant for US FDI in the EU (and for EU FDI in the USA). All of this suggests that horizontal (market-oriented) FDI between developed trade blocs is not significantly motivated by labour costs. This would imply that the location of production is mainly dictated by transport costs, and the need for proximity to the market, including the effect of NTBs. However, within an economic area, investment of a rationalised production character is attracted to those locations that offer specific skills at the best value.

Market Concentration

The idea of oligopolistic rivalry as a determinant of US FDI in continental developed Europe has a long pedigree, and originated with Hymer (1960). Indeed, the first statistical investigation of the relationship between market concentration and FDI was conducted on US FDI in Europe, by Knickerbocker (1973). Unlike the bulk of research on US FDI in Europe, the starting point for this body of work is market conditions in the home country, rather than in the host.

In econometric work, Wallis (1968) first put forward the argument that the motive of defensive investment might be the underlying cause of EU inward FDI from the USA. He proposed that the explanatory power of this motive was often wrongly attributed to trade barrier related changes. The basic notion forms part of the industrial organisation thesis that FDI follows trade between trade blocs, to resolve conflict between producers. More recently, Culem (1988) has invoked the same idea to rationalise his unexpected finding that EU market size does not attract US inward FDI, although in this case the result is probably an outcome of the maturing of foreign affiliates.

Knickerbocker's (1973) finding, on Harvard data, has been extensively criticised. He found an association between US oligopoly structure and temporal clustering in the establishment of foreign affiliates abroad. The leading accusation is that this work did not discriminate between alternative hypotheses within the theory of the MNE. It also ignored hypotheses on the effects of innovations in international communications and on foreign market size (Buckley and Casson, 1976). Similar criticisms can be made of Flowers' (1976) study, which found in favour of the same oligopolistic reaction hypothesis on data for Canadian and European FDI into the USA. However, this study did successfully test for the existence of source country differences in the pattern of FDI.

In the context of the EU, there are clear sources of instability along each of these lines: the enlargement of the EU; the breakdown of stability in industries arising from over-capacity during recession; internal de-regulation and market liberalisation; and the external growth of NTBs. For this reason the explanatory power of the hypothesis is likely to be periodic, peaking during periods of instability, and then waning over time. Naturally, the discovery that entry timing can be explained does not furnish a complete explanation of FDI, because FDI might have occurred in the absence of entry clustering. However, Graham (1974, 1978) (who extended the analysis to retaliation by European firms through defensive FDI) and Flowers (1976) do strive to show that, in the cases of their data, the simple foreign market growth and product cycle arguments could not account adequately for FDI.

The Role of Financing Decisions

In the theory of the MNE, the ownership of production abroad is driven by transaction cost considerations, arising at the firm, industry, and country level (Buckley and Casson, 1976, 1985; Dunning 1977, 1993). With ownership structure determined by the need to exercise control, it follows that the burden of any adjustment in the financing of firms' FDI positions abroad typically falls on debt finance rather than on equity. The attention afforded by research on FDI (and that on the MNE) about how the MNE chooses to finance foreign operations has been very modest (however see, for example, Gilman, 1981).

Although Culem (1988) found the effect of relative interest rates to be insignificant for US FDI in the EU, the most comprehensive study of the financing decision is that of Boatwright and Renton (1975). This research concerned the UK rather than the EU, and found that balance of payments outflows and inflows were related, respectively positively and negatively (through the refinancing of FDI) to the relative foreign to domestic rate of interest (proxying the comparative marginal costs of borrowing). The short-run impact of interest rate changes on FDI flows were found substantially to exceed the long-run steady state effects, which suggests that much of the total FDI flows generated are intended to exploit short-lived international differentials (see Grubel, 1982).

Exchange Rate Changes

To date the statistical literature on FDI into the EU has not covered any substantial hypothesis on exchange rates, although Scaperlanda and Balough (1983) and Lunn (1983) have advocated its inclusion. Empirical work on this topic has focused on the USA (Bailey and Tavlas, 1991; Caves, 1990; Cushman, 1985; Ray, 1989). This empirical work seems to favour a negative sign for a host (US) exchange rate appreciation (Stevens, 1993). However, the underlying problem is that the effect on FDI flows is the net outcome of several influences, which work in opposition to each other. Indeed, Stevens (1977) developed three alternative models to demonstrate that the effect of a dollar devaluation on FDI could assume any sign whatever. Nevertheless, it is certainly desirable to include a suitable variable, especially for the period since 1973, when the Bretton Woods System of pegged exchange rates came to an end. It would also be necessary to include the impact of the OPEU oil price rises. However, empirical work is a long way from approaching the issue of the impact on FDI of the EU's efforts to stabilise exchange rates.

Capital Controls

Most research shows that, for the developed countries at least, capital controls have had little effect on aggregate outward FDI. The debate over the effect of capital controls nevertheless continues. Specifically, these controls refer to the US voluntary (1965–7) and mandatory (1968–72) capital controls program (Lunn, 1980, 1983; Scaperlanda and Balough, 1983; Scaperlanda and Mauer, 1973).

Lunn (1980) found no role for his capital controls dummy variable in restraining manufacturing foreign affiliates' plant and equipment expenditures. However, Scaperlanda and Mauer (1973) reported some evidence to the contrary, where a capital controls variable showed the expected negative impact on aggregate, but not on manufacturing, FDI. Further work by Scaperlanda and Balough (1983) also found that capital controls restrained total US FDI in the EU, on data for 1953–72 (though not for manufacturing FDI, nor plant and equipment expenditures alone for this and later data periods). Unfortunately, it is perfectly possible that the outflow of capital from the USA might naturally have tended to fall over the period of the controls. The study of the UK's FDI by Boatwright and Renton (1975) similarly found that dummy variables for foreign exchange controls introduced in 1965 and 1966 were insignificant, with no effect on either the real or financial components of FDI.

The Statistical Evidence Reviewed

It seems evident that market size has been paramount in promoting new entry, notably around the time of the creation of the EU. Subsequently, market growth has become the leading determinant of the later expansion of FDI once most foreign affiliates were established, and is strongly linked to rationalised FDI. The sparse work involving wage costs suggests that high transport costs from the USA to the EU make the decision whether or not (and how much) to invest in the EU insensitive to relative EU to US wage costs. However, within the EU rationalised FDI strategies seek out the locations of key factor of production and minimum wage costs.

The role of oligopolistic rivalry could be considered more important than the rather select body of research on the topic suggests. Mark I integration may well have been seen as a form of aggression by EU states and their firms against US producers, causing uncertainty and conflict. After investing in the EU, US MNEs had a voice (via lobbying) in the decision-making of the EU, and had an interest, in conjunction with native EU firms, in internal EU NTB reduction and in non-tariff protection against imports from third countries, principally Japan. Several studies invoke the importance of uncertainty over trade policy in the decision of third country firms to invest in the EU (e.g. UN-TCMD, 1993; Milner and Allen, 1992), though none go further to integrate firm strategy and government decision-making. Therefore, the contribution of the oligopolistic rivalry approach would appear to offer some explanation of business strategy and of the timing of FDI, but clearly it must be used in conjunction with other approaches.

The effects of relative interest rates are felt more within the balance of payments than in terms of employment and output. Nevertheless, these effects bear witness to the integrated behaviour of multinationals in the face of internationally segmented capital markets. They also demonstrate the edge enjoyed by the internal capital markets of these firms over the external market, so adding to the advantages of multinationality. The modest recognition given to financial factors highlights the neglect of exchange rates. In fact, the only work on foreign exchange and FDI flows to the EU has been that on capital controls. However, an imperceptible effect should be expected for these now redundant measures. The absence of significant inter-industry research means that certain standard structural hypotheses and variables from the theory of international business (such as technology intensity) are as yet not in evidence. To this extent, in the terminology of the eclectic paradigm (Dunning 1977, 1993), research has largely failed to specify any appropriate variables for ownership advantages.

US FDI FLOWS TO THE EU, 1950–91

Over the 40-year period of the data now available, US FDI has shifted towards the countries of the EU. Table 10.3 presents some basic dimensions on the importance of the various incarnations of the EU in US FDI. Clearly, the inclusion of the UK in the EU has the effect of considerably bolstering the EU share throughout. The embodiment of the EU, with 12 members, commanded 105 per cent of the European total. This would indicate that non-EU Europe hosted a negative FDI stock from the USA. The cause of this disinvestment is most likely to be the refinancing of the existing FDI stock with alternative funds to those of the parent firm.

The first thing that is evident from Figure 10.1 is the long-run cyclical nature share of the EU(6) in aggregate outward US FDI. At first sight, it is rather surprising that the cycles are features when the data are expressed as regional proportions. This variation is also evident in the raw data. In fact, the cyclical pattern was discernible in the data used by Scaperlanda (1967, 1968) and by Wallis (1968), and is visible in the charts presented by both. In his test of the tariff discrimination hypothesis, Scaperlanda found no significant difference between the rate of increase in the EU's share of US FDI abroad and that of non-EU Europe, standing as the control. However, re-estimation by Wallis succeeded in finding such a difference. In Scaperlanda's (1967) work the apparent shift in the full 1951–64 data period compared with the subperiod 1951–8 can be entirely attributed to the ending of a trough in the FDI cycle, which occurred for EU and non-EU countries alike. Therefore the impression of no significant difference between the full period time trend for each region (the experiment and the control) was inevitable, given the short period of the data and the pronounced amplitude of the cycle.

The re-estimation of Scaperlanda's findings by Wallis (1968) simply ex-

Table 10.3   US FDI stock in the EU as a percentage of total US FDI in the World and in Europe, 1950–91

	EU(6) as a percentage of		EU(9) as a percentage of		EU(12) as a percentage of	
	World	*Europe*	*World*	*Europe*	*World*	*Europe*
1950	5.40	36.77	11.12	75.68	..	..
1977	21.02	49.06	43.24	100.92	45.15	105.39
1991	22.73	45.45	47.52	95.03	49.49	98.98

Note: Signifies that data are not available.
.. Not available

Source: US Department of Commerce data tape.

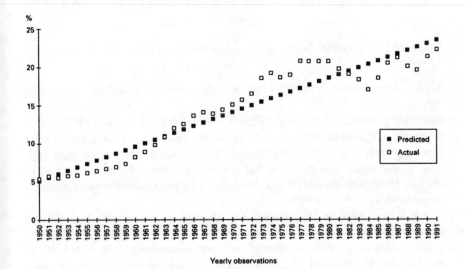

Figure 10.1 US FDI in the EU (6) as a percentage of the world, for all industries, 1950–91

Source: Author's data, from US Department of Commerce data tape.

tended the earlier error of failing to discern a cycle. Breaking the data into 1951–8 and 1959–64 subperiods, Wallis found a significant increase in the slope coefficient. Unfortunately, the turning point (minimum) in the cycle just happened to have preceded the formation of the EU, with a period of growth following immediately in its wake, in 1958–60. The apparent decline in the non-EU slope coefficient with respect to time (Wallis, 1968) was mainly the result of the greater dispersion in the non-EU data. It is

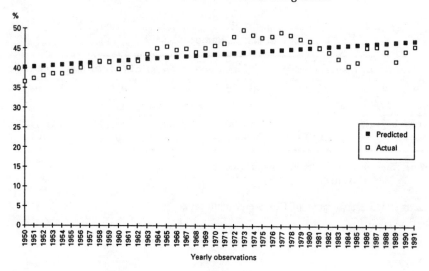

Figure 10.2 US FDI in the EU (6) as a percentage of Europe, for all industries, 1950–91

Source: Author's data, from US Department of Commerce data tape.

therefore pointless to update the early work of Scaperlanda (1967, 1968) using the original methodology, because the instability in the model over time is plainly not due to structural shifts, but rather to some omitted variable, or variables. The question that remains is: what induces the cycles? In the late 1960s, the answer to this question was a prerequisite for any progress in research on US FDI in the EU.

It has been seen in this chapter that the answer was partly furnished in the recasting of research to include market related variables, although the earlier errors were never recognised, or never acknowledged. As noted above, the fact that the cyclical variation occurs also for the EU(6) expressed as a percentage of Europe (Figure 10.2) indicates that there is some omitted variable either specific to the EU, or that strongly influences the proportions of investment flowing to the different regions of the world. A very similar cyclical pattern applies also to EU(9), also with a cycle length of around 5–8 years, centring around 7 years.

Of the hypotheses advanced in the earlier sections, none can logically be excluded from this overview of the data. However, what must stand out is the probable importance of market growth. More precisely, the relative growth of regional markets, such as the EU, as compared with the rest of the world. The fact that the cyclical pattern applies across the EU and the non-EU, in more or less the same phase, suggests such a common factor. However, since 1963, the EU(6) has represented the biggest geographical concentration of US FDI growth within Europe, overtaking the UK in 1963. In other

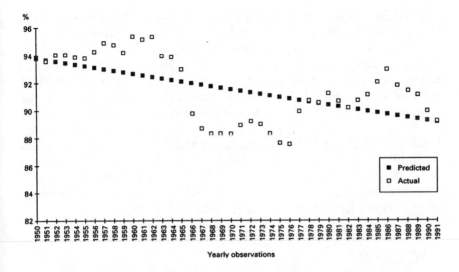

Yearly observations

Figure 10.3 US FDI in the EU (9) as a percentage of Europe, for manufacturing industry, 1950–91

Source: Author's data, from US Department of Commerce data tape.

words, US FDI is more strongly linked to growth in the EU market than to growth in the rest of Europe. For this reason, the EU share of FDI to Europe exhibits the major part of the cycle. Why should this be? The most compelling answer is that, owing to market integration, a given degree of growth in the EU generates more inward FDI than in the non-EU. EU internal barrier reduction renders corporate integration and rationalised investment more profitable than elsewhere, so bolstering the EU's share of FDI.

The apparent business cycle is likely to be that common to the developed world. For this reason, the financing issue remains very pertinent. The outflows of US FDI to Europe will depend on the availability of finance from the USA, as well as on European market fortunes. A downturn starting in the USA would be transmitted to Europe via a reduction in FDI outflows, as well as through trade. In addition, it should be expected that local (EU) market demand conditions will directly influence FDI via the demand for investment. The underlying international nature of the cycle means that there should be some trace of it in existing studies. Some evidence of such a common international factor comes from Culem's (1988) study. This finds a widespread positive correlation of the residuals between hosts for each source country, and between source countries for each host. This sign of a significant omitted variable (or variables) applies to several transatlantic equations.

Focusing on the manufacturing sector confirms the above impressions.

Although the business cycle dominates the data, Figure 10.3 shows that there has been a trend downwards in the EU(9) share of US manufacturing FDI in Europe. A greater dispersion of investment between countries has been underway. This trend is likely to be caused by shifts in industrial structure and relative labour costs within the European continent. Indeed, the share of the EU(9) in world-wide US FDI has been steadily rising; however, the collective share of other European countries has been rising faster. In fact, this reorganisation and rationalisation of investment within Europe has led to the relative growth in US manufacturing FDI in the most recent members of the EU(12). In contrast with the EU(9), the EU(12) has steadily increased its overall share of US manufacturing FDI in Europe. It thus appears that the propensity of the EU to redraw its boundary has enabled it to maintain its grip on inward FDI into this major industrial sector.

CONCLUSIONS

There has been progress in research on the determinants of US FDI into the EU. However, it has mainly taken the form of refinements to a relatively narrow and myopic literature. Within the literature on FDI capital flows, the importance of financial behaviour has been only infrequently recognised. Although the different types of FDI (e.g. import substituting, rationalised, etc.) cannot be observed directly, the significance of the factors that drive them can be easily evaluated (i.e. trade barriers and market size, and market growth, respectively).

The literature affords confirmation of the other real determinants of capital formation abroad – host labour availability and costs. The findings suggest that the first entry of US MNEs in the EU was primarily driven by market size, in particular by the creation of the EU, and by tariff discrimination. Later FDI flows appear to have been expansions and rationalisations of existing investment, which are responses to market growth. The evidence on the completion of the Single European Market (SEM) under Mark II integration suggests that established US affiliates will respond by integration servicing strategies throughout the EU. Service industries are also under a similar imperative. The recent trends in FDI inflows include an increasing component from the service sector. In many service industries, liberalisation and de-regulation have increased access to foreign firms, which are newly able to respond to EU market size. In the service sector, FDI follows market opportunities especially promptly, because the nature of production processes is often highly specific to the location of the market.

The impact on US FDI of the widening of the EU, through the entry of the southern European States of Spain and Portugal, has been quite positive. That of Greece has been less so because of domestic economic and political uncertainties during the 1980s (UN-TCMD, 1993). The relocation of manufacturing production within the EU to these countries has probably enabled the EU to maintain its competitive position relative to industrialising countries. The impact of internal EU NTB reduction is expected to be greater on intra- and extra-EU FDI inflows than Mark I integration, both because of the enhanced effective discrimination against third countries and because of the impetus to EU income generation. Past EU external trade policy, including the application of NTBs (in partial substitution for tariff protection), may have maintained the incentive for non-native firms to invest in the EU. Nevertheless, internal market integration will favour a pan-EU investment strategy on the parts of firms of all national origins.

As has been seen, during the Mark I period US MNEs dominated total inward FDI flows to the EU. The evidence from Mark I integration is that US firms increased their degree of corporate integration (for instance, as measured by intra-group trade). Following the start of the Mark II period, EU firms accounted for an increasing share of total flows, and have been catching up with the lead given by US firms in treating the EU as a single market for production. In contrast with more recent US FDI, much intra-EU FDI represents new entry rather than expansionary investment. This is more reactive to market size and the opening up of markets, and the rise in intra-EU FDI suggests that native EU firms have responded more vigorously to the prospect of Mark II than they did to Mark I integration. These offensive and rationalised FDI strategies are, by their nature, likely to be continuing medium- and long-term patterns of behaviour, linked to falling internal barriers.

Although US FDI has been, and still is, highly orientated towards the EU, the formal evaluation of the impact of EU creation and enlargement has been beset with methodological and data problems. However, the cyclical nature of US FDI seems to confirm that US MNEs are more responsive to the business fortunes in the EU than elsewhere in Europe, furnishing further evidence that they are treating the EU market as an integrated whole. The evidence of this chapter is that over the 40-year period to the early 1990s, the phases of EU market integration have caused the responsiveness of US FDI to market growth to be greater for EU countries than for non-EU Europe. This supports the view that integration has been, and will continue to be, a reality in the eyes of foreign direct investors.

Note

1. Hard-core non-tariff barriers are the most entrenched and formalised in nature. These include import prohibitions, voluntary export restraints (VERs), variable levies, MFA restrictions, and non-automatic licensing (World Bank, 1987).

References

Bailey, M.J. and Tavlas, G.S. (1991) 'Exchange rate variability and direct investment', in M. Ulan, (ed.), *The Annals of the American Academy of Political and Social Science: Foreign investment in the United States*, vol. 516 (July), pp. 106–17.

Bandera, V.N. and White, J.T. (1968) 'US direct investments and domestic markets in Europe', *Economia Internazionale*, 21 (1), pp. 117–33.

Boatwright, B.D. and Renton, G.A. (1975) 'An analysis of United Kingdom inflows and outflows of direct foreign investment', *Review of Economics and Statistics*, 57, (4), pp. 478–86.

Buckley, P.J. and Casson, M.C. (1976) *The Future of the Multinational Enterprise* (London: Macmillan).

Buckley, P.J. and Casson, M.C. (1981) 'The optimal timing of a foreign direct investment', *Economic Journal* 92 (361), pp. 75–87, reprinted as Chapter 5 in P.J. Buckley and M.C. Casson, *The Economic Theory of the Multinational Enterprise* (London: 1985 Macmillan).

Buckley, P.J. and Casson, M.C. (1985) *The Economic Theory of the Multinational Enterprise* (London: Macmillan).

Buckley, P.J., Berkova, Z. and Newbould, G.D. (1983) *Direct Investment in the UK by Smaller European Firms* (London: Macmillan).

Cantwell, J.A. (1988). 'The reorganisation of European industries after integration: selected evidence on the role of multinational enterprise activities' in J.H. Dunning, and P. Robson, (eds), *Multinationals and the European Community* (Oxford: Blackwell), pp. 25–50.

Caves, R.E. (1971) 'International corporations: the industrial economics of foreign investment, *Economica*, 38 (February), pp. 1–27, reprinted as Chapter 11 in J.H. Dunning (ed.), *International Investment* (Harmondsworth: 1972 Penguin Books).

Caves, R.E. (1990) 'Exchange rate movements and foreign direct investment in the United States', in D.R. Audretsch and M.P. Claudon, (eds), *The Internationalization of US Markets* (New York: New York University Press) pp. 199–229.

Cecchini, P. *et al.* (1989) – *1992: the Benefits of a Single Market* (Aldershot: Wildwood House).

Clegg, J. (1993) 'Investigating the determinants of service sector foreign direct investment', Chapter 5 in H.J. Cox, Clegg and G. Ietto-Gillies (eds), *The Growth of Global Business* (London: Routledge), pp. 85–104.

Commission of the European Communities (CEU) (1988) *The Costs of Non-Europe*, vols 4, 5, 6, 7 (Luxembourg: Office for Official Publications of the European Communities).

Culem, C.G. (1988) 'The locational determinants of direct investments among industrialised countries', *European Economic Review*, 32 (4), pp. 885–904.

Cushman, D.O. (1985) 'Real exchange rate risk, expectations, and the level of direct investment', *Review of Economics and Statistics*, 67, pp. 297–308.

Dunning, J.H. (1977) 'Trade, location of economic activity and the multinational enterprise: a search for and eclectic approach', Chapter 12 in B. Ohlin, P.-O. Hesselborn and P.M. Wijkman, (eds), *The International Allocation of Economic Activity* (London: Macmillan), reprinted and revised as Chapter 2 in J.H. Dunning, *International Production and the Multinational Enterprise* (London: Allen & Unwin (1981), and as Chapter 1 in J.H. Dunning, *Explaining International Production* (London: Unwin Hyman, 1988).

Dunning, J.H. (1993) *Multinational Enterprises and the Global Economy* (Wokingham: Addison-Wesley).

Dunning, J.H. and Robson, P. (1988) 'Multinational corporate integration and regional economic integration', in J.H. Dunning and P. Robson, (eds), *Multinationals and the European Community* (Oxford: Blackwell), pp. 1–23.

Eurostat (1994)

Evans, P. and Walsh, J. (1994) 'The EUI guide to the new GATT' (London: Economist Intelligence Unit).

Flowers, E.B. (1976) 'Oligopolistic reactions in European and Canadian direct investment in the United States', *Journal of International Business Studies*, 7 (2), pp. 43–55.

GATT (1980) *The Tokyo Round of Multilateral Trade Negotiations, Volume 2, Supplementary Report* (Geneva: GATT), p. 37.

Gilman, M.G. (1981) *The Financing of Foreign Direct Investment: A Study of the Determinants of Capital Flows in Multinational Enterprises* (London: Frances Pinter).

Goldberg, M.A. (1972) 'The determinants of US direct investment in the EEU: comment', *American Economic Review*, 62 (4), pp. 692–9.

Graham, E.M. (1974) 'Oligopolistic imitation and European direct investment in the United States', Harvard Graduate School of Business, unpublished DBA dissertation.

Graham, E.M. (1978) 'Transnational investment by multinational firms: a rivalistic phenomenon', *Journal of Post Keynesian Economics*, 1 (1), pp. 82–99.

Grubel, H.G. (1982) 'The theory of international capital movements', Chapter 1 in J. Black and J.H. Dunning, (eds), *International Capital Movements* (London: Macmillan).

Hine, R.C. (1985) *The Political Economy of European Trade: An introduction to the Trade Policies of the EEU* (Brighton: Wheatsheaf).

Hymer, S. (1960) 'The international operations of national firms: a study of direct foreign investment', PhD. Thesis; (Cambridge, MASS: MIT Press, 1976).

Knickerbocker, F.T. (1973) *Oligopolistic Reaction and the Multinational Enterprise* (Boston: Harvard University Press).

KPMG Peat Marwick (1989) *EU 1992: Strategic Implications for American Business* (London: KPMG Peat Marwick) (June).

Lunn, J. (1980) 'Determinants of US direct investment in the EEU: further evidence', *European Economic Review*, 13 (1), pp. 93–101.

Lunn, J. (1983) 'Determinants of US direct investment in the EEU: revisited again', *European Economic Review*, 21 (3), pp. 391–3.

Mayes, D.G. (1985) 'Factor mobililty', in A.M. El-Agraa (ed.), *The Economics of the European Community* (London: Macmillan).

Milner, C. and Allen, D. (1992) 'The external implications of 1992', in D. Swann, (ed), *The Single European Market and Beyond: A Study of the Wider Implications of the Single European Act* (London: Routledge).

Mundell, R.A. (1957) 'International trade and factor mobility', *American Economic Review*, 47 (3), pp. 321–35.

Ray, E.J. (1989) 'The determinants of foreign direct investment in the United States: 1979–1985', in R. Feenstra, (ed.), *Trade Policies for International Competitiveness* (Chicago: University of Chicago Press).

Scaperlanda. A.E. (1967) 'The EEU and US foreign investment: some empirical evidence', *Economic Journal* (March), pp. 22–6.

Scaperlanda. A.E. (1968) 'The EEU and US foreign investment: some empirical evidence – a reply', *Economic Journal* (September), pp. 558–68.

Scaperlanda, A.E. and Balough, R.S. (1983) 'Determinants of US direct investment in the EEU: revisited', *European Economic Review*, 21 (3), pp. 381–90.

Scaperlanda, A.E. and Mauer, L.J. (1969) 'The determinants of US direct foreign investment in the EEU', *American Economic Review*, 59 (3), pp. 558–68.

Scaperlanda, A.E. and Mauer, L.J. (1972) 'The determinants of US direct investment in the EEU: reply', *American Economic Review*, 62 (4), pp. 700–4.

Scaperlanda, A.E. and Mauer, L.J. (1973) 'The impact of controls on United States direct foreign investment in the European Economic Community', *Southern Economic Journal*, 39, pp. 419–23.

Stevens, G.V.G. (1977) 'Comment', in P.B. Clark, D.E. Logue and R.J. Sweeney (eds), *The Effects of Exchange Rate Adjustments* (Washington, DC: US Government Printing Office), pp. 183–8.

Stevens, G.V.G. (1993) 'Exchange rates and foreign direct investment: a note', *International Finance Discussion Papers*, 444 (April) (Washington, DC: Board of Governors of the Federal Reserve System).

Swedenborg, B. (1979) *The Multinational Operations of Swedish Firms: An Analysis of Determinants and Effects* (Stockholm: Almqvist & Wicksell).

United Nations Centre on Transnational Corporations (UNCTC) (1990) 'Regional economic integration and transnational corporations in the 1990s: Europe 1992, North America, and developing countries', *UNCTC Current Studies*, Series A, 15 (New York: UN).

United Nations Transnational Corporations and Management Division (UN-TCMD) (1993) 'From the Common Market to EU 92: regional economic integration in the European Community and transnational corporations', Department of Economic and Social Development (New York: UN).

US Department of Commerce (various issues) *Survey of Current Business* (Washington: DC).

Wallis, K.F. (1968) 'The EEU and US foreign investment: some empirical evidence re-examined', *Economic Journal* (September) , pp. 717–19.

World Bank (1987) *World Development Report, 1987* (Oxford: Oxford University Press).

11 The Creation and Application of Technology by MNEs' Subsidiaries in Europe

Marina Papanastassiou and Robert Pearce

INTRODUCTION

Recent decades have seen increases of overseas R & D operations, first in US multinational enterprises (MNEs) and later in those from Japan. Substantial parts of this growth have taken the form of laboratories, controlled by these MNEs, located in Europe.[1] Furthermore European MNEs have a strongly-established commitment to the performance of R & D in Europe outside of their home country. This chapter argues that this growth of MNE R & D not only serves the obvious fundamental purpose of enhancing a firm's competitiveness in the European market, but does so in a way that should be seen as also an integral part of the firm's global strategy for sustained long-term development. In fact an argument of the chapter is that Europe can be seen as a middle level in the strategy of these firms, being perceived as a key region in the formulation of *global* strategy but also acknowledging the persistence of *national* needs and characteristics as potentially relevant to the effective implementation of European policies.

The argument and analysis to be developed may be seen as reflecting two factors that are likely to underpin much of the policy of MNEs, and reflect crucial elements in their pursuit of international competitiveness. First, MNEs are increasingly aware that making the most effective use of the resources available to them world-wide involves not only optimally efficient use of current productive resources, but also the full development of creative resources in overseas facilities. Secondly, innovation remains a central factor in the way MNEs seek to sustain and enhance their position in their industries.[2] Thus, these companies are likely to be increasingly committed to a global approach to innovation, which is motivated both by the *needs* of globalised competitiveness and by the decentralised *availability* of valuable creative inputs.[3]

There is extensive evidence[4] that technology is frequently a key ownership

207

characteristic of MNEs, which provides vital support for their international operations when turned into a significant competitive advantage through effective combination with other ownership characteristics (e.g. management, marketing). It would not be accurate, however, to suggest that possession of a strong centralised ability to create technology then makes the internationalisation of production easy and cheap. Technology should not be taken to have a strong public goods nature in MNEs, in the sense that knowledge that is already commercially efficient in one environment can then be implemented competitively in other locations at very little extra cost, and thus underwrite an effective globalisation of operations. Thus Teece (1976, 1977) provided important early documentation of the resource costs of technology transfer within MNEs and the effect on these costs of the need for various types of adaptation when such technology is applied to new conditions. As MNEs, pursuing a globalised approach to competitiveness, become increasingly aware that a strong ability to react to distinctive market needs in different areas or countries is often a vital facet of such competitiveness, these costs of transfer are likely to gain in magnitude.

However, a new element is entering into the global technology programmes of MNEs. As these companies become embedded in particular host country environments, they become increasingly aware of, and willing to work with, the technical strength and capacities available in these countries. Such local scientific resources may have always been useful in helping to increase the effectiveness of technology transfer in MNEs, by taking part in its adaptation to local market and production conditions. Nowadays, however, decentralised R & D in MNEs frequently plays roles[5] that go beyond the effective use of established technology, taking ambitious positions in global programmes which involve both the creation and commercial implementation of new knowledge. The crucial issue and challenge for international technology organisation in MNEs is thus moving from technology transfer to technology creation.

The strategic changes implied by the emergence of decentralised creativity in MNEs are also reflected in the various roles that their subsidiaries can take (Pearce, 1992; Papanastassiou and Pearce, 1993). The traditional import-substitution type of subsidiary can be described as a truncated miniature replica (TMR). By focusing on the supply of the MNE's established product range to their host country markets, these subsidiaries tend to be very truncated in their functions, especially lacking any capacity for in-house creativity.

Once the subsidiaries move to an export-oriented role, one option is that of the rationalised product subsidiary (RPS). This type of facility specialises in the cost-effective supply of limited parts of the MNE's product range, but by still being tied to established products, its creative scope is again constrained. The process of evolution of subsidiaries may then extend to regional (or world) product mandate (RPM/WPM) operations, which have the permission and creative resources to develop and supply new products, often within the context of the group's view of innovation, as outlined earlier in this section.

EMPIRICAL EVIDENCE

The survey analysed in the subsequent sections of this chapter covers 145 subsidiaries of MNEs operating in Europe.[6] 71 of these subsidiaries belonged to US parent MNEs, 24 to Japanese parents, 46 were subsidiaries of a European MNE operating in a country other than its home country, and four had Canadian parents. The survey covers subsidiaries in four countries, the UK (99 subsidiaries), Belgium (20), Greece (16) and Portugal (10).[7]

We can observe at this stage that results from the survey tend to confirm two assumptions about the behaviour of the MNE subsidiaries in Europe that underpin the broad analytical perspectives of the chapter. First, it emerges that the majority of MNEs do tend to perceive the activities of individual subsidiaries as part of their regional operations (itself in turn an element in their global strategy), rather than as being autonomously focused on their host country markets (though this does not mean that local market and production conditions cannot have a significant influence on the location and development of such subsidiaries). Thus, of 144 respondents to a question on market orientation only 44 (30.6 per cent) said that their host country market was their only one. Subsidiaries of Japanese MNEs were least likely to supply only their host country, with only 12.5 per cent seeing this as their exclusive market. It therefore seems likely that the relatively recent arrival in Europe of Japanese MNEs has caused them to react, from their initiation, to the needs of a wider competitive perspective. Despite the older vintage of many of their subsidiaries, US MNEs also adopt the wider view, with only 24.3 per cent of their respondents focused exclusively on their host-country market. Whereas the more recent US subsidiaries may have been established with this viewpoint, others may have needed to restructure their approach to find a role in the new European competitive environment.[8]

By contrast with Japanese and US subsidiaries, 50 per cent of the subsidiaries of European MNEs operating in countries other than their parent did perceive their host country as providing their only market. Two factors may contribute to this. First, it may be that European companies are more able to detect important differences between national markets in the region than US or Japanese enterprises, and are more willing to allow their individual subsidiaries to focus on responding to the particular needs of the markets of the countries they operate in. This reflects their geographical proximity, reflected in lower cultural distance, and therefore greater understanding of these differences. Another important factor is that many such investments outside of the home country within the EU may be to overcome protectionism, e.g. nationalistic buying policies. Where this motive prevails, the projects are likely to serve national markets only. The second factor is that whilst US and Japanese MNEs may be less responsive to differences in national markets in Europe, they may be more responsive to differences in production conditions. Thus, having opted to supply a product range aimed at the overall European market, these MNEs can choose a limited number of specialised, export-oriented, production sites to supply it from. They can then make this production choice through a quite subtle evaluation of a range of relevant factors reflecting on different potential supply locations. By contrast with this optimising approach, European MNEs may adopt a more satisficing view of the location of export-oriented plants to supply wider markets. Thus, there may be a historically- and culturally-derived tendency to keep such operations in the group's home country until very strong evidence emerges that a plant elsewhere in Europe could supply the products more efficiently. This may then tend to limit the number of export-oriented subsidiaries European MNEs have set up in the region outside their home country.

Industries where subsidiaries were relatively likely to focus on their host country markets include petroleum (57.1 per cent of respondents), pharmaceuticals and telecommunications (50 per cent of respondents each), metal manufacturing and products (42.9 per cent) and mechanical engineering (38.5 per cent). In most of these cases the likelihood of distinctive consumer tastes, government regulations and procurement or the need to customise products for industrial purchasers, stimulates subsidiaries to concentrate efforts on local responsiveness to a particularly extensive degree. Subsidiaries in the UK (27.6 per cent of respondents) were less likely to focus on the local market than those in the other three countries (37.0 per cent). Generally the markets of exporting subsidiaries were very wide ranging. Thus, of the 100 subsidiaries that did not focus on their home country market, 97 included EU countries in their target markets, 92 included non-EU European countries and 84 of them markets outside Europe.

In Table 11.1 information is provided on an alternative perspective on market orientation, with data on percentage of production exported. Generally, the number of respondents reporting zero exports is lower than would have been suggested by the numbers noted above as indicating that their host country market is their only one. It seems likely that subsidiaries which report positive but small amounts of exports may perceive these as sporadic and ad hoc, rather than representing a sustained and active commitment to particular foreign markets, and therefore as not compromising their essentially dominant local market orientation. These figures again show Japanese subsidiaries to be the most strongly export oriented, and those of European MNEs clearly least so. Subsidiaries in the UK are substantially more export oriented than those in the other host countries covered by the survey. Amongst the industries that report notable export orientation are industrial and agricultural chemicals, electronics and electrical appliances, and automobiles.

Two other questions relating to the trade of subsidiaries may also be briefly

Table 11.1 Percentage of production exported by MNE subsidiaries in Europe

	0	0.1–10.0	10.1–25	25.1–50	50+	Total
By industry						
Food and drink	22.2	66.7	11.1			100.0
Industrial and agricultural chemicals	9.1	18.2	4.5	27.3	40.9	100.0
Pharmaceuticals and consumer chemicals	31.6	26.3	5.3	15.8	21.1	100.0
Mechanical engineering	33.3		16.7	8.3	41.7	100.0
Electronics and electrical appliances[1]	20.6	14.7	5.9	17.6	41.2	100.0
Automobiles	14.3			28.6	57.1	100.0
Metal manufacture and products	14.3	28.6	28.6		28.6	100.0
Petroleum	28.6	42.9			28.6	100.0
Other manufacturing[2]	11.1	16.7	5.6	27.8	38.9	100.0
Total	19.7	19.7	7.0	17.6	35.9	100.0
By home country						
USA	14.7	17.6	7.4	19.1	41.2	100.0
Japan	8.3	4.2	4.2	20.8	62.5	100.0
Europe[3]	34.8	30.4	6.5	13.0	15.2	100.0
Total[4]	19.7	19.7	7.0	17.6	35.9	100.0
By host country						
UK	18.8	10.4	10.4	19.8	40.6	100.0
Other[5]		21.7	39.1		13.0	26.1
	100.0					
Total	19.7	19.7	7.0	17.6	35.9	100.0

1. Includes computers and telecommunications.
2. Includes building materials, instruments, rubber, miscellaneous.
3. Covers subsidiaries of European MNEs in countries other than their home country.
4. Includes subsidiaries of Canadian MNEs.
5. Subsidiaries in Belgium, Greece, Portugal.

Source: Marina Papanastassiou data base.

reported as reflecting on the nature of their position in their group's European operations. First, when asked what proportion of their exports went to other parts of the MNE group, 37.9 per cent of respondents said that none did, whilst another 23.3 per cent said less than 10 per cent, 13.8 per cent between 10 per cent and 50 per cent, and 25 per cent over half. Secondly, 51.8 per cent of respondents said that none of their exports were intermediate products (e.g. components, goods needing further processing), while another 14.9 per cent said that less than 50 per cent were of this type, though 33.3 per cent said that over half their exports took this form. Pharmaceuticals and electronics were the most notable industries with an above-average

propensity to include intra-group exports. However, neither of these industries showed a strong orientation towards intermediate products in their subsidiaries' exports. This may suggest that in these industries', MNEs use a
region-wide sales network to market a range of products, with individual
subsidiaries specialising in the production (and perhaps development) of particular items in the range. Intermediate products were particularly significant in the exports of subsidiaries in automobiles, industrial and agricultural
chemicals, and metals and metal products, though in none of these industries were intra-group exports especially prevalent.

US and Japanese subsidiaries were quite comparable in their commitment
to both intra-group and intermediate product exports. The subsidiaries of
European MNEs, however, were somewhat less inclined to include intra-
group exports and distinctively the least likely to be involved in intermediate products trade. This is again in line with the view that European MNEs
seem less likely than their US and Japanese competitors to use subsidiaries
in the region as part of a network of specialising supply facilities. Subsidiaries in the UK were quite notably more oriented towards both intra-group
and intermediate product exports than those in the other three countries. A
conventional interpretation of this pattern would be that these UK subsidiaries are low cost based operations specialising in the production of inputs as
part of a region-wide network. However, an alternative, more positive, role
might also be hypothesised to explain this exporting behaviour by UK subsidiaries. Thus, it may be that UK operations often take a leading creative
position in a MNE's European activities (i.e. RPM status), with the production facility's interdependent supply role then reflecting a key central position rather than a peripheral dependent one.

The second premise that can be investigated immediately from the survey
is that overseas subsidiaries play roles in a global innovation strategy that
require them to implement extensive independent technological creativity in
support of their own operations. Thus, responding subsidiaries were asked if
any technological work was carried out (a) in a properly constituted R & D
laboratory with a permanent staff of scientists, or (b) less formally by members of the engineering unit during the process of production. Overall, 118
subsidiaries replied to the question, of which only two specified that neither
type of work was relevant (though clearly this may be the position of some
of the non-respondents to this question). Of these, 54 said they relied entirely
on an R & D laboratory, 40 said they were solely dependent on the less
formal source and 22 that they utilised both. Thus 64.4 per cent of the 118
respondents (or at least 52.4 per cent of the full sample) incorporated the
work of an R & D lab in their operations. Table 11.2 provides more detail
of the position of the types of technological inputs, by industry and home
country of MNE and host country of subsidiary.

Table 11.2 Sources of technological work carried out for MNE subsidiaries

	Source[1] (%)		
	A	B	C
By industry			
Food and drink	55.5	22.2	22.2
Industrial and agricultural chemicals	52.4	19.0	28.6
Pharmaceuticals and consumer chemicals	57.1	28.6	14.3
Mechanical engineering	33.3	44.4	22.2
Electronics and electrical appliances[2]	38.5	50.0	11.5
Automobiles	33.3	58.3	8.3
Building materials	50.0	25.0	25.0
Metal manufacture and products	40.0	40.0	20.0
Petroleum	66.7	33.3	
Other manufacturing[3]	50.0	14.3	35.7
Total	46.6	34.5	18.9
By home country			
USA	44.8	29.3	25.9
Japan	37.5	62.5	
Europe[4]	48.7	33.3	18.0
Total[5]	46.6	34.5	18.9
By host country			
UK	44.9	34.6	20.5
Other[6]	50.0	34.2	15.8
Total	46.6	34.5	18.9

1. Respondents were asked 'Is any technological work carried out for your subsidiary:
   A – in a properly constituted R & D laboratory with a permanent staff of scientists;
   B – less formally by members of the engineering unit during the process of production?;
   C – covers respondents who used both A and B.
2. Includes computers and telecommunications.
3. Includes building materials, instruments, rubber, miscellaneous.
4. Covers subsidiaries of European MNEs in countries other than their home country.
5. Includes subsidiaries of Canadian MNEs.
6. Subsidiaries in Belgium, Greece, Portugal.

Source: Marina Papanastassiou data base.

Roles and Motivation of Subsidiary R & D

In the survey, MNE subsidiaries in Europe were asked to evaluate the importance of various types of work in their R & D labs. As Table 11.3 shows, both development of new products and adaptation of the product or production process play extensive roles, with the former emerging into the rather more prominent position that would be implied by the implementation of global innovation strategies. An especially notable example of a strong orientation towards development rather than adaptation occurs for US MNEs' subsidiaries in electronics and electrical appliances, where the average response for adaptation was only 1.25 compared with 3.00 for development. This is likely to reflect quite basic differences in key technological characteristics (e.g. radio and television transmission standards) between areas, which indicate that an adaptable global product cannot be defined in many sectors of the industry, so that fundamental redesign (i.e. independent development) of a product concept is normally required for key regions.

Two industries in which notably strong development work is complemented by an above-average commitment to adaptation as well, are industrial and agricultural chemicals and mechanical engineering. This suggests that in these industries globally competing firms develop product ideas to meet the broad characteristics of major markets, but are then prepared also to adapt them further to conform to the detailed requirements of the individual industrial customers that are likely to be prevalent in both industries. In food, drink and tobacco a predictably strong role for adaptation combines with a somewhat below-average importance for development. This may indicate that MNEs in these industries leave the most distinctive elements of local tastes to national firms, and try to compete in wider markets through globally known products, which can quite often be centrally developed but then need some adaptation to increase their acceptability in individual markets. The results also imply that the potential for centrally-derived products that only need subsequent adaptation, rather than localised development, exists strongly in the petroleum industry.

It therefore becomes clear that in certain industries, at least, extensive taste heterogeneity in Europe demands adaptation work that differentiates products to be supplied throughout the region. Along with results to be reported subsequently, this underlines that the reality of a Single European Market (SEM) often still falls well short of the formal vision.

In pharmaceuticals and consumer chemicals' MNEs both development and, to some extent, adaptation are of below-average prominence in overseas laboratories. This comparative centralisation of creative work may seem surprising in view of the relative local market-orientation of subsidiaries already noted and the well known influence of government regulations and often distinctive national consumer preferences in this industry. It may be that, due to an unusually high concern with commercial secrecy in pharmaceuti-

Table 11.3 MNE subsidiaries' evaluation of the importance of various types of work in their laboratories

	Average response[1] Type of research		
	A	B	C
By industry			
Food and drink	2.88	2.63	1.38
Industrial and agricultural chemicals	2.80	3.00	1.75
Pharmaceuticals and consumer chemicals	2.40	2.27	2.20
Mechanical engineering	2.60	3.00	1.40
Electronics and electrical appliances[2]	2.13	2.85	1.50
Automobiles	2.17	2.67	1.80
Metal manufacture and products	3.00	2.67	1.67
Petroleum	2.67	1.33	1.67
Other manufacturing[3]	2.58	2.75	1.75
Total	2.52	2.69	1.69
By home country			
USA	2.53	2.81	1.77
Japan	2.22	3.00	1.56
Europe[4]	2.56	2.38	1.67
Total[5]	2.52	2.69	1.69
By host country			
UK	2.47	2.82	1.66
Other[6]	2.62	2.38	1.76
Total	2.52	2.69	1.69

Type of research

A – Adaptation of the product or production process.
B – Development of a new product.
C – Provision of scientific knowledge to a broader research project organised by the MNE group.
1. Respondents were asked to evaluate each type of work as either, 'important', 'relatively important'; 'not important'. The average response was then calculated by allocating responses of 'important' the value 3, 'relatively important 2 and 'not important' 1.
2. Includes computers and telecommunications.
3. Includes building materials, instruments, rubber, miscellaneous.
4. Covers subsidiaries of European MNEs in countries other than their home country.
5. Includes subsidiaries of Canadian MNEs.
6. Subsidiaries in Belgium, Greece, Portugal.

Source: Marina Papanastassiou data base.

cals,[9] firms may desire to centralise as much of the development and product innovation stages[10] as possible. Then, to a greater extent than in many industries it may, indeed, be possible to centralise the creation of the product variants that will meet the needs of specific foreign markets. Thus, the relevant government regulations that stimulate the need for such variants may be set down in precise documentation that can be effectively communicated to a central laboratory in the group, and elements of consumer preference (e.g. for drugs in capsule, tablet or liquid form) may also be easy to discern and communicate. This may lessen the need for the sustained 'face to face' interaction between development/adaptation labs and regional or national markets that may be necessary to improve performance in other industries.

It is indicated in Table 11.3 that R & D labs of US and Japanese MNEs' subsidiaries in Europe tend to be rather more focused on development, and less on adaptation, than those that European MNEs set up outside their home country. Thus, the US and Japanese labs are likely to have a primary role to develop an original European version of a centrally-derived new product. The persistence of quite extensive adaptation in these labs may then involve either further refinement of the new European product for individual national markets, or adaptation of existing products (already established in markets outside Europe) to take effective supplementary positions in the firm's European product range. The most likely reason for the smaller role for development in the R & D labs of European MNEs outside their parent country[11] is a preference for carrying out the main work of creating major new European products in their home country facilities. Indeed, given the availability of this option, the fact that development is still prominent in these companies' 'overseas' labs in Europe indicates a quite notable willingness to decentralise such work. This may be a response to the capacity of other European countries in relevant areas of scientific knowledge and research capabilities. The higher level of adaptation carried out by their subsidiaries complements their more extensive local market orientation observed earlier, and is likely to again reflect a greater ability to discern, and respond to, differences in consumer tastes between national markets in the region than their US or Japanese counterparts.

MNE subsidiaries in the UK emerge as rather more likely to use their R & D units for development than are those located in the other three host countries. Conversely, labs in the other countries are more likely to undertake adaptation than those in the UK. In addition to the fact that strong UK based development may lead to the creation of products that already tend to some extent to conform to UK conditions, the smaller and often distinctive markets of the other countries may have a stronger propensity to require adaptation of products conceived in a wider European context. More generally, this development orientation of UK labs' operations supports the earlier suggestion that the apparently interdependent position of UK subsidiaries, as reflected in their trade patterns, may reflect a role of creative leadership rather than technological dependency (i.e. RPM activity).

By contrast with the prevalence of the types of work associated with the implementation of the market responsive elements of a global innovation strategy, the labs surveyed in Table 11.3 show a much more limited propensity to supply scientific knowledge to the group-level pre-competitive R & D projects that aim to create the new background knowledge from which new product concepts derive. The strong tendency of the pharmaceutical labs to provide scientific knowledge to broader MNE group research projects supports the interpretation of their limited commitment to development and adaptation. Thus the apparent tendency for centralised R & D to take responsbility for all stages in the creation of new ranges of products in pharmaceutical companies also allows them scope to acquire specialised research inputs from overseas labs to support the centrally controlled and coordinated programme.

Sources of Technology in Subsidiaries

Indications of the technological independence or interdependence of MNEs' European subsidiaries was obtained in a question which investigated three possible sources of the technology used in their operations. As reported in Table 11.4, it is clear that technology imported from elsewhere in the MNE group plays a pervasive role in the operations of European subsidiaries. This imported group technology may take a form embodied in current products and production processes, in which case it is likely to be subjected to adaptation in subsidiaries. Or, alternatively, it may take the disembodied form of the knowledge behind a new product concept, so that the responsibility taken by local subsidiaries will be to achieve its development into a fully-defined product appropriate to European needs. Generally, established host country technology emerges as a much less relevant source of technology. One way in which the third source, the results of R & D carried out by the subsidiary, can constitute an input into its technology would be if the lab undertook a sustained and autonomous programme, developing a product from its own quite basic research. On the other hand, this R & D could also be considered to help provide a source of technology if it complemented that imported from elsewhere in the group by carrying out the work needed to render it effective in the European markets (i.e. by adapting products or completing the development of product concepts). It might be expected that R & D involved in product development would be rated by respondents as having greater relevance as a source of technology than that involved in adaptation

The results of Table 11.4 thus clearly emphasise the view that MNE subsidiaries often contribute to the overall competitiveness of their group by applying existing technology in ways that respond more fully and effectively to their own segment of the global market, which here can be the individual

Table 11.4 Sources of technology used by MNE subsidiaries in Europe

	Average response[1] Source of technology		
	A	B	C
By industry			
Food and drink	2.78	1.75	1.88
Industrial and agricultural chemicals	2.27	2.00	2.05
Pharmaceuticals and consumer chemicals	2.56	1.77	1.86
Mechanical engineering	2.64	1.91	1.60
Electronics and electrical appliances[2]	2.53	1.48	1.82
Automobiles	2.25	2.00	2.20
Metal manufacture and products	2.50	1.83	1.67
Petroleum	2.83	1.33	1.50
Other manufacturing[3]	2.65	1.83	1.95
Total	2.52	1.77	1.88
By home country			
USA	2.46	1.93	1.95
Japan	2.73	1.57	1.76
Europe[4]	2.60	1.61	1.82
Total[5]	2.52	1.77	1.88
By host country			
UK	2.41	1.91	1.96
Other[6]	2.86	1.46	1.70
Total	2.52	1.77	1.88

Sources of technology

A – Technology imported from elsewhere in the MNE group.
B – Established host country technology.
C – Results of R & D carried out by the subsidiary.
1. Respondents were asked to evaluate each source of technology as either, 'the main source' 'a secondary source'; 'not a source'. The average response was then calculated by allocating responses of 'main source' the value of 3, 'secondary source' 2, and 'not a source' 1.
2. Includes computers and telecommunications.
3. Includes building materials, instruments, rubber, miscellaneous.
4. Covers subsidiaries of European MNEs in countries other than their home country.
5. Includes subsidiaries of Canadian MNEs.
6. Subsidiaries in Belgium, Greece, Portugal.

Source: Marina Papanastassiou data base.

host country, or a wider area in Europe. Further aspects of this were investigated in two questions reported in Table 11.5. The first of these asked respondents that used imported MNE technology and/or established host-country technology to evaluate the extent to which they adapted this to suit their current needs. Overall, only 20.6 per cent of respondents said they adapted technology extensively, though a further 66.3 per cent did so to some extent. In the light of our view of the importance of local market responsiveness in the MNEs' global strategies, one interpretation of this result is that where established (embodied) technology would need more than moderate adaptation to meet distinctive conditions, the firms usually opt for a more substantial step in technological progress. This may then involve RPM subsidiaries developing new products from recently created group technology, rather than limited evolution of an older generation of products.

The second question reported in Table 11.5 relates to possible reasons for carrying out adaptation of established technology. Clearly the desire to make the product more suitable for the subsidiaries' markets was the most widely pervasive motive. Of two possible reasons for adaptation relating to the production process there seemed to be rather more concern to make alterations that would achieve a more suitable scale of production than to adjust in ways that would make a more appropriate use of local factor proportions.

In Table 11.4 it is revealed that subsidiaries in the UK are less likely to use imported technology, and more likely to use established host-country technology and their own R & D, as sources of knowledge inputs to their operations than are subsidiaries in the other three countries. Though this pattern occurs for US and Japanese subsidiaries in the UK, it is most strongly exemplified in the subsidiaries of European MNEs, at least with regard to the roles of imported technology and own R & D. Thus, these European subsidiaries provided an AR of 2.32 for imported MNE group technology in the UK compared with 2.90 in the other countries, whilst the comparative values for results of their own R & D were 2.00 and 1.61. This suggests that the European MNEs' subsidiaries in the three other countries may be mainly concerned with the effective implementation of established product and process technology in their host country market focused operations, whilst the subsidiaries in the UK may be allowed a more creative right to use their more extensive resource base in development work aimed at wider exploitation.[12] In some cases the UK subsidiaries may have a substantially autonomous scientific position, mandated to develop products for wider markets using mostly their own knowledge in a self-sufficient and locally integrated manner. Alternatively, the UK subsidiaries may complete the development of products as their role in an integrated group-wide European R & D programme, by taking up technology created elsewhere in their MNEs' operations. In such a case, the relatively low AR for imported group technology may reflect a tendency for respondents to evaluate such imported 'intermediate'

Table 11.5 Extent, and motives for, adaptation of MNE subsidiaries in Europe

	Average response			
		Reason for adaptation[2]		
	Extent of adaptation[1]	A	B	C
By industry				
Food and drink	1.78	2.88	2.25	2.38
Industrial and agricultural chemicals	2.19	2.68	1.76	1.35
Pharmaceuticals and consumer chemicals	2.13	2.31	2.00	2.23
Mechanical engineering	1.82	2.55	1.20	1.60
Electronics and electrical appliances[3]	2.17	2.59	1.42	1.63
Automobiles	2.09	2.83	1.71	2.20
Metal manufacture and products	2.00	2.40	1.40	2.00
Petroleum	1.83	2.50	2.00	2.50
Other manufacturing[4]	2.16	2.63	1.79	1.93
Total	2.08	2.58	1.69	1.85
By home country				
USA	2.07	2.71	1.63	1.90
Japan	2.14	2.40	1.47	1.86
Europe[5]	2.08	2.50	1.88	1.80
Total[6]	2.08	2.58	1.69	1.85
By host country				
UK	2.07	2.57	1.57	1.81
Other[7]	2.15	2.62	1.94	1.94
Total	2.08	2.58	1.69	1.85

1. Subsidiaries that used imported MNE technology and/or established host country technology were asked if they adapted this to suit their current needs, 'extensively'; 'to some extent'; 'not at all'. The average response was then calculated by allocating responses of 'extensively' the value 3, 'to some extent' 2, and 'not at all' 1.
2. The reasons for adaptation were:
   A – To make the product more suitable for our markets.
   B – To make suitable use of local factor proportions.
   C – To achieve a more suitable scale of production.
Respondents were asked to evaluate each reason as either, 'important'; 'relatively important'; 'not important'. The average response was then calculated by allocating response of 'important' the value 3, 'relatively important' 2, and 'not important' 1.
3. Includes computers and telecommunications.
4. Includes building materials, instruments, rubber, miscellaneous.
5. Covers subsidiaries of European MNEs in countries other than their home country.
6. Includes subsidiaries of Canadian MNEs.
7. Subsidiaries in Belgium, Greece, Portugal.

Source: Marina Papanastassiou data base.

technology less strongly than that already embodied in products and processes, since they may perceive it as incomplete and of, at that stage, undetermined commercial relevance.

One rather more detailed result may nevertheless be worthy of comment. This is that the least export-oriented group of subsidiaries, those of European MNEs in the other countries (i.e. non-UK), are the ones with the strongest reaction to the two process adaptation motives covered in Table 11.5. Thus, adaptation of processes both to increase their suitability for local factor proportions and to achieve a more suitable scale of production were rated at ARs of 2.06 for these subsidiaries.[13] This is in line with the previously argued view (Behrman and Fischer, 1980; Pearce, 1989; Papanastassiou and Pearce, 1993) that local market focused subsidiaries that apply existing technology are more likely to need such process adaptation than cost based export-oriented operations that also produce established products.[14] Thus, export markets are more likely to be large enough to allow a subsidiary to use existing processes at an optimum scale than would the host country market alone. Also, where an MNE is implementing an export-oriented subsidiary as part of specialised cost based facilities, it can select locations whose factor proportions are in tune with existing production processes, whereas a local market operation might need to correct such a mismatch.

Subsidiaries' Host Country Scientific Links

A clear theme of the earlier analysis is that overseas subsidiaries of MNEs play an interactive role in the creative activity of the overall group. Thus, a global competitive MNE is likely to have a pervasive dominant technological trajectory which will influence the evolution of the operations of each of its subsidiaries. These subsidiaries, however, often pick up this underlying technology and apply their own resources (managerial and marketing, as well as scientific) to it, in order to implement the second phase of a global innovation strategy as competitively as possible in their own market area. Though this clearly implies a very strong demand-side (i.e. market based) influence on the decision to set up R & D facilities targeted at a local market, it has also been shown that in a large regional market, such as Europe, where such a facility is located may depend to some extent on supply-side factors, notably the quality of the local science base. Where these R & D subsidiaries play a role in the supply of basic research to the pre-competitive phase of a MNE's global innovation programme, availability of quality scientific inputs is likely to be an even more influential factor. Thus, alongside their integration into the wider operations of the MNE, these R & D labs are also likely to interact significantly with other elements of the scientific community in their host countries.

As has been observed elsewhere (Papanastassiou and Pearce, 1994b), an effective interdependence between a MNE subsidiary's technological work and host country institutions may have sustained benefits for both which go beyond the solution to short-term problems. Thus, where a MNE subsidiary moved its R & D role forward from adaptation of existing products to the more challenging one of product development, local scientific linkages and inputs should expand considerably. Therefore, local scientific inputs assist the subsidiary in undergoing a substantial creative transition in its capabilities and ambitions. However, it is also likely that in many cases the local scientific institutions involved may benefit considerably from such links in terms of substantial evolution of their own scope and capacities. This may come about not only through access to the scientific knowledge of the MNE (which may complement their own) and the chance to learn from the opportunity to help deal with new scientific challenges, but also from an enhanced familiarity with work within wider and more ambitious programmes with more clearly perceived commercial perspectives. Thus, sustained technological collaborations of this type with MNEs may also lead to a creative transition in indigenous scientific capacity, broadening its knowledge, its organisational scope and vision, and its commercial perceptions. From this change, local science may also enhance its ability to make a useful contribution to the dynamism of indigenous firms.

Some aspects of the interaction of MNEs' subsidiaries with the local science base through collaborative research were investigated in the survey through a question reported in Table 11.6. Though collaborations with local universities were quite widespread, with 59.3 per cent of respondents reporting that they had such links, they seem, rarely, to be particularly intensive, with only 14.4 per cent of respondents rating such collaborations as extensive. In the case of collaborations with independent research labs, only 3.7 per cent of respondents reported that such links were extensive, whilst 66.7 per cent had established no such research connections. These first two types of host country institutions seem to be the most likely to encapsulate a country's areas of particular strength in pure and basic research, and would, therefore, be expected to be most likely to attract MNEs seeking such inputs into the pre-competitive stages of their research programmes.

Industry research labs will obviously be working in the area of science most applicable to their industry, but with perhaps a much clearer perception than independent labs of how this relates to commercial needs, and especially to the characteristics of their country of location. These may then prove to provide a more plausible collaboration for product development-and/or adaptation-oriented MNE labs. Only 3.7 per cent of respondents considered collaborations with such industry labs to be extensive, and 63.9 per cent omitted them. Research collaboration with other firms were described as extensive by only 6.8 per cent of respondents, whilst only a further 31.1 per cent implemented them to a more moderate degree. Such research alliances with other firms could occur at the pre-competitive stage, with the partners both providing specialised and complementary basic research in-

Table 11.6 MNE subsidiaries' evaluation of their collaborative research with local institutions

	Average response[1] Research collaboration			
	A	B	C	D
By industry				
Food and drink	2.00	1.63	1.22	1.38
Industrial and agricultural chemicals	1.86	1.47	1.61	1.84
Pharmaceuticals and consumer chemicals	1.88	1.50	1.20	1.13
Mechanical engineering	1.67	1.44	1.63	1.17
Electronics and electrical appliances[2]	1.44	1.05	1.21	1.48
Automobiles	1.86	1.18	1.36	1.27
Metal manufacture and products	1.50	1.25	1.50	1.25
Petroleum	1.40	1.25	1.50	1.25
Other manufacturing[3]	1.93	1.90	1.69	1.62
Total	1.74	1.37	1.40	1.45
By home country				
USA	1.81	1.41	1.43	1.50
Japan	1.42	1.17	1.21	1.33
Europe[4]	1.73	1.42	1.44	1.39
Total[5]	1.74	1.37	1.40	1.45
By host country				
UK	1.69	1.34	1.40	1.54
Other[6]		1.84	1.44	1.39
	1.25			
Total	1.74	1.37	1.40	1.45

Collaborations

A – With universities.
B – With independent research laboratories.
C – With industry research laboratories.
D – With other firms.

1. Respondents were asked to evaluate each type of collaboration as 'extensive', 'moderate' or 'non-existent'. The average response was then calculated by allocating responses of 'extensive' the value 3, 'moderate' 2, and 'non-existent' 1.
2. Includes computers and telecommunications.
3. Includes building materials, instruments, rubber, miscellaneous.
4. Covers subsidiaries of European MNEs in countries other than their home country.
5. Includes subsidiaries of Canadian MNEs.
6. Subsidiaries in Belgium, Greece, Portugal.

Source: Marina Papanastassiou data base.

puts. Alternatively the other firm might provide local knowledge that assists with the suitable development of a MNE's product concept.

A CASE STUDY

The case study deals with a European electronics MNE for which information is available on two UK subsidiaries and one each in Belgium and Portugal. All the subsidiaries serve their national markets, but for the Portuguese subsidiary it is its main market, indicating import-substituting behaviour. The other three subsidiaries show a definite export-oriented behaviour covering a wide range of international markets but especially European. However, export orientation does not mean identically motivated operations as they can be either regional or world product mandate subsidiaries (RPM/WPM), or rationalised product subsidiaries (RPS), or even truncated miniature replicas (TMRs) in a creative transition towards becoming RPMs or RPSs.

Thus, export orientation, although it is normally a more dynamic attitude compared to that of import substitution, can itself be characterised by the different forms that it takes, though these can be perceived as stages that are relatively static (RPS) or dynamic/evolutionary (RPM or WPM). Time is definitely one element that can help classify the export behaviour of a subsidiary, but also accumulation of data on sales, personnel, product diversification, to name but a few, can provide a more integrated picture of the market orientation of a company. Overall, market orientation is an important characteristic that can assist not only an understanding of the activity of individual subsidiaries within the MNE group but also their importance to the industry of the host country.

An important element in this is the preference of most subsidiaries (as noted earlier) to possess an R & D lab. The R & D lab is associated with the dynamism of a subsidiary as expressed through the creation of new products or the adaptation of existing ones or alterations in the production process. All four of the subsidiaries possessed R & D facilities, with three of the units being established as fresh installations and the other acquired as part of a takeover. The export-oriented behaviour of the Belgian and UK subsidiaries can be a sign of their labs' serious adaptation of existing products, or creation of new products, for international markets. The R & D lab in the case of the Portuguese subsidiary indicates alterations in production processes in response to the cheap available labour.

The main point here is that in all four subsidiaries the parent company has provided for their support by an R & D lab. This can be easily explained by the fact that electronics is a very dynamic and 'daily evolving' sector, with strong European, US and, of course, Japanese competitors. This is further reflected in the fact that in all the subsidiaries the labs are found to interact with other sources of technology.

For the Belgian subsidiary the R & D lab's own results act as the major source of technology, with the secondary support of both imported technology and host country technology. This R & D lab was acquired, and as a matter of strategy it would not be wise to under-estimate the importance of the acquired lab or perceive its acquisition as a sideline. Also host country results may be inherited from the previous ownership of the laboratory. The UK subsidiaries use all possible sources of technology, but attribute varying relative importance to the different sources, indicating that subsidiaries can have independent managerial attitudes as they can be involved in different product lines. Generally differing significance is given to the priority of each source, not only for the UK subsidiaries but for all those of the group, indicating different views on efficiency of supply of technology, as the role of each subsidiary differs and as each host country possesses different characteristics which influence the shaping of technology use.

Regarding the extent of adaptation, the Belgian subsidiary makes full use of its own R & D personnel by extensively adapting the external technology supply. The other subsidiaries in the other two countries also adapt, but only to a more moderate degree. The extent of adaptation also gives us an indication of the sort of export orientation and of the gravity of the role of each subsidiary and R & D lab in the host country industry and the MNE group. The main purpose of adaptation for all the subsidiaries is to make their products suitable for their markets. This is in line with the fact that most of the subsidiaries export and each one plays a specialised role in the group. Thus, their production covers needs beyond the national and represent the flag of the company in wider markets, which makes the role of the subsidiaries very complicated, with wider responsibilities. However, even in the case where the national market plays the major role, we see that the parent company takes this market seriously, despite its size, as its subsidiary may later serve other markets and must be dedicated to international standards. Further, even if the subsidiary serves only its national market, in an interrelated world a wrong attitude in one market can undermine the reputation of the company in other countries (via the media).

The responsibilities of the subsidiaries often extend to creation of new products. However, the concept of a new product seems to vary from subsidiary to subsidiary. Scientists or engineers in their labs may see particular work on an established product or process as significant enough to classify it as a different product if its efficiency increases notably in comparison to the current version. Thus, variations of an established product may be perceived as different products, as the changes that have occurred give it a different appearance and market potential even if its essential function is unaltered. In all our subsidiaries examined the major influence on the creation of a new product is the availability of scientific personnel. Capable scientists are an important asset to each company. Companies may accumulate them, if they can afford it, in order to be prepared for future competition. Also, as every company is interested in future markets, for three of the four subsidiaries, increased competitiveness in the European market is reported as an important factor in creating a new product.

The character of each subsidiary was noted earlier. Although all of them have some sort of export orientation, the Portuguese form can be classified as an RPS as its exports are limited to intermediate products supplied to other parts of the MNE group. This can explain why the other three companies, which are variants of the RPM type, view their role of deriving new products as part of the global vision of their parent company strategy. The Portuguese RPS, with its main clients in the national market and within the MNE itself, does not see increased competitiveness and a global view on innovation as part of its existence, as the nature of this subsidiary is more or less externally defined. This indicates its position in a sort of hierarchy, but without underestimating the contribution of its role.

In examining the spillovers to the host country economy via subsidiaries' links with local suppliers and scientific exchanges, at first glance the evidence is mixed. The Portuguese and Belgian subsidiaries have very strong links with local suppliers, who provide them with technical advice. The UK ones seem to have the least possible links with their local surroundings, with just one collaboration with a university. The Belgian subsidiary has the strongest links with local research facilities, which it inherited from its previous ownership.

The position of any subsidiary in an MNE group may be subject to tensions and change, and the potential for this may be discerned amongst the subsidiaries described here. The Belgian subsidiary, through its previous local ownership, still benefits the local market, so it would not be wise for the parent company to diminish the role of this newly acquired subsidiary as a matter of policy towards the host country. Maybe after a certain time has passed, in a process of rationalisation of its activities, the subsidiary will go through a more substantive adjustment process. The Portuguese subsidiary's role is mainly to supply the host country market efficiently with a high-quality standard product, but it also supplies inputs to other parts of the MNE group. Although its role in the group therefore seems very stable, it does not mean that the management would not seek a different role, especially as it has a large research laboratory.[15] Finally the UK subsidiaries, although they differ between themselves in some respects, both seem to be playing an increased role in the MNE group, despite which neither seems to have a deep relationship with local factors, either subcontractors or research institutions. This once more demonstrates that the industrial development of the UK is very uncertain, as the country is being exploited for what it can offer but the feedback is small.

From this point of view, the Portuguese subsidiary offers more to the host country in the form of help for creative infrastructure, but plays a less fundamental role in the MNE group. Frustration, however, may be felt by the two UK subsidiaries as the personnel wants to see itself participating in more challenging roles. The Belgian subsidiary may need to protect its traditional local links and develop a new role around them to establish its position in the group hierarchy.

CONCLUSIONS

This chapter has sought to investigate aspects of the approach of MNEs to the European market against the background of a particular view of evolving trends in their strategic behaviour. The perceived international business context is one in which increasingly intense competitive pressures in many industries mean that MNEs need to regularly introduce new products, to respond to differentiated national or regional needs and tastes, and to produce goods in a cost-effective manner. Whilst the sustained relevance of the use of specialised RPSs to pursue efficient production is fully recognised, this chapter has been more concerned to delineate the emerging trend in MNEs to use creative (RPM/WPM) subsidiaries in order to respond to the distinctive needs of particular markets and, at its most ambitious level, to implement a global innovation strategy.

The evidence indicates that whereas Europe plays a role in MNEs' *global* strategies, national markets still often play particular roles in their *European* strategy. We have seen that whereas MNEs' often *develop* products for the European market as part of a global approach to innovation, there is frequently additional motivation to *adapt* these products further in order to refine them to meet national needs. Thus whilst European integration can, or should, provide similar standards that secure consumer safety, it cannot standardise tastes and resources.

Thus, in many sectors it appears that the reality of the Single Market is one of increased scope for integration between national markets that nevertheless often retain significant idiosyncratic taste characteristics. The evidence suggests that MNEs perceive competitive dangers in any attempt to override these market differences and frequently adapt products to respond to them. However, even while MNEs retain this willingness to differentiate products in this way, use of the enhanced freedom of movement of goods within the EU may become relevant. Taken with increased flexibility of production and improved communications, it may become possible to derive a product to meet the needs of one national market but produce it elsewhere in the EU. Such a response to national market needs means the use of national subsidiaries, with the potential of retaining the cost problems of traditional import-substitution operations, may then be avoided. The Single Market may yet provide MNEs with the ability to combine responsiveness to differentiated tastes within the EU with the scope for increased production efficiency that is opened up by freedom of trade.

Another important issue is the commitment of management, not only to its subsidiary but also to the other parts of the group. All companies want to look forward to a better role in the European context. It seems that European integration may sometimes be perceived by firms as involving only legislative and financial procedures, which in some cases can facilitate their work but in others may contradict their desire to preserve and develop their individual subsidiaries' character within the group.

Notes

1. See Pearce and Singh (1992, pp. 58–64), JETRO (1993, p. 3), Papanastassiou and Pearce (1994a).
2. In an analysis of issues perceived as important by technology management executives in US, Japanese and Swedish multitechnology companies, 'pressure for more frequent introduction of new generations of products', 'pressure for shorter innovation lead times', 'shorter market lifetimes of products' were all seen as of above-average significance (Granstrand and Sjolander, 1992).
3. For discussion of a global innovation strategy see Papanastassiou and Pearce (1994c). Important conceptualisation of possible global approaches to innovation have emerged from the work of Bartlett and Ghoshal (1989, 1990).
4. See Pearce (1993, pp. 32–4) for a review and discussion.
5. For earlier typologies of overseas labs and their roles see Ronstadt (1978, 1977); Hood and Young (1982); Haug *et al.* (1983); Hakanson (1981); Cordell (1971, 1973); Pearce (1989), Papanastassiou and Pearce (1993).
6. The study was carried out by Marina Papanastassiou in 1992/3.
7. Questionnaires were sent to 313 subsidiaries in the UK, providing a response rate of 31.6 per cent, and to 220 in the other three countries for a response rate of 20.9 per cent.
8. See Pearce (1992).
9. See Pearce and Singh (1992) for evidence that security concerns are not generally a major factor operating against decentralisation of R & D.
10. It has been shown that decentralised R & D units play a notably significant role in the pre-competitive (basic research) stages of R & D in pharmaceuticals (Pearce and Singh, 1992).
11. In fact, development is more important in the UK for those subsidiaries (AR of 2.73) than adaptation (2.50). Nevertheless, this figure for development is below that for all subsidiaries in UK, whilst that for adaptation is above that for all subsidiaries.
12. In support of this perspective, the market-orientation data of Table 11.1 shows that 40.0 per cent of European MNEs' subsidiaries in UK exported over 25 per cent of their sales, compared with 14.3 per cent of those in the other countries. Further, the data covered by Table 11.3 reveals that European MNE subsidiaries in the UK reported average responses of 2.73 for product development and 2.50 for adaptation, whilst those in the other countries reversed the ratings with ARs of 1.91 and 2.62 for the two roles.
13. This compares, for example, with comparable values of 1.69 and 1.53 for European MNEs' subsidiaries in the UK, or 1.85 and 1.87 for US subsidiaries in these three host countries and 1.67 for and 1.67 Japanese subsidiaries there.
14. Obviously subsidiaries that export products for which they have development

responsibility will seek to create suitable production technology as a part of this development process.

15. Taggart's (1993) analysis of MNEs' subsidiaries in Scotland led to the suggestion that 'there may be a link between the type of R & D a subsidiary carries out and the future direction of subsidiary and/or corporate strategy'. A similar argument is developed by Andersson and Pahlberg (1993).

References

Andersson, U. and Pahlberg, C. (1993) 'Technology development and its implications for subsidiary influences in international firms', in V.C. Simoes (ed), *International Business and Europe after 1992*, vol. 2, proceedings of the 19th Annual Conference of the European International Business Association (Lisbon: CEDE).

Bartlett, C.A. and Ghoshal, S. (1989) *Managing Across Borders: The Transnational Solution* (Boston: Harvard Business School Press).

Bartlett, C.A. and Ghoshal, S. (1990) 'Managing innovation in the transnational corporation', in C.A. Bartlett, Y. Doz and G. Hedlund (eds), *Managing the Global Firm* (London: Routledge).

Behrman, J.N. and Fischer, W.A. (1980) *Overseas R & D Activities of Transnational Companies* (Cambridge, Mass.: Oelgeschlager, Gunn & Hain).

Cordell, A.J. (1971) *The Multinational Firm, Foreign Direct Investment and Canadian Science Policy* (Ottawa: Information Canada).

Cordell, A.J. (1973) 'Innovation, the multinational corporation: some policy implications for national science policy', *Long Range Planning*, 6(3), pp. 22–9.

Granstrand, O. and Sjolander, S. (1992) 'Internationalisation and diversification of multitechnology corporations', in O. Granstrand, L. Hakanson and S. Sjolander (eds), *Technology Management and International Business* (Chichester: Wiley).

Hakanson, L. (1981) 'Organisation and evolution of foreign R & D in Swedish multinationals', *Geografiska Annaler*, 63B, pp. 47–56.

Haug, P., Hood, N. and Young, S. (1983) 'R & D intensity in the affiliates of US-owned electronics companies manufacturing in Scotland', *Regional Studies*, 17, pp. 383–92.

Hood, N. and Young, S. (1982) 'US multinational R & D: corporate strategies and policy implications for the UK', *Multinational Business*, 2, pp. 10–23.

JETRO (1993) *The 9th survey of European Operations of Japanese Companies in the Manufacturing Sector* (Tokyo: JETRO).

Papanastassiou, M. and Pearce, R.D. (1993) 'The globalisation of innovation and the role of research and development in multinational enterprises', paper prepared for Institute Française des Relations Internationales, mimeo.

Papanastassiou, M. and Pearce, R.D. (1994a) 'The internationalisation of research and development by Japanese enterprises', *R & D Management*, 24(2), pp. 155–65.

Papanastassiou, M. and Pearce, R.D. (1994b) 'Host-country determinants of the market strategies of US companies' overseas subsidiaries', *Journal of the Economics of Business*, 1(2), pp. 199–217.

Papanastassiou, M. and Pearce, R.D. (1994c) 'The creation and application of technology by MNEs' subsidiaries in Europe, and their role in a global-innovation strategy', *Discussion Papers in International Investment and Business Studies*, 184 (University of Reading, Department of Economics).

Pearce, R.D. (1989) *The Internationalisation of Research and Development by Multinational Enterprises* (London: Macmillan).

Pearce, R.D. (1992) 'World product mandates and MNE specialisation', *Scandinavian International Business Review*, 1(2), pp. 38–58.

Pearce, R.D. (1993) *The Growth and Evolution of Multinational Enterprise* (Aldershot: Edward Elgar).

Pearce, R.D. and Singh, S. (1992) *Globalising Research and Development* (London: Macmillan).

Ronstadt. R.C. (1977) *Research and Development Abroad by US Multinationals* (New York: Praeger).

Ronstadt. R.C. (1978) 'International R & D: the establishment and evolution of R & D abroad by seven US multinationals', *Journal of International Business Studies*, 9(1), pp. 7–24.

Taggart, J.H. (1993) 'Strategy conflict in the MNE: parent and subsidiary', paper presented at 14th annual conference, European International Business Association, Lisbon (mimeo).

Teece, D.J. (1976) *The Multinational Corporation and the Resource Cost of International Technology Transfer* (Cambridge, Mass.: Ballinger).

Teece. D.J. (1977) 'Technology transfer by multinational firms: the resource cost of transferring technological knowhow', *Economic Journal*, 87 (June), pp. 242–61.

12 Transatlantic Perspectives on Inward Investment and Prospects for Policy Reconciliation

Stephen Young, Neil Hood and Cameron Hood

INTRODUCTION

There is greatly increased interest in government and academic circles concerning the prospects for multilateral foreign direct investment (FDI) rules along the lines of a 'GATT for Investment'. The recently completed Uruguay Round negotiations brought FDI issues within the domain of the General Agreement on Tariffs and Trade (GATT) and its successor the World Trade Organisation (WTO), and in the Organisation for Economic Cooperation and Development (OECD) discussions are continuing on the possibility of a Multilateral Agreement Investment (MAI). The feasibility of further multilateral FDI policy developments clearly depends upon similarities of interests between major actors, and since the European Union (EU) and the USA account for about 70 per cent of the world stock of inward investment (UN-TCMD, 1993), agreement between these two parties will be critical. This chapter, therefore, attempts to review and evaluate the results of studies on the impact of FDI into the EU and the USA, as well as comparing and contrasting existing and proposed policies, in an attempt to ascertain the possibilities for policy reconciliation in the longer term.

INWARD INVESTMENT IN THE EU AND THE USA

Inward investment has a long history on both sides of the Atlantic. Mira Wilkins identified Singer as the first modern US multinational, noting its initial moves into the UK in the 1850s (Wilkins, 1970; see also Bostock and Jones, 1993). In regard to the reverse flow, J. & P. Coats (now part of Coats Viyella) was the pioneering British manufacturing company in America whose initial expansion abroad preceded that of Singer, while British headquartered insurance companies inaugurated their US branches in 1851.

The most recent and large scale phase of US FDI into Europe began over 40 years ago and in the recent period, at least, relationships have been chiefly benign: manufacturing investment has mostly been in high technology industries and involved greenfield projects where economic benefits may be more obviously assumed. The boom in FDI into the USA was more recent and took a different form with a higher proportion of acquisitions (see, for example, Young and Hood, 1980): just over 60 per cent of outlays were spent on acquisitions in 1982–3, but 80–90 per cent in the years 1986–90 before falling back in the early 1990s (Caves, 1993; US Department of Commerce, 1993); much of this was highly visible, involving leading brand names in a number of sectors and prominent property investments.

Recent data on the inward and outward investment positions of the EU and the USA are summarised in Tables 12.1–12.3. As at 1992 the outward investment stake of the EU totalled $844mn, as compared with a figure of $767m. for inward investment; the equivalent figures for the USA were $489m. and $420m respectively (Table 12.1). The EU and the USA are the largest investors in each other's markets: the EU accounted for 52 per cent of the total stock of FDI in the USA in 1992, while America represented approximately 26 per cent of FDI into the EU in that same year. Manufacturing industry is especially important in transatlantic investment, while petroleum FDI from the EU represents a very high proportion of the sectoral total in the USA. Interestingly, EU investment into America is surpassed by Japan in the real estate sector only. Despite this latter point, much of the debate in the United States has revolved around the impact of Japanese FDI. Data on Japanese investment, summarised in Table 12.3, reveal that the cumulative capital inflow into North America was more than double that into Europe at end 1993 and flow data show a widening gap, confirming that North America continues to be the preferred location.

From its earliest period – pre the Second World War – Japanese investment into the USA has been trade related (Wilkins, 1989, 1990; Caves, 1993), and studies by Kogut and Chung (1991) and Hennart and Park (1992) have shown the significant positive effect of quantitative trade restrictions on the levels of this FDI from Japan. Thomsen (1993) argues that trade barriers may not be driving Japanese investment into Europe and at best merely serve to accelerate a process clearly underway. Statistics on trade between Japan and the EU and the USA indicate that the trade imbalance is little different in the two areas, which might seem to suggest that stronger protectionist forces in the USA at least partially account for differences in recent FDI flows; certainly Japanese inward investment into America has been intricately bound up with the continuing problems between the two countries on trade relations, market access and balance of payments issues. There is perhaps further confirmation of this suggestion from Table 12.3, which presents the industry breakdown of Japanese FDI in Europe and North America: manufacturing investment represents a higher proportion of the total in North

Table 12.1 FDI inward and outward stock for the EU and the USA, 1980, 1985, 1990 and 1992

	Inward stock ($USmn)				Outward stock ($USmn)			
	1980	1985	1990	1992	1980	1985	1990	1992
EU	175 810	212 068	678 678	767 429	206 003	271 056	707 316	843 894
of which								
France	22 617	33 392	86 513	119 198	23 604	37 077	110 126	160 897
Germany (W)	36 630	36 926	119 619	129 606	43 127	59 909	151 581	178 682
Italy	8892	18 977	57 985	62 740	6970	16 301	56 105	68 718
Netherlands	19 167	25 071	33 188	83 733	42 116	47 810	108 438	131 730
Spain	5141	8939	66 276	97 888	1226	2076	14 987	23 322
UK	63 014	62 561	203 905	173 254	80 729	101 195	229 308	221 197
USA	83 046	184 615	394 911	419 526	220 178	251 034	431 689	488 767
Share of world total (%)								
EU	35.0	28.4	39.8	39.4	40.7	40.2	42.9	43.7
USA	16.5	24.8	23.2	21.5	43.5	37.2	26.2	25.3

Notes: See UNCTAD (1994), Annex Tables 3 and 4.

Source: UNCTAD (1994).

Table 12.2 FDI position at year end 1992, EU in USA and USA in EU

EU outward FDI in USA ($ USmn)	All industries of which	Petroleum	Manufacturing	Banking and financial services	Real estate
EU total	219 539	27 301[a]	95 938	29 338[b]	10 408[c]
of which					
France	23 808	3233	14 121	414	105
Germany (W)	29 205	-172	15 050	3498	1 071
Netherlands	61 341	12 373	21 442	10 133	4 611
UK	94 718	11 863	42 208	13 378	4 414
EU as share of total FDI in USA (%)	52.3	70.8	60.2	43.2	29.5
USA outward FDI in EU ($ USmn)					
EU total	200 535	17 305[d]	88 841[e]	56 472[f]	n.a.
of which					
France	23 257	n.a.	13 975	2 700	n.a.
Germany (W)	35 393	2111	20 951	6 667	n.a.
Netherlands	19 114	1 465	7 216	5 064	n.a.
UK	77 842	13 153	20 328	34 560	n.a.
EU as share of total FDI from USA (%)	41.2	31.3	47.4	36.9	n.a.

Notes: a Excludes Belgium, Ireland, Luxembourg.
    b Excludes Belgium, Denmark, Ireland, Italy, Spain for some items.
    c Excludes Ireland.
    d Excludes Denmark, France, Greece, Portugal.
    e Excludes Belgium, Denmark, Greece, Portugal for some items.
    f Figures for banking and financial services also include real estate.
    n.a. not available.

Source: US Department of Commerce (1993).

Table 12.3 Japanese FDI, cumulative total, 1993, Europe and North America

Industry/region	Europe [a]		North America [a]	
	Amount ($ USmn)	% of total	Amount ($ USmn)	% of total
All industries	83 637	100.0	184 868	100.0
Manufacturing of which	19 372	23.2	54 514	29.5
Electric machinery	5675	6.8	14 152	7.7
Non-manufacturing of which	61 859	74.0	128 637	69.6
Banking and Insurance	30 677	36.7	25 181	13.6
Real estate	10 265	12.3	42 611	23.0

Note: a All industries total includes manufacturing and non-manufacturing plus balancing figures relating to branch openings/expansions and real estate acquisitions.

Source: JETRO.

America. What is also interesting is the significant share of total FDI into real estate in North America, partly explaining the greater visibility of foreign investment in the latter area.

THE IMPACT OF INWARD INVESTMENT IN THE EU AND THE USA

As a consequence of the factors outlined above, the subject of the impact of inward investment has attracted much more attention in the USA than in the EU in recent years. Some of the writings on the subject in the USA have been almost hysterical, with apocalyptic claims of 'a colony in the making' (Prestowitz, 1988, p. 308), while anti-Japanese sentiment was fuelled by best selling novelist Michael Crichton in *Rising Sun* (1992). The most influential work from an academic and policy perspective is more balanced, and the approach taken here at both American and European ends emphasises orthodox economic analyses. In Europe, the work of authors such as Dunning (UK), Van Den Bulcke (Belgium), Simoes (Portugal), Michalet (France) and others is well known (see the contributions of these authors in Dunning, 1985). In the USA, prominent recent contributions include those of Graham and Krugman (1991); Reich (1991a); Glickman and Woodward (1989); Wilkins (1989);[1] and Tyson (1992).

It is important to acknowledge initially that there are important areas of similarity in the findings on the two sides of the Atlantic. The respected US work of Graham and Krugman (1991) concludes that:

A careful assessment of the evidence on FDI in the United States does not justify tremendous worry about its economic effects. Most of these effects are in fact beneficial. (p. 84)

The comparisons with the conclusions of the Steuer Report on the UK (Steuer *et al.* 1973) are worth noting:

concerns over the multinational firm and inward investment on the grounds of monopoly power, technology and the balance of payments are not well founded. At the same time, some drawbacks have been indicated, as well as a substantial amount of uncertainty with respect to . . . [the] findings. (p. 12)

In both regions there is a recognition of the fundamental importance of competitiveness, and therefore of public and private investment in education and training, and communications infrastructure to attract and retain high value added investments of whatever nationality: the argument was popularised in the USA in Reich's 'Who is Us?' (1990; see also his follow-up 'Who is Them?', 1991b). Similarly, concerns have been expressed in both areas about the higher import propensities of inward investors, (especially the Japanese in the US case); and in America the benefits of increased domestic sourcing have been seen as being diluted by the *keiretsu* procurement policies of Japanese investors.

There are also a number of notable divergencies in conclusions concerning impact, as highlighted in Table 12.4. As pointed out previously the dominance of the acquisition entry route and the alleged 'fire-sale' of US assets has been widely discussed in America and fears expressed even by balanced writers. In the EU, there was a huge amount of cross-border activity of all types in the run up to the commencement of the Single Market. Many of the acquisition projects were, however, intra-European as non-EU companies sought entry into the Union and EU companies restructured to enhance competitiveness. While specific cases have raised concerns, and doubts have been raised about the effects of takeovers in Less Favoured Regions (LFRs) (Ashcroft and Love, 1993) and more generally (Hamill and Castledine, Chapter 5 in this volume), less attention has been paid to the acquisition issue in the EU than in the USA. Of course in some Continental European countries hostile takeover bids are difficult because of company law, the small size of capital markets and the long-term aims of banks and institutional shareholders (Woolcock, 1991). The UK and USA are more similar in terms of relatively open markets for takeover activity.

A related area of divergence concerns wage and value added differentials between indigenous and foreign firms. With the high level of acquisitions, no systematic differences exist on an ownership basis in the USA. In European countries, foreign affiliates generally record higher productivity ratios

Table 12.4 The impact of inward investment in the EU and USA, major areas of divergence

EU	Economic effects	USA
• Acquisition entry and expansion an 'issue' in specific cases only • Wages and value added generally higher in foreign firms • Impact of inward investment in LFRs a cause for concern (linked to effects of SEM and progress to EMU) • Long-term developmental impacts of inward investment limited at country/regional level • Focus on the nature of the MNE subsidiary and its impact • Japanese investment has had a favourable demonstration effect on management practices in EU industry • Limited comment on transfer pricing or tax avoidance issues		• High level of acquisitions and acquisition price a concern for some writers • No systematic differences • Inward investment reinforcing growth of Sunbelt states • Little discussion or evaluation • Little discussion (but see Reich, 1990) • Concerns over Japanese *keiretsu* procurement practices, and displacement effects on indigenous industry, e.g. in autos • Results of some work consistent with transfer price manipulation

	Political effects	
• Discussion of political economy of inward investment varies between EU countries		• Political influence of foreign firms a potential source of economic costs

	National security effects	
• Little systematic discussion or evaluation		• Important concerns relating to technology dependence, etc.

and pay higher wages than their indigenous competitors – the French case may be an exception (Michalet and Chevallier, 1985). The favourable demonstration effects of Japanese management and labour practices on indigenous firms have been widely acknowledged in Europe, but rather less so in the USA, where Glickman and Woodward (1989) remarked on the uneven labour relations record of the Japanese.

The regional impacts of inward investment are also perceived substantially differently in the EU and USA. Glickman and Woodward's (1989) work on the regional aspects of FDI in America confirms earlier studies in highlighting the Sunbelt state bias in new plant and expansion activity. While they raise various negative aspects, the general conclusion is that inward investment is reinforcing the growth of the Sunbelt states on the back of their good market access, low labour costs and low levels of unionisation ('right-to-work' laws having a significant influence in regard to the latter). Among less favoured regions (LFRs) (essentially regions in peripheral EU countries), there are strong and continuing concerns about the 'embeddedness' of MNE subsidiaries (Amin *et al.* 1994) and their long-term impact (Young, Hood and Peters, 1994). Part of the difference in attitudes and approaches undoubtedly stems from the fact that the EU is comprised of sovereign nations: individual countries and regions thus seek fully integrated business operations, whereas multinationals may exploit differential national advantages by spatially separating different business functions. The position is further complicated by Single Market effects and the potential impacts of economic and monetary union in the Union, with fears that the LFRs may lose out from the process of integration in which MNEs will have a major role (Young and Hood, 1993). Some of the same fears are in fact beginning to surface in connection with the debate on the North American Free Trade Agreement (NAFTA). There has been considerable discussion in newspaper articles, TV broadcasts and unpublished papers on the effects of FDI (inward and outward) and trade on the economies of particular states and regions in the USA, with each congressman having to be convinced that it would be of benefit to his locality.[2] As an aside, the whole question of regional adjustment in the USA and EU is an extremely interesting one. Because of greater flexibility, especially in terms of labour migration, convergence between states in the US is a good deal more advanced than between regions in the Union (Shepley and Wilmot, 1992): there are no persistent divergencies of unemployment rates from the national average, and *per capita* income levels are rather similar. In the circumstances the potential centrifugal or centripetal effects of MNEs in the EU are much greater.

The other major issues, which have been stressed more strongly in America than in Europe, concern the political and national security implications of rising foreign involvement in the respective economies. In the USA, there are claims that Japanese firms, for example, have an excessive influence on the political process, but research is still lacking. In the EU it is difficult to discern consistent views on this topic, the position being complicated by divergent attitudes between countries and over time and the incident-specific/case related nature of any discussions. National security concerns have scarcely been raised in Europe (hardly surprising perhaps, given the technological and military dependence of the area) whereas these are paramount in the USA, especially linked to the wider theme of competitiveness in high technology industries. Even balanced writers acknowledge possible problems associated with foreign affiliates as a 'fifth column' and there are worries that the US affiliate's link with the parent could be broken when the US is militarily dependent on critical items or technologies. Fears are also expressed about the effects of foreign takeovers in high technology industries such as semiconductors on US commercial and defence interests.

Overall, it is apparent that there are significantly different economic and political perspectives on a range of inward investment issues on the two sides of the Atlantic, which inevitably feed into policy, as the following sections reveal.

INWARD INVESTMENT POLICY IN THE EU AND THE USA

The fact that both the EU countries and the USA are members of multilateral organisations like the GATT, WTO and OECD, and general support for the principles of free trade and investment means that policies and especially actions towards FDI *per se* do not differ greatly in many respects. Since the two blocs are the major investors in each other's markets, they have a mutual interest in open and free markets. And they are subject to the arbitrage pressures which have seen a process of gradual convergence of FDI policies world-wide. In highlighting policy similarities and differences, it is important to recognise initially that there is no FDI Policy in the EU. There does not even exist a current statement of principles governing Union attitudes to foreign direct investment and multinational enterprises (Young and Hood, 1993; Brewer and Young, 1994). There are many policies in areas like competition, internal trade and factor movements, research and technology, and regional and social affairs which impact upon MNEs. In each of these, either the EU or its member states may have 'competence' or competence may be shared. This issue of competence has come to the fore with the introduction of the principle of 'subsidiarity' into EU law by Article 36 of the Treaty of European Union (the Maastricht Treaty) of 1992, essentially allowing member states to challenge European Commission competence where there is uncertainty about the allocation of responsibilities and to limit any extension of Commission powers. Furthermore, there are no mechanisms for policy coordination on FDI matters, meaning that policy conflicts may occur and indeed some policy issues may 'fall through the cracks' (Brewer and Young, 1994). While not the same level of problem, there are also certain difficulties in the USA with the sub-Federal level of policy. As Woolcock (1991) has pointed out, the US Congress is disinclined to pass legislation which binds states on matters of foreign commercial policy and, for example, the 'national treatment' provisions (that is, foreign firms should not be subject to greater burdens or be granted greater privileges than domestic companies) of the OECD Codes of Liberalisation of Capital Movements and of Current Invisible Operations, do not commit state regulators in the USA.

In respect of policies dealing with FDI *per se*, some member states of the EU still have a variety of controls, principally on inward investment. These rules chiefly relate either to takeovers from outside the country concerned or the EU or sectoral measures in regulated or sensitive industries (where, additionally, reciprocity requirements may prevail). The Commission has for some time attempted to ensure the removal of the most discriminatory of these, such as the authorisation procedures for FDI in France and definitions of control, and UK equity limitations on foreign ownership in British Aerospace plc and Rolls Royce plc (Brewer and Young, 1994). The pattern of sectoral restrictions in the USA is generally similar to that in most EU countries relating, for example, to banking, broadcasting and telecommunications, energy, mining, fishing and both air and maritime transport. Individual US states have the means to impose certain restrictions on investors, too, and these cover some of the same sectors, as well as land, where 30 states restrict foreigners or foreign corporations from owning land (OECD, 1992).

Despite the fact that

> the United States has long been a staunch defender of a liberal and transparent policy towards foreign direct investment, grounded on the principles of national treatment and non-discrimination. (OECD, 1992, p. 31)

National security concerns and a desire to obtain reciprocal treatment led to the passing of the Exon–Florio provision of the 1988 Omnibus Trade and Competitiveness Act. This

> permits the President to intervene with respect to a merger, acquisition or takeover that, in the President's judgement, might threaten the national security of the United States. The Exon–Florio provision is administered by the Committee on Foreign Investment in the United States (CFIUS). (OECD, 1992, p. 32)

However, out of 700 cases notified in the four years to Summer 1992, only one proposed acquisition was blocked and this did not involve an OECD member (Tyson, 1992).

Liberalisation of FDI regimes took place in both the EU and USA in the 1980s and early 1990s as part of general liberalisation trends, as part of the process of deregulation and privatisation and, in the case of the EU, as a component of the process of regional integration. However, this liberalisation has often been accompanied by greater reciprocity requirements (with differing definitions), which provide the basis for greater tensions between the EU and USA (and amongst other countries too). In respect of the EU, the principle of reciprocity is provided for in the Second Banking Directive (adopted on 15 December 1989), requiring reciprocity of treatment in order to obtain a 'single licence' to undertake the whole range of banking activities within the area of the Union. Similar measures are being contemplated for financial services in the USA.

There is not scope in this chapter to review all other areas of policy which impact upon FDI and where differences exist between EU and US approaches. Some comment is, however, necessary on the incentives offered to attract inward investment, which in the EU represent one component of measures designed to assist economic and social cohesion and redress regional imbalances. Despite formal adherence to the principles of 'national treatment', the incentives offered at state and local level in the USA and at regional level in the EU are widely believed to discriminate in favour of inward investors, if only because incentives are targeted towards the latter and MNEs possess greater bargaining power. Inter-state bidding wars have been reported frequently, and probably occurred most intensely and publicly for various automobile investments in America. In the EU, the Commission has set ceilings on the regional incentives (mainly capital grants) that can be offered by member states in an attempt to limit the intensity of competitive bidding. Nevertheless, other incentives may be available in the form of labour related subsidies and infrastructure improvements, and monitoring and enforcement arrangements vary between countries. In the EU, cross-border rationalisation has become another area for competitive bidding in the 1990s. It has been alleged by Graham and Krugman (1991, p. 138) that foreign governments differ from US practice in their propensity to match incentive offers with performance requirements as part of a greater willingness to engage in targeted industrial policy. It is doubtful if this is true in an EU context except for large Japanese investments (where again automobiles is an illustration). Where competitive bidding does differ in the EU is in the range of measures open to national governments. In the recession conditions of the early 1990s economic nationalism was much discussed, with so-called monetary, fiscal and social 'dumping' alleged as a means, *inter alia*, of enticing inward investment (Young and Hood, 1993). For an author such as Safarian (1991) the conclusion was that it would

> be difficult, if not impossible, for the EC to develop the kind of coordination needed. . . . to assure net economic gain for the Community from strategic trade and investment policy. (p. 199)

It is important, finally, to draw attention to trade policy issues which have investment consequences, and especially to the application of anti-dumping legislation where the USA has been much more active than the EU. In the 10 years to end June 1993 the USA initiated 483 anti-dumping cases compared with 252 for the EU, and in the last three of these years the number of cases initiated in America was nearly three times as great as in the EU (*Financial Times*, 1993); these have an influence on FDI even if their motives were different (but see Thomsen, 1993). These differences in levels of activity in the EU and USA may be reduced in future as decisions on Union anti-dumping duties will be taken by the Council of Ministers on a simple majority basis from 1994 (*Financial Times*, 1994a): previously decisions could be blocked by a qualified minority, which was commonly made up of free trade-oriented nations like Germany, the UK, the Netherlands and Denmark.

US POLICY PROPOSALS

In considering policy proposals emerging on the basis of the analysis of economic and political impact, this section focuses exclusively on US measures.

This is a reflection, as noted earlier, of the generally positive contribution of FDI in the EU, of the lack of interest and involvement of academics and other analysts in the policy process, and of the issue based (as opposed to company based) approach to policy in both the EU as a whole and member states. By comparison, US concerns have elicited a wide range of new policy ideas as summarised in Table 12.5. These address themselves to the range of potentially negative impacts, and include recommendations for stronger screening and blocking powers for acquisitions, actions to require reciprocity of treatment, a ban on state and city level competitive bidding for inward investment and/or performance requirements to be imposed on firms receiving investment incentives. The Glickman and Woodward (1989) work, with its emphasis on regional impacts and policies, addresses some issues which are at the forefront of attention in Europe too, particularly in their call for plant closure legislation and exit policies. The proposal was to double the required notice for closures among large US and foreign firms from 60 to 120 days; and to provide aid for dislocated workers in the form of job training with income support during training, education and relocation assistance, and help with job counselling, job search and job placement. The authors also argued that cities suffering from large-scale plant closures should be eligible for federal government adjustment assistance. Glickman and Woodward acknowledged that this was not simply a problem in the USA but in Europe too as companies rationalised in the Single Market, and their proposals have a European parallel in the Protocol on Social Policy annexed to the Maastricht Treaty.

Reflecting their view that the only valid economic fears relate to the national security argument, Graham and Krugman (1991) have put forward proposals to maintain specific activities and technologies under domestic ownership and control, signalling therefore the undesirability of takeovers from outside the USA. Where activities or services were monopolised by foreign firms, the suggested solution was compulsory licensing to a domestic producer, or mandatory foreign investment allied to local content requirements (including provision that R & D capabilities be maintained in the USA), or the promotion of a domestic 'national champion' as a second source supply base. Similar arguments have been presented by Tyson (1992) as part of her 'cautious activist agenda' for US policy in high technology industries.

What is most interesting from the perspective of this chapter, however, is the attention being paid in the USA (as in the EU indeed) to multilateral policy actions and especially to the idea of a 'GATT for Investment'. As is well known, the 1948 Havana Charter proposed an International Trade Organisation (ITO) as one organisational component of an international system of cooperation and regulation which would have complemented the IMF and the IBRD. The ITO would have had much more extensive authority than the GATT including provisions concerning FDI, but the proposal foundered (Kline, 1993). The revival of interest in multilateral policy reflects the fact

Table 12.5 US policy proposals

National Policy and Inward Investment	See summaries in Encarnation (1992) and Graham and Krugman (1991)
Organisational arrangement • 'Board of Knowledgeables' to approve all foreign purchases irrespective of size	Forbes (1988) (see also Tolchin and Tolchin, 1988; Prestowitz, 1988) Glickman and Woodward (1989)
• Multinational Investment Review Agency and Department of Research (MIRADOR) as an information, watchdog and screening agency of Federal government	
Disclosure • As above, plus strong sentiment among some in Congress in support of increased disclosure	
Screening • As above but including other writers – screening (and blocking powers) would operate for both foreign acquisitions and new establishments	Glickman and Woodward (1989) Rohatyn (1988)
• Monitoring of foreign oligopolistic control in high tech industries	Tyson (1992)
• Stronger competition policy to discourage uncompetitive practices and unproductive merger and acquisition activity	Glickman and Woodward (1989)
Reciprocity • Foreign-controlled firms in the USA would be subject to same treatment under US law that US firms receive abroad	Prestowitz (1988), and others
• US/Japanese joint enforcement of anti-trust laws with regard to *keiretsu* behaviour	Bergsten and Noland (1993); Tyson (1992)
• Selective reciprocity for trade policy in high tech industries	
State and local policies • US Investment Representative to bar state and cities from bidding for investment	Reich (1991a)
• Objections to state incentives as 'subsidies to business'	Ulan (1991)
Performance requirements • Performance requirements to be imposed on firms receiving investment incentives	Glickman and Woodward (1989)
• Performance requirements on Japanese firms to improve economic benefits for US economy	Prestowitz (1988)
• While rejected in general, specific possibilities associated with investment in industries linked to national security interests	Graham and Krugman (1991)
Exit policy and plant closing legislation • Uniform national standard for plant closures and layoffs for large firms, e.g.	Glickman and Woodward (1989)

120-day advance notice of plant closure,
job severance pay, adjustment assistance
to workers and communities

National security
- Graham and Krugman (1991) reject most　　　Graham and Krugman (1991)
  of above in favour of multilateral policy
  action and domestic national security
  policies
  Latter would include domestic ownership
  and control of some activities and banning
  of takeovers; in other sectors, mandatory
  investment plus performance requirements

National Policy and US Competitiveness

- Public sector investment in commercial　　　Reich (1990)
  R & D; upgrading and expanding the
  national infra-structure; increased
  expenditures on education and training

Multilateral Policy and FDI

- GATT for investment: major item on　　　Reich (1990);
  agenda of most influential writers,　　　Graham and Krugman (1991);
  reflecting need for US to consider　　　Bergsten (1988);
  implications of outward investment　　　Bergsten and Noland (1993)
  policies on inward investment and
  vice versa

---

that the USA is now not only the major outward direct investor but also the largest single host nation to inward direct investment, requiring consideration of the implications of its outward FDI policies on inward FDI and vice versa. There are also strongly political elements in this new found interest, especially the aim of improving access to the Japanese market, and controlling the alleged undesirable elements of Japanese investment in the USA. The time is believed to be opportune given moves to common policies on a minilateral[3] (e.g. North American Free Trade Agreement (NAFTA) and EU Single Market) basis and generally more open investment policies around the world. Thus NAFTA, according to Gestrin and Rugman (1994), has substantially liberalised North American investment regimes, establishing a clear, rules based framework for the impartial treatment of FDI. Rules on performance requirements, which are more stringent than those emerging from the Uruguay Round agreements, and an investor–state dispute settlement mechanism have been established.

Some of the ideas emerging from the USA as constituents of multilateral policy action include the following:

- Granting of right of establishment and national treatment to foreign affiliates in host countries

- Acceptance of home nation rights and responsibilities in terms of protection of property abroad
- Commitment by MNEs that subsidiaries obey the laws of jurisdictions in which they are located
- Compliance by MNEs with specified international, non-discriminatory rules on disclosure and reporting (applying to all enterprises above a certain size)
- Restrictions on the use of performance requirements – basically forbidding new performance requirements and banning or phasing out existing requirements except, for example, those necessary for reasons of national security
- Limitations on the use of investment incentives
- Strengthening of competition policy (linked to *keiretsu* behaviour, as discussed earlier, to global joint venture activity, and to hostile foreign acquisitions).

The way in which such elements might be included within a multilateral policy structure is perceived differently by different authors. Graham and Krugman (1991) seem to foresee an international accord covering all the above issues (except mergers and restrictive business practices), with an additional framework to include other aspects such as taxation, anti-trust, pollution and environmental standards, security export control, product safety and liability standards, etc. These latter issues would be the subject of consultation and cooperation among national authorities, which might or might not be embodied in codes. To Kline (1993) the way ahead was seen initially in the formulation of a comprehensive voluntary code for multinational business, using the voluntary OECD Code (OECD, 1976; see also OECD, 1992) as a starting point, but extending its geographical coverage and its scope. The proposed UN Code of Conduct was rejected as a way forward because of concern over 'ghosts from the past' (UNCTC, 1990). Recognising that the same difficulties in achieving a political consensus will delay progress on any new comprehensive multilateral policy approach, Kline (1993) calls for 'practical mechanisms to reduce intergovernmental friction and resolve disputes over particular policy differences' (p. 162); while others are more focused and see the intermediate situation as involving an attack on key elements such as trade related investment measures (TRIMs), despite the limited progress made during the GATT Uruguay Round negotiations.

PROSPECTS FOR TRANSATLANTIC INWARD INVESTMENT
POLICY

As pointed out in the introduction to this chapter, FDI issues are currently high on the agendas of both the GATT/WTO and the OECD. The latter has had an FDI remit since its inception, but the OECD has entered a new phase in its history through its discussions of a Multilateral Agreement on Investment (MAI), and a decision was taken in summer 1995 to move ahead to formal negotiations. FDI issues are also formally within the remit of the GATT/WTO as a result of the Uruguay Round agreements. Upon ratification of these agreements and the formal establishment of the WTO, member governments' FDI measures in services will be subject to WTO discipline through the General Agreement on Trade in Services (GATS); and disputes concerning investment matters will be subject to the new WTO dispute settlement procedures (Brewer and Young, 1994, 1995). There are questions about whether the OECD or WTO (or perhaps even the World Bank) would be the most appropriate organisational base: the view within the European Commission seems to be that agreement on a higher standard of rules and in a shorter period of time would be easier within the relatively more homogeneous group of OECD nations, although in the long term the WTO forum was preferable; American preference is apparently to operate through the OECD, but the USA is unlikely to take an assertive and activist position on FDI discussions before the next Presidential election (Brewer and Young, 1995).

The policy categories that have become standard concerns in multilateral FDI discussions concern, first, the liberalisation of government restrictions on the entry and treatment of foreign direct investors; second, investment protection obligations including provisions on expropriation, compensation and transfer of funds; and, third, dispute settlement procedures. All of these policy categories are covered in some way in existing multilateral agreements in the GATT/WTO and OECD. The devil, as always, lies in the details. Focusing solely upon liberalisation, to date this has been linked chiefly to the issues of the right of establishment, national treatment and most favoured nation treatment. There is much work to be done in extending and clarifying these principles and in gradually rolling back existing restrictions. For example, the OECD's National Treatment instrument (OECD, 1993) does not prohibit reciprocity measures, but rather treats them as one type of exception to National Treatment. As earlier comments revealed, a creeping extension of reciprocity provisions raises the prospect of policy conflict between the EU and the USA.

However, if progress is to be made towards a wider multilateral investment agreement, negotiations will have to extend into policy areas relating to specific aspects of firms' conduct and behaviour. According to authors such as Ostry (1992) (see also Brewer and Young, 1995), these areas might include competition policy, R & D policy and financial market regulations as well as issues like public procurement, state ownership and privatisation, and both incentives and disincentives and performance requirements. Woolcock (1991) has considered a number of these in a trade policy context as non-tariff barriers and has highlighted the potential for tension or conflict between the EU and the USA. In the field of public purchasing, a GATT Code on Procurement Practices exists to deal with trade aspects, but it has had rather limited effect and there are big differences between the EU and US approaches and positions. The EU introduced a number of Directives aimed at liberalising procurement, and extended these as part of the Single Market programme to include both central and local government, public and private utilities and services. Efforts are also being made to ensure effective compliance, which is still a major problem. In the USA, by contrast, there are numerous restrictions on open public purchasing, many of which are based on national security. The 1937 'Buy America' Act (revised in the 1988 Omnibus Trade and Competitiveness Act) provides a range of price preferences for US products in most federal purchasing and in sectors like transportation and power; 37 states also have 'Buy America' legislation. On the basis of these different approaches, Woolcock (1991) notes significant differences in negotiating positions in trade policy, with the EU seeking to extend its comprehensive regime to multilateral level, while the USA has a much narrower focus. Similar problems would clearly arise in FDI negotiations.

As regards competition policy, the principal issues concern the similarities and differences between policies in the two regions, extra-territoriality in US and European Union law and coordination and conflict resolution. Comanor *et al.* (1990) have suggested that the pace of enforcement has accelerated in the EU at the same time as the effectiveness of antitrust enforcement has declined in the USA. Given the concerns about the impact of foreign acquisitions in both areas, there would seem to be a need for further study, the results of which could then form the basis for perhaps widening the criteria by which takeovers are judged. To avoid non-discrimination any revisions to competition law would need to apply to all takeovers, domestic and foreign. In respect of potential conflicts, Neven and Siotis (1993) have identified a number of instances where anti-trust bodies in USA, Europe and third countries might reach a different decision regarding particular foreign investments, although the general view is that the objectives of US and EU authorities are reasonably similar, except in respect of the use of industrial policy arguments in Union law. The major issue is, thus, extra-territoriality where both US and EU laws extend in principle beyond national borders. Criticisms of the application of US extra-territorial provisions have led to greater flexibility over time, and the present position is that courts on both sides of the Atlantic have taken into account the interests of foreigners but are not committed to do so. The view seems to be that a centralisation of competition policy involving the USA and EU might not be appropriate, but that attempts should be made to improve the coordination of the present decentralised policies by designing objective criteria to allocate jurisdictions (Neven and Siotis, 1993). Competition policies in both areas are, of course, far from perfect (see, for example, recent criticisms of EU competition law by the Confederation of British Industry, *Financial Times*, 1994b); but the introduction of stronger screening and blocking powers for foreign takeovers in the USA as advocated by several writers would clearly be unhelpful and would hamper subsequent efforts to improve integration or coordination of policies between the USA and the EU.

The potential for policy difficulties between the USA and the Union (and indeed between states and countries within these regions) undoubtedly exists for investment incentives and performance requirements. At American insistence, reflecting the views summarised earlier in this chapter, TRIMs were explicitly included on the agenda of the Uruguay Round negotiations (for a full discussion of TRIMs, see UNCTC, 1990). Local content requirements had in fact been found to be contrary to Article III (national treatment) of the GATT in an earlier case involving the Canadian Foreign Investment Review Agency (Greenaway, 1993). In the Uruguay Round the incompatibility of certain TRIMs with Article III as well as with Article XI (prohibition of quantitative restrictions) was confirmed (GATT, 1993). The offending TRIMs included measures which required particular levels of local procurement by an enterprise ('local content requirements') or which restricted the volume or value of imports ('trade balancing requirements'). The agreement required mandatory notification of all non-conforming TRIMs and their elimination within two years for developed countries, with a Committee on TRIMs monitoring the implementation of these commitments.

In relation to the GATT performance requirements, the view in the EU is that these are trade measures, and that any such measures relating, for example, to the local content of Japanese investors in the EU are bilateral and voluntary. Yet performance requirements, and especially performance requirements linked to investment incentives, would need to be included in any FDI agreements. The performance requirements provisions of NAFTA go beyond those of the Uruguay Round agreements, but, as Gestrin and Rugman (1994) point out, government support, linked to the location of production, the training and employment of workers, the conduct of R & D, etc. is permitted. In a sense, this is not far away from the EU position on investment incentives which are basically an arm of regional policy. In reviewing the current situation, the present authors have argued the case for greater transparency, greater guidance on acceptable forms of incentives, greater monitoring, and regular reviews of assisted areas (Young and Hood, 1993). Within such a guided framework, it should be possible to reduce the overall level of incentives; the aim would be to lower overall costs to Union and national taxpayers and to avoid the implicit discrimination which arises because some countries (e.g. Portugal) that are permitted to offer the highest rates of grants sometimes cannot afford to do so. Once again this might be acceptable in principle to the USA. On the other hand, there is now great interest in the EU in going much further, with the aim of improving the economic benefits associated with multinational activity which to date have been shown to be primarily short-term and static. The present authors have suggested, for example, that:

there should certainly be attempts to link incentives to the nature of the project as a form of performance requirement (rationalised production affiliates vs. world product specialist affiliate, at the extreme). Essentially, the EU would sanction different types of FDI attraction activity in different groupings of countries beyond joint aid ceilings as a control. These proposals would require much tighter control over regional incentives at Community level, which is necessary to avoid a destructive competitive bidding that benefits only TNCs. (Young and Hood, 1993)

Similar arguments have been presented by Amin *et al.* (1994). Their view is that current levels of regional subsidy (automatic and discretionary) should be cut back in order to reduce competitive bidding for short-term, cost based investment projects, with discretionary awards being tied to 'quality of investment' targets. The Amin *et al.* (1994) belief is that different targets should be set for different types of LFR. So in the 'more advanced' LFRs like Scotland and Ireland, awards might be weighted in favour of rewarding promising spin-offs in the research and supplies linkage potential of inward investment, while in 'less advanced' LFRs like Portugal, the weighting might be biased towards task multiplicity, local decision-making autonomy and skill formation. These viewpoints are clearly different to some of the thinking in the USA, although it has also been suggested within the EU that in the weakest regions consideration might be given to the linking of Union financial assistance for FDI to the condition that no delocalisation occurs within a certain period of time; this is not too far away from the thinking of Glickman and Woodward (1989) regarding exit policy and plant closing legislation.

On a number of the above issues, it might seem that differences in views on the two sides of the Atlantic are not so fundamental as to cause insuperable difficulties. According to Woolcock (1991), the chief problems relate rather to more philosophical issues such as, first, the role of the state in the economy: recent pronouncements on, for example, industrial policy in the EU still reveal stronger socio–political objectives than would be acceptable in the USA. Secondly, it is suggested that the degree of intrusiveness of new regulations in matters such as public procurement in the EU would be unacceptable in America. And thirdly, as noted at the beginning of this section, there is the thorny problem of handling the sub-federal level of regulations and policy in the USA. Even the NAFTA agreement does not appear to prevent individual states from pursuing policies which limit market access.

It is indeed interesting to compare the EU and NAFTA in terms of FDI regimes. Despite the debate over Member State versus EU competence on FDI matters and the absence of an EU FDI policy, there are views in the European Commission that Article 73 of the Treaty on European Union (the Maastricht Treaty) of 1992 could provide the legislative basis for a legal code on FDI or policy harmonisation (Brewer and Young, 1994). The continuing Single Market programme meantime has substantially liberalised goods and services and factor movements across frontiers. NAFTA bears little comparison to the EU. Despite the view of Gestrin and Rugman (1994, p. 92) that:

> New ground has been broken in terms of establishing clear rules, enforceable dispute settlement mechanisms and increased transparency

the fact remains that there are very important exceptions in the FDI rules. A number of sensitive sectors, especially in Mexico, are excluded, the USA maintains its national security provisions under the terms of the Exon–Florio amendment, existing restrictions in the automotive industry will be very gradually phased out, and tight rules of origin exist for particular industries designed to reduce import competition (on an inter-regional basis) for vehicles, textiles, electronics and machine tools. Gestrin and Rugman (1994) observe of the latter that

> their potential to serve protectionist goals and a beggar-thy-neighbour type of quest for manufacturing capital and employment should be considered more carefully. (p. 93)

CONCLUSIONS

This chapter takes a wider view than many others in this volume and underlines the importance of considering European issues within a wider transatlantic and indeed global perspective. There is much debate as to whether regional trade blocs in the world economy are likely to retard or promote global free trade: the pragmatic view of the present authors is that they will facilitate trade liberalisation within defined blocs and thereafter increase pressure on other blocs and other nations and in the process assist freer trade globally. A similar conclusion might be reached in respect of inward investment policy, where developments in the EU and USA/NAFTA have led to greater internal liberalisation, and where now, operating through GATT/WTO and OECD fora, there are hopes of wider liberalisation. Of course the trend towards increased reciprocity requirements is a concern, but such provisions may be regarded as bargaining positions, the outcome of which ultimately may be freer international direct capital movements. Of more concern is the fact that because economic impacts are (or are perceived to be) different in the EU and the USA, as are policy philosophies, progress towards liberalisation on detailed issues will be difficult. It may be, indeed, that resolution of particular internal difficulties will be necessary before broader international agreements are possible: the problem of the sub-federal level of policy in the USA and that of national government versus EU competence needs to be resolved. From an EU perspective only, it may be concluded that just as a Single Market in goods and services is still more of a vision than a reality, so at an international investment level much remains to be done in policy terms to facilitate FDI flows while seeking to improve the contribution of that investment and encouraging economic and social cohesion.

Notes

1. For space reasons the detailed review of studies on the impact of FDI into the USA has been omitted. Interested readers should consult Young, Hood and Hood (1994).
2. We are grateful to Mira Wilkins for drawing our attention to this topic and for suggesting academic contacts in the USA. At the time of writing no systematic studies on the anticipated effects of NAFTA by state and region had been identified.
3. The term 'minilateralism' is used in the context of trade liberalisation in Yarbrough and Yarbrough (1992).

References

Amin, A. *et al.* (1994) 'Regional incentives and the quality of mobile investment in the less favoured regions of the EC', *Progress in Planning* (January).

Ashcroft, B. and Love, J. (1993) *Takeovers, Mergers and the Regional Economy* (Edinburgh: Edinburgh University Press).

Bergsten, C.F. (1988) *America in the World Economy : A Strategy for the 1990s* (Washington, DC: Institute for International Economics) (November).

Bergsten, C.F. and Noland, M. (1993) *Reconcilable Differences? United States–Japan Economic Conflict* (Washington, DC: Institute for International Economics) (June).

Bostock, F. and Jones, G. (1993) 'The Growth of Foreign Multinationals in British Manufacturing 1850–1962', University of Reading *Discussion Papers in International Investment and Business Studies*, Series B VI (181) (Department of Economics, University of Reading) (September).

Brewer, T. and Young, S. (1994) 'European union policies and the problems of multinational enterprises', paper presented at European International Business Association Annual Conference (Warsaw) (December), *Journal of Trade* (forthcoming).

Brewer, T. and Young, S. (1995) 'Towards a new multilateral framework for FDI: issues and scenarios', *Transnational Corporations*, 4(1).

Caves, R.E. (1993) 'Japanese investment in the United States: lessons for the economic analysis of foreign investment', *The World Economy*, 16 (3), pp. 279–300.

Comanor, W.S. with George, K., Jenny, F. and Waverman, L. (1990) 'Conclusions for competition policy', in W.S. Comanor, *et al. Competition Policy in Europe and North America : Economic Issues and Institutions* (Chur: Harwood Academic Publishers).

Crichton, M. (1992) *Rising Sun* (New York: Alfred Knopf).

Dunning, J.H. (ed). (1985) *Multinational Enterprises Economic Structure and International Competitiveness* (Chichester: John Wiley).

Encarnation, D.J. (1992) *Rivals Beyond Trade* (Ithaca: Cornell University Press).

Financial Times (1993) 'Negotiations down in the dumps over US draft' (25 November).

Financial Times (1994a), 'EC to scrap many quotas in overhaul of import regime' (9 February).

Financial Times (1994b) 'A Burden on Business', (1 February).

Forbes, M.S. (1988) 'Fact and comment', *Forbes* (25 January), p. 17.

General Agreement on Tariffs and Trade (GATT) (1993) 'News of the Uruguay round of multilateral trade negotiations', Information and Media Relations Division of the GATT (Geneva) (14 December).

Gestrin, M. and Rugman, A.M. (1994) *The North American Free Trade Agreement and Foreign Direct Investment, Transnational Corporations*, 3 (1), pp. 77–95.

Glickman, N.J. and Woodward, D.P. (1989) *The New Competitors* (New York: Basic Books).

Graham, E.M. and Krugman, P.R. (1991) *Foreign Direct Investment in the United States*, (Washington, DC: Institute for International Economics), 2nd edn.

Greenaway, D. (1993) 'Trade and foreign direct investment', *European Economy*, 52, pp. 103–128.

Hennart, J.-F. and Park, Y.-R. (1992) 'Location, governance and strategic determinants of Japanese manufacturing investment in the United States', *Working Paper* (Champaign, Ill: College of Commerce and Business Administration, University of Illinois).

Kline, J.M. (1993) 'International regulation of transnational business: providing the missing leg of global investment standards', *Transnational Corporations*, 2 (2), pp. 153–64.

Kogut, B. and Chung, S.J. (1991) 'Technological capabilities and Japanese foreign direct investment in the United States', *Review of Economics and Statistics*, 75, pp. 401–13.

Michalet, C.A. and Chevallier, T. (1985) 'France', in J.H. Dunning (ed.), *Multinational Enterprises, Economic Structure and International Competitiveness* (Chichester: John Wiley) pp. 91–125.

Neven, D. and Siotis, G. (1993)'Foreign direct investment in the European Community: some policy issues', *Oxford Review of Economic Policy*, 9 (2), pp. 72–93.

Organisation for Economic Cooperation and Development (OECD) (1976) *International Investment and Multinational Enterprisess* (Paris: OECD).

Organisation for Economic Cooperation and Development (OECD) (1992) *Committee on International Investment and Multinational Enterprises. Feasibility Study of a Wider Investment Instrument* (OECD: Paris) (19 November)

Organisation for Economic Cooperation and Development (OECD) (1993) *National Treatment for Foreign-Controlled Enterprises* (OECD: Paris).

Ostry, S. (1992) 'The domestic domain: the new international policy arena', *Transnational Corporations*, 1 (1), pp. 7–26.

Prestowitz, C.V. Jr (1988) *Trading Places. How We Allowed the Japanese to Take the Lead* (New York: Basic Books).

Reich, R.B. (1990) 'Who is Us?', *Harvard Business Review*, 68 (1), pp. 53–64.

Reich, R.B. (1991a) *The Work of Nations* (London: Simon & Schuster).

Reich, R.B. (1991b) 'Who is Them?', *Harvard Business Review*, 69 (2), pp. 77–88.

Rohatyn, F. (1989) 'America's economic dependence', *Foreign Affairs*, 68 (1), pp. 53–65.

Safarian, A.E. (1991) 'Firm and government strategies', in B. Bürgenmeier and J.L. Muchielli (eds), *Multinationals and Europe 1992*, (London: Routledge), pp. 187–203.

Shepley, S. and Wilmot. J. (1992) 'Europe: core vs periphery', *Towards the 21st Century*, 4 (London: Credit Suisse First Boston).

252 *Transatlantic Perspectives on Inward Investment*

Steuer, M.D. *et al.* (1973) *The Impact of Foreign Direct Investment on the United Kingdom* (London: HMSO).

Thomsen, S. (1993) 'Japanese direct investment in the European Community', *The World Economy*, 16 (3), pp. 301–15.

Tolchin, M. and Tolchin, S. (1988) *Buying into America* (New York: Times Books).

Tyson, L.D. (1992) *Who's Bashing Whom?* (Washington, DC: Institute for International Economics).

Ulan, M. (1991) 'Should the US restrict foreign investment?', *The Annals of the American Academy of Political and Social Science*, 516 (July), pp. 117–25.

UNCTAD (1994) *World Investment Report 1994* (New York and Geneva: UN).

United Nations Centre on Transnational Corporations (UNCTC) (1990) UNCTC Current Studies Series A, 16, *The New Code Environment* (New York: UN).

UN-TCMD (1993) *World Investment Report 1993* (Geneva: UN).

US Department of Commerce (1993) *Survey of Current Business* 176 (3), United States General Printing Office (Washington, DC).

Wilkins, M. (1970) *The Emergence of Multinational Enterprise: American Business Abroad from the Colonial Era to 1914* (Cambridge, Mass: Harvard University Press).

Wilkins, M. (1989) *The History of Foreign Investment in the United States to 1914* (Cambridge, Mass: Harvard University Press).

Wilkins, M. (1990) 'Japanese multinationals in the United States: continuity and change 1870–1990', *Business History Review*, 40, pp. 585–629.

Woolcock, S. (1991) *Market Access Issues in EC–US Relations* (London: Royal Institute of International Affairs/Pinter).

Yarbrough, B.V. and Yarbrough, R.M. (1992) *Cooperation and Governance in International Trade* (Princeton: Princeton University Press).

Young, S. and Hood, N. (1980) 'Recent patterns of investment by British multinational enterprises in the United States', *National Westminster Bank Review* (May).

Young, S. and Hood, N. (1993) 'Inward Investment Policy in the European Community in the 1990s', *Transnational Corporations*, 2 (2), pp. 35–62.

Young, S., Hood, N. and Peters, E. (1994). 'Multinational enterprises and regional economic development', *Regional Studies.*, 28, (7) pp. 657–77.

Young, S., Hood, N. and Hood, C. (1994). 'Transatlantic perspectives on inward investment and prospects for policy reconciliation', Strathclyde International Business Unit, *Working Paper*, 94/3 (Glasgow: University of Strathclyde) (August).

13 Regional and Global Issues in International Business

Peter Buckley

This book is evidence of the growing importance of regional issues within international business (see also Mirza, forthcoming). This summary chapter attempts to focus on the conflicts brought about by regionalisation and globalisation in the context of the world economy.

A SIMPLE MODEL OF THE WORLD ECONOMY

Figure 13.1 shows a highly stylised picture of the global economy. It attempts to focus attention on the different degrees of integration across various types of market. It suggests that financial markets are largely unified globally so that world financial markets can, for many purposes, be regarded as a single market. Markets for goods and services are differentiated on a regional basis, with 'single markets' either existing or emerging across identifiable regions. The European Union (EU) 'Single Market' is the best example of such a convergence but, over time, it may be rivalled by developments throughout the Americas based on the expansion of NAFTA and by initiatives in Asian regions. Such regional markets are becoming increasingly uniform in regulation, standards, codes of practice (e.g. anti-trust) and business behaviour and so they offer increasing possibilities of economies of scale in production and distribution across the market but are substantially differentiated by these factors (and possibly by a common external tariff (CET)) from other regional markets. Some commentators (including Young *et al.* in Chapter 12 in this volume) are reasonably sanguine that regional trade liberalisation is a step towards world free trade. Others are not so sure and see 'Fortress Europe' as an outcome of inward-looking integration policies – a model likely to be followed by other regions. Labour markets, however, remain predominantly national. Governments wish to regulate their own national labour market and to differentiate it (protect it) from neighbouring labour markets even within regional economic units. Many of the current difficulties in governmental regulatory policies stem from the difficulties arising from the attempt to pursue independent labour market policies in the context of regional goods and services markets and a global capital market. Perhaps the best example is the UK's 'opt out' from the

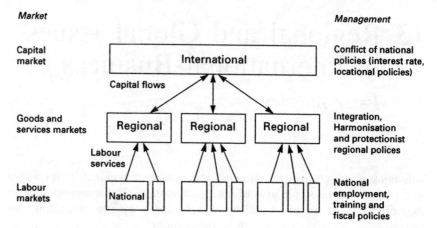

Figure 13.1 Internationalisation of firms – conflict of markets

Maastricht Treaty's 'Social Chapter'. This is a clear attempt to pursue a different labour market policy from the majority of the Member States of the EU. The UK's desire for a more unregulated labour market is, of course, linked to its attempt to remain the favoured location for foreign direct investment (FDI) into the EU.

In contrast to the problems of governments attempting to protect a national economic space, multinational enterprises are perfectly placed to exploit the differences in the international integration of markets. The existence of an international market for capital drives capital costs to a minimum. The existence of regional goods and services markets enables firms to exploit economies of scale across 'single markets'. Differentiated labour markets enable costs to be reduced by locating the labour intensive stages of production in cheap labour countries. Horizontal integration is facilitated by regional goods and services markets, vertical integration by differentiated labour markets and the spatial distribution of key raw materials.

Policy decisions by governments and regional bodies must confront these realities if they are to have any chance for success. As chapters in the book have illustrated, policies on employment, on control of monopoly (and takeovers) and cartels (even those under the more attractive title of alliances), on technology policy and regulatory issues are bedevilled by the fact that many of the key variables are outside the control of any individual political unit.

EAST AND CENTRAL EUROPE

The end of the 'cold war' and the liberalisation of East and Central Europe have brought great opportunities for international business (Buckley and Ghauri, 1991). The same events potentially threaten to destroy stability in the world economy. The management of a course through this rough sea is a primary task of the global community. One key element is the role of FDI in aiding the regeneration of the shattered economies of East and Central Europe. FDI represents a package of resources including capital, technology, management and organisational skills. Each of these is sorely needed in emergent economies. What is perhaps even more important is the transformation of business culture – from producer-dominated to consumer-responsive and from robber baron, Mafia-style opportunism to responsible long-term planning. Foreign direct investment can be a major conduit for such a transformation (Casson, 1994). The joint venture can thus become a role model in transforming emergent economies. The extent to which inward investors can assume such a role will be a major determinant of the future development of the economies of East and Central Europe. The strategies of privatisation and buyouts discussed in this book are technical devices which provide the means for a fertile, honest business culture to develop but, as the authors show, these are only planks in a wider programme of fundamental reform.

THE EXCLUDED – REGIONS AND DEVELOPING COUNTRIES

As with all partial changes, regional integration has very different effects on those included in the emerging blocks and those outside them. The successful regional bodies, essentially NAFTA and the EU, in the developed world are paralleled to only a limited extent in the developing world. Mercosur (Mercosul) in Latin America and ASEAN in Asia are role models for developing country integration. There are many more moves towards integration, particularly within Asia, but the ability of countries to integrate at vastly different levels of economic development has yet to be fully tested. The extension of NAFTA to Mexico is such a test, as is the potential accession of Chile and the ability of the APEC (Asia Pacific Economic Cooperation) forum to achieve concrete results is of immense importance.

The avenues for development of the developing world will be considerably reduced should regionalism become 'closed' rather than open to widening trade (Garnaut and Drysdale, 1994).

CONCLUSIONS

The implications of 'Europe in transition' for international business are immense at several levels. First, for Europe itself, the integration project has economic and political ramifications, which affect the lives of all EU citizens. Second, for the potential applicants around the Mediterranean, through Central and Eastern Europe (and because of Russia) through to the Pacific, the degree of openness to new entrants will determine the political and development prospects for more than one continent. A crucial issue here is the cultural and religious diversity of the future EU. Is the EU to be synonymous with Christendom of old? The potential accession of Turkey poses an immediate question of relevance to the whole of North Africa and, potentially, the Middle East and Israel. Third, is the EU to be defined in opposition to other regional blocs? Competition between regions is to some degree inevitable but the future can also be cooperative as well as competitive. The consolidation of regions can be a move away from free trade as well as a move towards a barrier free trading world. Finally, the relationship between those in one or more 'rich men's clubs' and the remainder of the world is as problematic now as in the days of empire and colonialism. The issues discussed in this book can justly claim to be universal, and unresolved.

References

Buckley, P.J. and P.N. (eds) (1994) *The Economics of Change in East and Central Europe* (London: Academic Press).

Casson, M. (1994) 'Enterprise culture and institutional change in Eastern Europe', in P.J. Buckley and P.N. Ghauri, *The Economics of Change in East and Central Europe* (London: Academic Press).

Garnaut, R. and Drysdale, P. (1994) *Asia Pacific Regionalism* (Pymble, Australia: Harper Educational).

Mirza, H. (forthcoming) *Beyond Protectionism: The Strategic Responses of Transnational Firms to the Regionalisation of the World Economy* (Cheltenham: Edward Elgar).

Index

acquisitions *see* cross-border; foreign
Africa 2, 256
Albania 170, 177, 179, 180
Alchian, A.A. 156, 158
Alexander, N. 66
Allen, D. 197
Amin, A. 187, 236, 248
Aoki, M. 109, 157
APEC *see* Asia Pacific Economic
    Cooperation
Armenia 170, 175
ASEAN *see* Association of South
    East Asian Nations
Ashcroft, B. 91, 96, 235
Asia 253, 255
  competitiveness policy 12
  research and development spending
    as percentage of gross national
    product 8
  see also East
Asia Pacific Economic
    Cooperation 255
Asia-Pacific region 186
Association of South East Asian
    Nations 255
Australia 88, 90, 95
Austria 1
automatic teller machines (ATMs) 47,
    48, 49
autonomy effects 102
Azerbajian 170

Bailey, M.J. 196
balance of payments 28, 99–100
balance of trade 8, 28
Balough, R.S. 193, 194, 196, 197
Baltic states *see* Estonia; Latvia;
    Lithuania; Slovenia
Banders, V.N. 194
Banks, J.C. 109
Barney, J. 130
Beamish, P. 109, 119
Beddows & Co 48, 56
Behrman, J.N. 221
Belarus 170, 175, 181
Belgium 1, 9
  foreign acquisitions 90

home shopping 76
inward investment 234
multinational enterprises 187, 209,
    211, 213, 215, 218, 220, 223–7
    passim
retail financial service firms 43,
    44, 47, 48, 49, 53, 55
Ben-Ner, A. 151, 157, 159, 162
Benelux countries 36
Bennison, D. 66
Berger, A. 51
Bergsten, C.F. 242, 243
Berry, D.F. 161, 165
Berry, L. 45
Biggadike, R. 136
Blanchard, O. 164
Bleaney, M. 172
Bleeke, J. 118, 122
Boatwright, B.D. 196, 197
Boddewyn, J.J. 45
Bös, D. 150, 151, 172
Bostock, F. 231
Boutsouki, C. 66
Bowditch, J. 123, 124, 135
Brech, M. 91
Bretton Woods System 196
Brewer, T. 16, 238, 245, 248
British Industry Confederation 246
Brook, P. 17, 21, 23, 65–85
Buck, T. 18, 142, 145–65
Buckley, P.J. 19, 45, 46, 109, 115,
    193, 195, 196, 253–6
Building Societies Act 1986 43
Bulgaria 2
  privatisation 169, 170, 174, 175,
    177, 179, 181
Buono, A. 123, 124, 135
Burgess, R. 176
Burgman, R. 130, 139
Burt, S. 66
Burton, F. 1–19, 21–3, 83, 84,
    109–20
'Buy America' Act 239, 246
buyouts and Russian industry 145–65
  employee buyout 146, 151, 152–3,
    154, 156, 157, 158, 165
  employees as controllers 157–8

257

buyouts *cont.*
    employees as owners   158–60
    employees as owners and controllers
      160–4
    privatisation and corporate
      governance 146–53
    vouchers   151, 153–4, 156, 174

Canada
    Canadian Foreign Investment
      Review Agency   247
    foreign acquisitions   90
    foreign direct investment   195
    multinational enterprises   209, 211,
      213, 215, 218, 220, 223
Cantwell, J.A.   193
capital controls   196–7
Cartwright, S.   123, 124, 125, 134,
    135
Casson, M.C.   45, 109, 115, 143, 193,
    195, 196, 255
Castledine, P.   18, 83, 84, 87–107,
    235
Caves, R.E.   192, 196, 232
CCT *see* common customs tariff
Cecchini, P.   22, 42, 47, 62, 69, 187,
    190
Central Europe   18
    buyouts   145, 146, 148, 150, 151, 152
    competitiveness policy   12
    cross-border cooperation   11
    foreign direct investment   255
    see also   privatisation
CET   *see* common external tariff
Channon, D.   125, 136
Chatterjee, S.   124, 125, 126, 128,
    129, 130, 134
Chevallier, T.   236
Chile   255
Chung, S.J.   232
Clegg, J.   18, 186, 189–203
Clinton, B.   26
Cockfield, Lord   62
Comanor, W.S.   246
common customs tariff   193
common external tariff   193, 253
competitiveness   7–10, 9–14, 125,
    239, 246
conduct   100–1
Contractor, F.J.   119
Cook, P.   18, 142, 143, 168–82
Cooper, C.   123, 124, 125, 134, 135

cooperative ventures in Spain and
      United Kingdom   109–20
    initial configuration   117–18
    motives for choice   113–17; local
      experience, harnessing of
      114–15; market integration
      contribution   116–17; resources,
      securing of and/or market
      access at reduced cost and risk
      115–16
    strengthening strategic positions in
      European Union markets   119
Coppins, B.   91
Corbett, J.   150
corporate governance   146–53
corporate policy   136–7
Correa, M.   129
Cowling, K.   129
Crichton, M.   234
Croatia   170, 174, 175, 177
Cronbach Alpha value   127, 130
cross-border acquisitions   122–37
    absorption integration   124, 131
    acquisition integration, form
      of   127–8
    acquisition performance   129–30
    autonomy, degree of   128–9
    competitive advantage   125
    control variables   130–1
    corporate policy implications
      136–7
    integration, form of   123–4
    integration types, classification
      of   129
    management style differences   123,
      127
    preservation integration   124, 131,
      132, 133, 135
    strategic interdependence   128
    symbiotic integration   124, 131–2,
      133, 135
cross-border cooperation   10–14
Cushman, D.O.   196
Customs Union   2
Czech Republic   2
    buyouts   150, 154
    privatisation   169, 170, 173, 174,
      176–81 *passim*
Czechoslovakia   2
    privatisation   169, 175
    see also   Czech Republic; Slovak
      Republic

Data Processing Directive 71
data protection provisions 76–7
Datta, D. 123, 126, 127, 129, 130, 134
Davies, R. 51, 53
Dawson, J.A. 66
De Meyer, A. 123
de-industrialisation 27–9
Delors, J. 3, 23, 26, 33, 34, 35
Demsetz, H. 150
Denmark 1, 4, 5, 9
  foreign acquisitions 90
  home shopping 66, 76
  inward investment 240
  retail financial service firms 43, 50
  unemployment 34
Derek, R. 76
Dess, G. 130
Dillman, D. 127
direct investment *see* foreign; inward; outward
distance selling 72–5
Distance Selling Directive 71, 73, 74, 76, 77
Dixon, R. 61
Drucker, P.F. 148, 151
Drysdale, P. 255
Dunning, J.H. 56, 91, 109, 191, 196, 198, 234

East Asia 8, 83
Eastern Europe 18
  buyouts 145, 146, 148, 150, 151, 152
  competitiveness policy 12
  cross-border cooperation 11
  foreign direct investment 255
  regional and global issues in international business 254–5
  see also privatisation
EBO *see* employee buyout
ECB *see* European Central Bank
Economic and Monetary Union 3–7
Economic and Social Committee 4–5
economy of European Union 21–3
ECU *see* European Currency Unit
educational expenditure 9
EFTA *see* European Free Trade Association
Eire 90
Emerson, M. 15

EMI *see* European Monetary Institute
employees
  as controllers 157–8
  as owners 158–60
  as owners and controllers 160–4
employment
  full 29–30
  Japan and United States 6
  policies for jobs 33–7
  and related effects 101–2
Employment Act 1991 177
EMS *see* European Monetary System
EMU *see* European Monetary Union
ERM *see* Exchange Rate Mechanism
Ernst, D. 118, 122
ESC *see* Economic and Social Committee
Estonia 2, 170, 175, 180, 181
Euro-Mediterranean Economic Area 2
Europe *see* Central; Eastern; European; Northern; Southern
European
  Banking Federation 7
  Central Bank 4, 35, 37
  Currency Unit 3, 105
  Free Trade Association 186
  Investment Bank 34
  Monetary Institute 4
  Monetary System 3, 15, 18
  Monetary Union 7, 236
European Union evolution 1–7
  Common Market 2–3
  Customs Union 2
  Economic and Monetary Union 3–7
  Single European Market 3
Evans, P. 190
exchange rate changes 196
Exchange Rate Mechanism 3, 4, 5
  unemployment 25, 28, 37
exchange rates 4

FDI *see* foreign direct investment
Filatotchev, I. 18, 142, 145–65
Financial Services Act 1986 43
financing decisions, role of 196
Finland 1, 95
Fischer, W.A. 221
Flowers, E.B. 195
Flynn, P. 34
Forbes, M.S. 242
foreign acquisitions in United Kingdom 87–107

foreign acquisitions *cont.*
  impact 91–4
  impact-survey results 96–102;
    employment and related
    effects 101–2; market structure,
    conduct and performance effects
    100–1; resource transfer
    effects 98–9; sovereignty and
    autonomy effects 102; trade and
    balance of payments effects
    99–100
  methodology 94–6
  policy implications 104–6
  results 102–3
foreign direct investment 14, 18, 19
  cooperative ventures 110, 120
  East and Central Europe 178–82,
    255
  foreign acquisitions 87, 88, 91,
    103, 106
  inward investment 235–50 *passim*
  multinational enterprises 185, 186,
    188
  retail financial service firms 45–6
  United Kingdom 254
  see also United States
foreign market servicing 44–6, 57–9
France 1, 10, 23
  cooperative ventures 117–18
  foreign acquisitions 88, 90, 95
  home shopping 66, 67, 76
  inward investment 233, 234, 236, 238
  retail financial service firms 42–3,
    46–55 *passim*, 57
  unemployment 29, 35, 36
Friedman, M. 26
Frydman, R. 150, 152, 164, 169

Garnaut, R. 255
General Agreement on Tariffs and
    Trade (GATT) 193, 231, 244,
    245, 246, 247
  inward investment 238, 241, 243,
    249
General Agreement on Trade in
    Services (GATS) 245
Georgia 170, 175
Geringer, M. 130, 132
Germany 9, 23
  buyouts 146, 149, 150, 151
  cooperative ventures 117–18
  East 1, 168, 172

home shopping 65, 66, 67, 71, 72,
    73, 74, 76, 77
  inward investment 240
  retail financial service firms 42,
    46, 51, 57, 61
  reunification 4
  unemployment 28, 30, 34, 35, 36,
    37
  West 1; foreign acquisitions 90,
    95; inward investment 233;
    privatisation 172; retail financial
    service firms 43, 47, 48, 50, 52,
    53, 54, 55; unemployment 29
Gestrin, M. 247, 249
Gilbert, R. 62
Gill, S. 68, 69
Gilman, M.G. 196
Gilson, R.J. 150
Glickman, N.J. 234, 236, 241, 242,
    248
globalisation 67–9
Goldberg, M.A. 193, 194
Gort, M. 136
Graham, E.M. 195, 234, 240, 241,
    242, 243, 244
Grahl, J. 67, 68–9
Greece 1
  foreign acquisitions 90
  foreign direct investment 202
  home shopping 66, 76
  multinational enterprises 187, 209,
    211, 213, 215, 218, 220, 223
  retail financial service firms 43,
    51, 52, 61
  unemployment 28
Green, S. 161, 165
Greenaway, D. 247
Greiner, L. 134
gross disbursements 181
gross domestic product 2, 4
  home shopping 65
  Japan and United States 6
  privatisation 175
  retail financial service firms 42
  unemployment 29, 35
Grubel, H.G. 56, 196

Halimi, S. 36
Hall, P. 129
Hamill, J. 18, 81–107, 235
Hansmann, H. 157
Hanweck, G. 51

Hare, P. 178
Harrigan, K.R. 116, 117
Haspeslagh, P. 122, 124, 125, 127–8, 129, 135
Havanna Charter 1948 241
Hebert, L. 130, 132
Hennart, J.-F. 232
Henning, C.R. 7
Hine, R.C. 190
Hirschman, A. 148
Hofstede, G. 123, 134
Hollander, S.C. 66
home shopping 65–85
    data protection provisions 76–7
    distance selling 72–5
    integration 71–2
    neo-liberalism and
        globalisation 67–9
    place in retail sector 67
    policies for consumer 69–71
    retailing 65–6, 69
Hong Kong 90
Hood, C. 19, 185, 231–50
Hood, N. 15, 19, 91, 187, 231–50
Hughes, A. 91
Hume, I. 175
Hungary 2
    privatisation 169, 170, 173–81
        passim
Hunt, J. 129
Hychak, T.J. 173
Hymer, S. 44

IBRD 241
IMF *see* International Monetary Fund
imports 190, 191
Industry Act 1975 104
integration, form of 123–4
interest rates 4
internal market policies 16–17
International Monetary Fund 37, 180, 181, 241
International Trade Organisation 241
investment *see* direct; inward;
    Multilateral
inward investment 9, 15, 231–50
    European Union and United
        States 231–40
    prospects 244–9
    United States policy
        proposals 240–4

Ireland 1, 5
    home shopping 76
    retail financial service firms 43, 47, 51, 53
Israel 256
Italy 1, 4
    foreign acquisitions 90
    home shopping 65, 66, 67, 71, 72, 73, 74, 76, 77
    inward investment 233
    retail financial service firms 43, 46, 48–55, 61
    unemployment 29
ITO *see* International Trade
    Organisation

Japan 2
    balance of trade 8
    buyouts 146, 149, 150, 151, 157
    cross-border cooperation 11, 14
    educational expenditure 9
    employment 6
    foreign acquisitions 90, 95, 107
    foreign direct investment 16, 190, 191, 197
    gross domestic product 6
    inward investment 232, 234, 236, 237, 240, 242, 244, 247
    labour productivity 6
    market share 7
    mergers and acquisitions 83
    multinational enterprises 185–6, 207, 209–11, 215–16, 218–20, 223–4
    patents 8
    research and development
        spending 8
    unemployment 25, 26, 28, 29, 34–5
Jemison, D. 122, 124, 125, 127–8, 129, 135
Jensen, M.C. 162, 163
Johanson, J. 45, 109
joint venture agreements 181
Jones, G. 231
Joyce, P.L. 91

Kacker, M. 66
Kalecki, M. 36
Kayser, G. 172
Kazakhstan 170, 175
Keynes, J.M. 36
Khandwalla, P. 127
Killing, J.P. 116

King, A.E. 173
Kirkpatrick, C. 18, 142, 143,
    168–82
Kitching, J. 122, 125, 127, 129, 130
Kitson, M. 36
Kline, J.M. 241, 244
Knickerbocker, F.T. 195
Kogut, B. 109, 113, 116, 119, 232
Korean War 31
Kornai, J. 148, 152, 153
Krugman, P.R. 234, 240, 241, 242,
    243, 244
Kusewitt, J. 125
Kyrgyzstan 170, 180

laboratories, importance of work 215
labour and privatisation 176–8
labour productivity 6
Latin America 12, 255
Latvia 2, 170, 175, 180, 181
Laurent, A. 123
Lawlor, E. 70–1
Lawrence, C. 61
Layard, R. 26
Lehn, K. 150
Leigh, R. 91
LFRs (less favoured regions) 236,
    237, 248
Likert-type scales 127, 128, 130
Lithuania 2, 169, 170, 175, 180, 181
Lopes, P.S. 174
Lorange, P. 119
Love, J.H. 91, 96, 235
Lovelock, C.H. 45
Lubatkin, M. 125, 129
Lunn, J. 192, 193, 194, 196, 197
Luxembourg 1, 5, 9
    foreign acquisitions 90
    home shopping 76
    retail financial service firms 43
    unemployment 35
Lyles, M.A. 119

Maastricht Treaty 3, 26, 254
    home shopping 70, 72, 75
    inward investment 238, 241, 248
    unemployment 34, 35
MacDonald, R. 30
MacDougall Report 35
Macedonia 170, 177
MAI *see* Multilateral Agreement on
    Investment

Malekzadeh, A. 124
management style differences 123,
    127
manufacturing versus service industry
    acquisitions 125
market
    access 115–16
    concentration 195
    integration 116–17, 191–2
    related variables 193–4
    share 7
    structure 100–1
Mattson, L.-G. 109
Mauer, L.J. 193, 194, 197
Mayer, C. 150
Mayes, D.G. 17, 193
McKinsey & Co 122, 129
Meckling, W.H. 162, 163
Mediterranean 2, 12
Mexico 255
Michalet, C.A. 234, 236
Michie, J. 7, 17, 21, 22–3,
    25–39
Middle East 2, 256
Miles, D. 148
Milner, C. 197
Mirvis, P. 124, 135
Mirza, H. 253
Mitterrand, F. 34, 36
MNEs *see* multinational enterprises
Moldova 170–1, 180
Monopolies and Mergers
    Commission 104
Montgomery, C. 125, 129, 130
Morgan, J. 61
Mullender, L. 60
Multilateral Agreement on
    Investment 231, 245
multinational enterprises 207–29
    adaptation, extent and motives
        for 220
    foreign acquisitions 87, 94, 96
    foreign direct investment 189,
        191–2, 194–7, 202, 203
    inward investment 236, 237, 238,
        239, 244
    laboratories, importance of work
        in 215
    production exports 211
    research and development 214–17
    research with local institutions 223
    scientific links 221–4

technological work 213
technology, sources of 217–21
Mundell, R.A. 192
Murrell, P. 148

NAFTA *see* North American Free
  Trade Agreement
Nahavandi, A. 124
NAIRU *see* non-accelerating inflation
  rate of unemployment
neo-liberalism 67–9
Netherlands 1, 9
  foreign acquisitions 90
  home shopping 76
  inward investment 233, 240
  retail financial service firms 43,
    47–53, 55
Neven, D. 246
'New Deal' 26
New Zealand 90
Nickell, S. 26–7
'1992' programme 21–2, 23
Noble, D. 18, 83, 84, 109–20
Noland, M. 242, 243
non-accelerating inflation rate of
  unemployment 26–7
non-binding Recommendation 73, 74
non-tariff barriers 190, 191, 194, 195,
  197, 203
Norburn, D. 122, 129
Normann, R. 125, 135–6
North America 8, 83, 232, 234
North American Free Trade
  Agreement 237, 243, 247, 248,
  249, 253, 255
North, D.J. 91
Northern Europe 31
Norway 2
NTBs *see* non-tariff barriers
Nuti, D. 161

Omnibus Trade and Competitiveness
  Act 1988 239, 246
Organisation for Economic
  Cooperation and Development
  (OECD) 19
  foreign direct investment 16
  inward investment 231, 238, 239,
    244, 245, 249
  multinational enterprises 187
  privatisation 178
  unemployment 25, 37

Organisation of Petroleum Exporting
  Countries (OPEC) 196
Ostry, S. 245
outward direct investment 14–15
outward foreign direct investment 9,
  15–16

Panić, M. 15, 91
Papanastassiou, M. 18, 185, 186,
  187, 207–29
Park, Y.-R. 232
Parkhe, A. 85
patents 8
Pearce, R.D. 18, 185, 186, 187,
  207–29
performance effects 100–1
personal equity plan (PEP) 51
Peters, E. 187, 236
Pinto, B. 175
Pioch, E. 17, 21, 23, 65–85
Poland 2
  privatisation 169, 171, 173–5, 177,
    179–81
policy agenda 30–2
Porter, M. 125, 128, 129, 130
Portugal 1
  foreign acquisitions 90
  foreign direct investment 202
  home shopping 66, 76
  inward investment 234, 247, 248
  multinational enterprises 187, 209,
    211, 213, 215, 218, 220, 223,
    224, 226
  retail financial service firms 43,
    51, 52, 55, 61
  unemployment 28
Prescott, K. 17, 21, 23, 41–63
Prestowitz, C.V. Jr 234, 242
price stability 4
Price Waterhouse 53
private sector development 174–6
privatisation in East and Central
  Europe 168–82
  foreign direct investment 178–82
  gross disbursements 181
  joint venture agreements 181
  labour and social security 176–8
  private sector development 174–6
  scale 168–74
  small-scale and large-scale 170–1
  unemployment 177
privatisation in Russia 146–53

Privatisation of State Owned
  Enterprises Law 178
production exports 211
public finances 4
Putterman, L. 159, 160, 161, 162

Quelch, J. 143

R&D *see* research and development
Rapaczynski, A. 169
Rathmell, J.M. 45
rationalised product subsidiaries 208,
  224, 226, 227
Ray, E.J. 196
Regan, W. 45
regional and global issues in
  international business 253–6
regional product mandate 187, 208,
  212, 217, 219, 224, 226, 227
Reich, R.B. 234, 236, 242, 243
Renton, G.A. 196, 197
research and development 18
  cooperative ventures 115
  cross-border cooperation 14
  foreign acquisitions 98–9, 102, 103
  inward investment 231, 234, 241,
    243, 245, 247
  with local institutions 223
  multinational enterprises 186–7,
    207–8, 212–17, 219, 221–2, 224,
    225
  spending 8, 21
  unemployment 35
resource transfer effects 98–9
resources, securing of 115–16
retail financial service firms 41–63
  competition 55–7
  demand 52–5
  foreign market servicing 44–6
  strategies 57–61
  supply 46–52
retailing 65–6
Robinson, R. 130
Robocx, S.H. 62
Robson, P. 17, 191
Roe, M.J. 150
Rohatyn, F. 242
Romania 2, 171, 174, 175, 177, 179,
  181
RPM *see* regional product mandate
Rugman, A.M. 118, 247, 249

Russia 18, 255
  privatisation 169, 173–4, 175, 177,
    178, 180, 181
  see also buyouts
Russian Federation 169, 171

Safarian, A.E. 240
Sales, A. 124, 135
Salmon, W.J. 66
Scaperlanda, A.E. 192, 193, 198,
  200
Scarpetta, S. 178
Scherer, F.M. 129
Schneider, S. 123
Schoenberg, R. 18, 83, 85, 122–37
Schwartz, G. 172, 174
scientific links 221–4
Scouller, J. 91
Second Banking Directive 1989 239
service industry versus manufacturing
  acquisitions 125
Seth, A. 129
Shackleton, M. 2
Shanley, M. 129
Sharp, M. 91
Shepley, S. 237
Shleifer, A. 150
Shore, G. 134
Shrivastava, P. 124
Simmonds, K. 62
Singh, A. 28
Singh, H. 125, 129
Single European Act 110, 119
Single European Market Act 3, 46
Siotis, G. 246
Slovak Republic 2, 169, 171, 178
Slovakia 177, 179, 181
Slovenia 2, 174, 175, 177, 179, 181
Smith, I.J. 91
social security and privatisation 176–8
South Africa 90
Southern Europe 15
sovereignty 102
Spain 1, 23
  foreign acquisitions 90
  foreign direct investment 202
  home shopping 66, 76
  inward investment 233
  mergers and acquisitions 83
  retail financial service firms 43,
    47–55 *passim*, 57, 61
  see also cooperative ventures

Standard Industrial
    Classification 126, 130, 132,
    136
Steuer, M.D. 91, 235
Stevens, G.V.G. 196
Stiglitz, J.E. 152
Stopford, J.M. 91
strategic interdependence 128
Sweden 1
    foreign acquisitions 90, 95
    foreign direct investment 194
    unemployment 31
Swedenborg, B. 194
Switzerland 2, 90

tariffs *see* General Agreement
Tavlas, G.S. 196
Teague, P. 67, 68–9
technological work 213
technology, sources of 217–21
Teece, D.J. 208
Thomas, D.R.E. 45
Thomsen, S. 232
TNCs 248
Tokyo Round 190
Tolchin, M. 242
Tolchin, S. 242
Tordjman, A. 66
trade
    effects 99–100
    policies 15–16
    related investment measures 244,
    247
    see also General Agreement;
    European Free; North American
    Free; Omnibus; World
Trautwein, F. 130
Treadgold, A. 66
Treaty on European Union *see*
    Maastricht
Treaty of Rome 1, 2–3, 21, 34
TRIMs *see* trade related investment
    measures
truncated miniature replicas 208, 224
Tschoegl, A. 56
Turkey 256
Turner, L. 91
Tyson, L.D. 234, 239, 241, 242

Ugeux, G. 61
Ukraine 175, 181
Ulan, M. 242

unemployment in Central and Eastern
    Europe 177
unemployment in global
    recession 25–39
    de-industrialisation 27–9
    full employment in future 29–30
    non-accelerating inflation rate of
    unemployment 26–7
    policies for jobs 33–7
    policy agenda 30–2
United Kingdom 1, 4, 5, 10, 18, 19,
    23, 253
    buyouts 146, 148, 149, 150, 151,
    158, 165
    cross-border acquisitions 122, 123,
    125, 126, 127
    foreign direct investment 196, 200
    home shopping 67, 76
    inward investment 231, 233, 234,
    235, 238, 240, 248
    labour market, unregulated 254
    mergers and acquisitions 83–5
    multinational enterprises 187,
    209–13, 215–16, 218–20, 223–7
    privatisation 168
    retail financial service firms 42–4,
    46–55 *passim*, 57, 60–1
    unemployment 25–6, 28–32, 34,
    35, 37
    see also cooperative ventures;
    foreign acquisitions
United States 2, 19
    balance of trade 8
    buyouts 146, 148–52, 158, 164, 165
    cooperative ventures 116
    cross-border acquisitions 123, 134
    educational expenditure 9
    employment 6
    foreign acquisitions 87, 88, 90, 95,
    105, 107
    foreign direct investment 16, 18,
    189–203; capital controls 196–7;
    exchange rate changes 196;
    financing decisions, role of 196;
    industrial country imports 191;
    market concentration 195; market
    integration 191–2; market related
    variables 193–4; statistical
    evidence 192–3, 197–8; tariff
    averages on total imports 190;
    wage and other cost factors
    194–5

United States *cont.*
  gross domestic product 6
  inward investment 231–47, 249
  labour productivity 6
  market share 7
  mergers and acquisitions 83
  multinational enterprises 186–7,
    207, 209–16 *passim*, 218–220,
    223, 224
  research and development
    spending 8
  retail financial service firms 43, 53
  unemployment 25, 26, 28, 31, 34, 35
  see also foreign acquisitions; North
    America
Uruguay Round 15, 190, 231, 243,
  244, 245, 247
Uzbekistan 175

Valentiny, P. 151, 155
van Brabant, J.M. 169
Van Den Bulcke, D. 2, 234
Vernon, R. 45
Vishny, R.W. 150
voucher scheme *see* buyouts

wage and other cost factors 194–5
Waldman, C. 66
Wallis, K.F. 195, 198–9
Walsh, J.P. 125, 190
Walter, G. 130

Walton, P. 129
Wang, Y. 148
Weber, J. 128
Welford, R. 41
White, J.T. 194
White, R. 66
Whitehead, M. 69
Wiedersheim-Paul, F. 45
Wilkins, M. 231, 232, 234
Wilkinson, F. 26
Williams, D.E. 66
Williamson, O.E. 109, 119, 158
Wilmot, J. 237
Wilson, V. 129, 130
Winters, L.A. 17
Woodward, D.P. 234, 236, 241, 242,
  248
Woolcock, S. 235, 238, 245–6, 248
World Bank 175
world product mandate (WPM) 187,
  208, 224, 227
World Trade Organisation (WTO) 19
  foreign direct investment 15, 16
  inward investment 231, 238, 244,
  245, 249
Wright, M. 18, 142, 145–65

Yamin, M. 1–19, 83–5, 141–3
Young, S. 1–19, 45, 91, 185–8,
  231–50
Yugoslavia 177